PENGU

FATHER BOB

Sue Williams is the author of a number of bestselling books, including *Mean Streets, Kind Heart: The Father Chris Riley Story*, *Women of the Outback* and *No Time for Fear: How a Shark Attack Survivor Beat the Odds* and, most recently, *The Girl Who Climbed Everest*. Her other books include *Peter Ryan: The Inside Story*, *Outback Spirit* and *Welcome to the Outback*. *And Then the Darkness*, about the disappearance of Peter Falconio, was shortlisted for a Golden Dagger Award in the UK and the Ned Kelly Awards in Australia. Sue worked in print and television overseas before moving to Australia in 1989 and has since written for many of our leading newspapers and magazines. She lives in Sydney's Kings Cross with her partner, writer Jimmy Thomson.

suewilliams.com.au

ALSO BY SUE WILLIAMS

Peter Ryan: The Inside Story

Mean Streets, Kind Heart: The Father Chris Riley Story

And Then the Darkness

Women of the Outback

Outback Spirit

No Time for Fear

Welcome to the Outback

Left for Dead

The Girl Who Climbed Everest

FATHER BOB

The Larrikin Priest

SUE WILLIAMS

PENGUIN BOOKS

PENGUIN BOOKS

UK | USA | Canada | Ireland | Australia
India | New Zealand | South Africa | China

Penguin Books is part of the Penguin Random House group of companies
whose addresses can be found at global.penguinrandomhouse.com.

Penguin
Random House
Australia

First published by Penguin Random House Australia Pty Ltd, 2013
This edition published by Penguin Australia Pty Ltd, 2017

1 3 5 7 9 10 8 6 4 2

Cover design by John Canty and Louisa Maggio
© Penguin Random House Australia Pty Ltd
Cover photograph by Monty Coles
Typeset in Sabon by Samantha Jayaweera,
Penguin Random House Australia Pty Ltd
Colour separation by Splitting Image Colour Studio, Clayton, Victoria
Printed and bound in Australia by Griffin Press, an accredited ISO AS/NZS 14001 Environmental Management Systems printer.

National Library of Australia
Cataloguing-in-Publication data:

Williams, Sue, author.
Father Bob: the larrikin priest / Sue Williams.
9780143571360 (paperback)

Maguire, Bob.
Catholic Church – Clergy – Biography.
Priests – Victoria – Biography.
Religion and culture.
Religion and politics.

270.092

penguin.com.au

MIX
Paper from responsible sources
FSC® C009448

And we are here as on a darkling plain
Swept with confused alarms of struggle and flight,
Where ignorant armies clash by night.

'Dover Beach' by Matthew Arnold, 1851

All that is required for evil to prevail is for
good men to do nothing.

Edmund Burke

CONTENTS

PART 3: THE TROUBLES

Foreword

Father Bob Maguire
AM, RFD

There's been a lot said, and written, about me over the years.

Some people have said I'm a saint; to others, I'm more the devil incarnate.

I've been called the 'sad' priest because so much of my work has been with the poorest, most marginalised, most desperate people in Australia today. To some I'm a 'bad' priest, because many of my ways of doing things are quite unconventional, although my interpretation of the gospels has always been absolutely orthodox.

And to many I might seem, at times, quite mad. They're the ones who only see me on TV, hear me on radio or read about me in newspapers, sounding off about the sorry state of my beloved Catholic Church around the world today, calling for those of us in religious life to be much more inclusive, and pontificating on the kinds of subjects priests don't usually dare to go near: sex 'n' drugs 'n' rock 'n' roll, abuse by clergy, contraception, gay marriage, crime, forgotten Australians and the dangers of hidebound clericalism.

Since I was ordained as a priest in 1960, I've seen many changes in both society and religious life. Vatican II has come and almost gone, and the Catholic Church has become mired in controversy over the abuse of youngsters in its care and its treatment of both offenders and their victims. For that, I apologise wholeheartedly, with every strand of my being. Nothing will ever wipe out the pain of those who suffered, or excuse their sickening betrayal by the Church, although I hope the Royal Commission can go even a little way to helping those victims.

At the same time, society has doubtless become more secular, more stressed and a great deal less forgiving of those who fall between the cracks.

My time as a priest, up until I was forced out of my church in South Melbourne after thirty-eight years working there, was all about creating a caring, sharing church, working in partnership with the neighbourhood and community to design a new model of collaboration and support. It was about a church working for the people, and by the people.

As a result, everything achieved during those years was never done by me alone, but was a real and meaningful expression of teamwork. That includes the pioneering work with street kids through Open Family, the formation of the Emerald Hill Mission to help older people who were struggling, the galvanisation of the parish to feed, clothe and assist the poor and, finally, the Father Bob Maguire Foundation to help those at both ends of the spectrum: granting scholarships to disadvantaged kids, helping with a refuge in Nepal for child victims of the global sex trade, and looking after those older Australians who otherwise might have given up all hope.

Of course, I've made mistakes along the way, but we've also enjoyed great successes.

Finally, as I still strive to continue my work, now without my parish but instead as part of a church without borders, harnessing technology to build a whole new pop-up congregation online through Church.tv, Twitter and my blogs, using traditional media to send my message and travelling around Melbourne to say mass and hold baptisms, weddings and funerals, I felt it was at last the right time to tell our story.

That's the good and bad, and warts 'n' all – both, as you may say, the saintly and the devilish.

And for the love of Jesus, now here it is.

Bob Maguire

PART 1

A HARD ROAD

1

The Day is Over

A lone bagpiper steps into an old church in an inner-city suburb of Melbourne, to the soaring refrain of 'Amazing Grace'.

As he makes his way up the aisle, the 1000-strong packed congregation rise, as one, to their feet. They turn and look behind the piper to see a short, bespectacled, snowy-haired man in flowing white and green vestments hurrying to the front of the church.

Immediately, the applause starts, and doesn't stop until he takes his place behind the pulpit and adjusts the microphone. Already, there's barely a dry eye in the house.

For this is Father Bob Maguire – battler, army veteran and for the last thirty-eight years the priest of this proud parish.

During that time, he's been the founder of both national and local charities to help the poor, a champion of efforts to democratise Catholicism in Australia, an outspoken campaigner for the rights of perhaps the most downtrodden of all in society, a one-man comedy turn and, along the way, a much-admired TV and radio personality.

He's received nationwide recognition for his work, too. As well as being the 2012 Victorian of the Year, he's also a Member of the Order of Australia, a Local Hero as part of the Australian of the Year awards and a long-time Australia Day Ambassador, in addition to winning an Ernst & Young Entrepreneur of the Year Award for social and community enterprises.

On the flipside, he's a man who also manages to outrage people. Some of the more traditional members of the Church have been appalled by his approach from time to time; he's been criticised by people as diverse as the Archbishop of Melbourne and one of the city's most influential shock jocks, and he once scandalised one of his old schoolteachers with his utterances from the pulpit. 'I'm embarrassed by him now!' says the elderly Christian Brother, shaking his head.

To others, however, he's seen as a 21st-century saviour of the Church, a man as saintly as he is entertaining, sitting on the limit of 5000 Facebook friends, with an astonishing 86 000-plus followers for his Twitter feed, regular radio and TV appearances, and his own Sunday night radio show on Triple J with media personality John Safran. 'He always puts others first,' says a long-time friend and follower from his parish of South Melbourne. 'Despite the fact that he gets to meet and greet and be a confidant of leading business, political, sporting and community people, his preference is to be mixing with the outsiders, the lost sheep. Because, as he tells us, that's where we'll find God.'

One of those lost sheep, a former drug-addicted street kid now living at a run-down boarding house, brightens visibly when she hears his name as she queues on a cold July night at one of the food vans he started. 'If it wasn't for Father Bob, I wouldn't be alive today,' she says. 'If Catholic priests were allowed to marry, I'd ask him tomorrow . . .'

But today, a bright Sunday morning in January 2012, is his bittersweet swansong. Aged seventy-seven, he's finally leaving the church he loves after being invited to retire by the Melbourne Catholic hierarchy, declining but then losing the fight to be allowed to stay on until he was ready to quit.

After a lifetime of service, he now has no idea where he'll go, what he'll do next, how he'll manage.

Yet as his last official mass begins with standing room only, he just can't help poking fun at himself, and at Church officialdom. He makes a reference to his co-celebrant also being moved on before he was perhaps ready. But he stops himself. 'Don't go there! Don't go there!' he warns, to uproarious laughter from the congregation, most of whom have been campaigning hard as The Bob Squad for their hero to remain. Then he cracks another joke about an Aboriginal smoking ceremony also having been planned, but not taking place. 'I was going to say, we ran out of puff,' he smiles.

And when he's forced to shuffle through his papers to find the page he wants, he sighs. 'That's why I've been moved on, you see,' he says. His voice rises an octave: 'I've lost me wits!'

He also mentions the Father Bob Maguire bobble-head

figurine still for sale to fund his continuing charity ventures. He recounts a conversation he had the other day when someone asked him, 'Don't you realise you're making a fool of yourself?' Father Bob laughs. 'I say, What's new? Now we'll do it for money, as Jesus said to his disciples.' He stops and chuckles. 'Don't look for the [Bible] passage,' he adds, playing with his audience. 'I don't think there is one!'

There are tributes from parishioners and friends, and another haunting rendition of 'Amazing Grace', this time from a member of the congregation who'd once been a contestant on 'The X Factor'.

Then another joke, which this time brings the house down. He'd been clearing out the presbytery ready for his move, he says, when he came across his birth certificate. 'I almost had a stroke,' he reports. 'I thought it said 1937, which meant I was only seventy-three . . . What do I do? Do I ring him [the Archbishop of Melbourne] up?' There's a gale of laughter, then cheering and clapping at the thought of a late reprise.

As the unconventional mass weaves its way to its conclusion, Father Bob is presented with a portable mass kit, so he can say mass wherever he is, some funds and a plaque for the wall of the church, inscribed with a tribute to him and one of his favourite sayings, 'No more us and them, just we'.

Finally, there's a standing ovation as everyone sings 'The Battle Hymn of the Republic': 'Glory! Glory! Hallelujah! Glory! Glory! Hallelujah! Glory! Glory! Hallelujah! His truth is marching on.' Father Bob stands to attention, like the old soldier he has always been, then straightens his white gown, the alb, and the green chasuble worn over it, and takes a deep breath.

There's a rousing chorus of Hip! Hip! Hooray! and then,

in another nod to Father Bob's heritage as the son of Scottish migrants, a Scottish pipe band steps out, playing the march 'The Black Bear', a tune traditionally played on a regiment's return to barracks, signalling the day is over.

As they lead the way for Father Bob Maguire out of his church and into a new life, not for the first time he wonders to himself how the hell he ended up in this position, and what on earth his future will hold.

2

A Mongrel Drunk and a Bully

The most chilling sound of young Bobby Maguire's childhood was his father's heavy footfall on the front doorstep, followed by the scratch of a fumbled key in the lock as he stumbled home from yet another drunken evening at the pub.

The family would hold their breath in fear, waiting to see just who would walk in. Sometimes it would be his dad in a genial mood, animated with ale and conversation, telling jokes, singing songs, reciting passages from Shakespeare and recounting funny anecdotes from his years spent at sea. More often, it would be a dark, smouldering stranger who didn't want to know his kids and could, with his temper on a hair-trigger, explode into violence at any moment.

It was their mum who was his usual target and she regularly endured savage beatings. The four children would cower in terror as their father lashed out in an alcoholic rage, frequently leaving his wife cut, bloodied and bruised. Even today, three-quarters of a century later, Bobby's older brother Jim can still picture the handprints of blood left smeared on the walls as she struggled to get away from him and out of the sight of the children.

At other times, their eldest sibling, Eileen, found herself on the wrong side of his fists, but Bobby, the baby of the family, has few memories of any of that. 'I think I probably just blocked it out,' he says now. 'But I do remember the only time my father communicated with me. He'd been away and when he came home, he beat me with his belt. He was always a bad drunk and that's the only time I can ever remember him taking any notice of me.'

Yet Jim, eight years older, recalls those times as if they happened yesterday. 'He would think nothing of giving our mother a backhander,' he says. 'Mum would be holding her hands to her face and to her nose, and she'd be all bloody. He was a total drunkard, a mongrel drunk and a bully. And he'd wake up the next morning and reckon everything was tra-la-la, as if nothing had ever happened.'

Their mother tried to hide her injuries as best she could, although doubtless the neighbours knew exactly what was going on. But this was Australia in the late 1930s, and they all had enough problems of their own to worry about. In the small working-class suburb of Thornbury, 7 kilometres north-east of Melbourne's CBD, most people were having to battle to get by. The memory of World War I, in which 16 000 of their fellow Victorians were killed, cast a dark shadow over the city, while the Great Depression that followed at the end of the '20s had sent demand for wool and wheat exports plummeting, and plunged the country into yet another crisis. Melbourne was hit the hardest and, at one point, unemployment touched 30 per cent.

The Maguires weren't, by any means, the only family struggling for survival, but they had significantly more to cope with than most. James Maguire's drinking loomed large. It had cost him his home once, back in Scotland, when his parents, frustrated and embarrassed by his escalating alcoholism, encouraged him to migrate to Australia where they hoped he'd be able to put his past behind him, and make a fresh start in a new land. Instead, his drinking was wreaking a terrible toll not only on him and his prospects, but now also on the life of the woman he'd married in Australia and, in turn, on their four children.

And their youngest, Bobby Maguire, took it harder than most. He developed into a quiet boy, introverted, fearful and gradually finding it harder and harder to find a reason to get up in the morning.

The Maguires – originally the McGuires – had first settled in Scotland back in the 1850s, when Bobby's great-grandfather, another James, had left his home in Ireland during the hard years of the potato famine, along with thousands of his starving countrymen. From the town of Bray, 20 kilometres south of Dublin, he'd caught the boat to Liverpool. A blacksmith by trade and experienced in working with iron, he found a job helping to build the railway at the start of its great expansion throughout Britain. He travelled north with the line to Glasgow, eventually settling with his Isle of Man–born wife Helenor in the suburb of Springburn in the city's north-east, a place known through its manufacture of steam railway engines as 'the workshop of the world'. It was an area perfectly suited to new migrants, and was very mixed, with middle-class houses and villas jostling for space next to sandstone tenements for the working classes. And while there were indeed jobs for the skilled, the strong and those with backgrounds favoured by employers, there was crushing poverty for others. The suburb was also home to Scotland's largest poorhouse, where paupers who couldn't support themselves were sent to break rocks and bundle firewood.

Irish Catholics made up a large number of those penniless families. Many had come to Scotland with nothing but the clothes they stood in, and the largely Presbyterian Scots frequently resented their arrival. Irish Catholics were considered by many to be a threat to Scottish nationality, and were routinely accused of drunkenness, crime and irresponsibility with money. Sectarian tensions flared even more sharply after the Irish Catholic uprising of 1916, the formation of the Sinn Fein and the Irish independence movement, and Catholics on the mainland were regularly discriminated against in jobs and housing, by both the Scots and the English.

It was against this background that James and Helenor's first-born son, again James, and his wife Ellen – Bob's grandparents – changed the spelling of the family name from McGuire to Maguire in a bid to camouflage its Irish origins. 'She thought they wouldn't do themselves any good being identified as Irish Micks [Catholics],' says Bob. 'So she wanted to do something to give her family an edge. It worked, too. From their start as an iron turner and a bonnet-maker, they went into business as newsagents and tobacconists and they did all right. They became socially upwardly mobile.' They ended up with two shops in Springburn and, from humble beginnings, became comparatively well-to-do, even buying their own home, something that was most unusual for an era in Scotland in which most, bar the land-owning rich, merely rented.

The couple had eleven children, of whom four died in infancy and a fifth at the age of nine from rheumatic fever. Most of the rest thrived. One son went on to become a lawyer, a daughter to own a wholesale warehouse with her husband, another daughter to marry a teacher who became a school headmaster, and another to marry a law clerk who also became a lawyer. The only one of their children who didn't do well was the one fast becoming the black sheep of the family: the eldest surviving son James, Bobby's dad.

With every passing year, the contrast between James and his siblings became more stark. For instance, James's younger brother, another Bob, was the one who went on to become a lawyer, a soldier, and a prominent member of the Catholic Young Men's Society. 'He was very successful,' says his son Des today, who himself ended up a Catholic priest, setting up the social services for the diocese of Glasgow. 'My father Bob had a highly developed conscience. But James, well, all the rest of the family saw him as the black sheep. It was a shame. He went to work at sea, and a seaman who drinks can easily go the wrong way.'

Yet James had started out well enough. Born in 1883, he developed into a smart boy academically, and a talented musician, winning prizes both for English language and violin at his Marist Brothers school. He had a real flair for words, a love of literature and a gift for performance. Following in the footsteps of his father, he loved declaiming passages from his favourite Shakespeare plays – *Hamlet*, *Macbeth*, *Othello* – and also the works of Scotland's national poet, Robert Burns. But when he left school at the turn of the century, he was unable to find work locally, and it seems it was then that he began his downhill slide. Again, he took his father's lead. The old man had always liked a tipple, and his son soon developed a taste for it too.

Finally, James chose the worst path possible for a man who liked to drink: he went to sea. Drinking had always been very much an occupational hazard of the seafaring culture, with many sailors binge-drinking whenever they hit shore, and James joined in with gusto. His problem was that he couldn't stop. It began when he joined the merchant navy, serving on a ship transporting passengers between Glasgow, the US and Canada. It continued through the outbreak of war in 1914, when the ship was used as a troop ship, bringing men, guns and stores from Canada. And it didn't even halt when he quit in 1916 and signed up to the Royal Navy. What's more, throughout his years at sea, his family fondly believed he was training to be an engineer. He was, in fact, serving as a lowly assistant cook and then as an assistant storekeeper.

By the time he was discharged from the Navy in 1918, having served on no fewer than six different ships in less than two years, he was drinking heavily and his family didn't know what to do with him. When questioned, he said that one of his ships had been torpedoed at sea, and the trauma had driven him to drink. Many privately doubted that story was true and it was later discovered that none of the ships on which he'd sailed had any record of ever having been attacked. As he alienated more and more friends and members of the family, they finally arrived at a solution: he should start a new life in the former colonies. The Australian Government at that time was subsidising the passage of migrants it deemed suitable under its White Australia policy, so it was decided James should make the move there, along with a number of other Scots in search of a better life.

James landed in Port Melbourne in 1922, at the age of thirty-nine. As soon as he arrived, he met up again with a local girl from back home in Springburn, Annie McLaughlin, who was six years younger. She was charmed by the handsome and charismatic ex-serviceman who recited poetry, quoted Shakespeare soliloquies, played the piano and sang in a beautiful, strong voice. She also loved the funny stories he told, although she could never be quite sure whether they were true or not. After a whirlwind romance, the couple married in November of the same year.

Annie was a sweet, gentle, pious young Catholic, who'd come over to Australia the year before hoping to better herself. The third of six children – five of them girls – to a brickmaker father and a mother who worked as a domestic, she hadn't had an easy life. Born in 1888, she was only twenty-six when her mother died of stomach cancer at the age of fifty. While her father by then had worked his way up to a job as a railway guard in Glasgow, there still wasn't much money to go round. 'But they would have had a bit of a working-class chip on the shoulder and the kind of bolshie attitude that comes from working in the brickworks,' says a cousin of the family, another priest, Father Willy Slavin. 'They would have been ambitious to get on in the world.'

So when Annie's younger brother Matthew announced he, his wife Grace and their new baby Molly were off for a new life in the promised land, Australia, she started thinking about migrating too. When they wrote back that things were going well, and her widowed father broke the news he'd decided to marry again, Annie, a dressmaker and milliner, and her older sister Margaret, known as Meg, realised they would no longer be needed to look after him, and decided to take the plunge. A year later, their younger sister Sadie joined them. 'We'd all been very poor back there, and they thought life would be better in Australia,' says Molly today. 'They came over hoping life would be easier.'

It was lonely starting off again in a new country, so it was only natural that Annie and her siblings socialised mostly with the people they'd known back home. James Maguire was on his own, so he similarly often sought out the company of Annie and her family. She would have been aware of his drinking but, flattered by his attention and enjoying his company, she'd already begun falling in love with him. Like generations of women before her, she doubtless ignored his bad habits in the fervent hope she'd manage to change him. In addition, Annie's family wasn't nearly as well off as James's, and she may well have imagined she was marrying up in the world. It didn't take long for her to realise that she'd actually done the exact opposite. On their wedding day, with her brother Matthew giving her away, James even turned up at the church half-cut.

The couple rented a small cottage in Darebin Road, Thornbury, and James, always so good at English, managed to find a job as a proofreader with *The Herald*, Melbourne's afternoon broadsheet newspaper, and wrote occasional sports reports for the twice-weekly *Sporting Globe*. For a while all seemed as if it would turn out well. The couple's first child, a girl they called Eileen, was born in 1923, and their second child, Kathleen, came the next year. Their first son arrived in 1926 and was christened James, immediately known as Jim. Another daughter, Marguerite, came along in 1929 but died after only seven months, from meningococcal meningitis. Annie was understandably distraught. 'That was very hard for her,' says Molly. 'Particularly on top of everything else.'

Finally, in 1934, eleven years after their first baby and eight years after their youngest, Jim, Annie had her last child, Bobby. Fourteen-year-old Molly was chosen to be his godmother and, in accordance with old Scottish custom, she walked with him in her arms all the way from his parents' home to the church for the christening, bravely trying not to notice the disapproving glances of passers-by who assumed she must be the under-age mother. 'I cringed when I saw them staring,' she says. But as the rest of the family gathered to mark Bobby's debut in the church, his father, after a hard night's drinking, didn't even turn up.

Young Bobby didn't have the happiest of childhoods. By the time he came along, the family was really struggling. James's drinking had been gradually growing worse, and the newspaper's hours didn't help. Back then, people in his position would generally start at 5 a.m. and have a break at about 10.30 a.m., when they'd head over to the Phoenix Hotel close by on Flinders Street for a 'heart-starter' before returning to the office. They'd then work through until 2 p.m. when the final edition came out, and adjourn back to the pub for the serious drinking of the day, up to the six o'clock swill – the last-minute heavy drinking until closing time. 'And when he had to write his sports stories, he did that mostly in the pub,' says Molly. 'He spent a lot of time in there. He was quite good when he wasn't drinking, but that wasn't very often.'

On payday, Annie often took her oldest child, Eileen, along with her to meet James as he left work to see if they could intercept him and take some of his wages before he spent it all on drink. 'Sometimes they'd manage it, but often they wouldn't,' says Eileen's daughter Peta Knights. 'As the oldest, Eileen had a pretty hard time. They were so short of money, she had to leave school at fourteen to go to work to earn a wage, when she'd won a scholarship to stay on, and dearly wanted to be a journalist. But it just wasn't possible.'

In the weeks where there was money, there'd be enough food to go round, and occasionally new clothes. But that was the exception. 'He often spent all his wages in the pub on grog and smokes when he left work, so he'd have nothing left by the time he came home,' says Jim. 'He was just a weak bludger. There often wasn't much food, but Mum would do her best and give us what there was, and only have something herself if there was anything left. And if there was nothing, then it was just bad luck.'

Despite trying to make ends meet and having an errant

husband and four children to look after, Annie was also taking in mending from neighbours and friends, and picking up some machining work at home to try to raise extra funds to pay the bills. Often, it still wasn't enough, and the family was forced to move house a number of times when the rent fell due and they didn't have the money to pay.

One time, they went to live in a weatherboard shack at bayside Black Rock, a particularly poor area where most families lived on credit with tradesmen and shopkeepers, according to local parish historians, scavenging wood from the foreshore scrub to provide heat in the winter. For the kids, though, that scrub was a delight. They'd revel in running down to the beach, and playing cowboys and Indians among the bushes. But with James now coming home drunk every day of the week, that wasn't to last. A number of times neighbours would knock on the family's door to let them know he was lying, drunk, in the gutter somewhere – from beer, wine or sometimes, even more desperately, Bay Rum, an oil used in the preparation of men's cologne and toiletries. It often fell to Jim to go out to find him, pick him up and half-carry, half-drag him back home.

'The neighbours there were probably twenty paces away, so they wouldn't have heard the violence indoors when he'd been drinking and made it home,' says Jim. Sometimes, he'd vent his rage on Eileen, too. 'She got the brunt of her father's anger, a lot,' says Peta. 'Much of the time it would be directed at her mum, but she had it tough too.'

James chose his victims carefully. He did hit Jim at first but when Jim grew in height and strength and stood up to him, he backed off. 'While he picked on Mum, I don't remember him attacking us so much,' says Jim. 'If he had, I think Mother would have stabbed him with a kitchen knife. She wouldn't have let him do that. We only survived because of her. She was a saint.'

And, of course, she couldn't leave her husband. A devout Catholic, she'd married for better or for worse, and she would never have dreamt of breaking her vows. Besides, how could she possibly survive on her own with four kids, and no form of social security whatsoever in those days? 'She would have gone from nothing to minus nothing,' says Jim, bluntly. 'And even with him, God knows how many houses we were kicked out of. He buggered it up each time.'

Already, this was all having a profound effect on Bobby's psyche. Living in such grinding poverty, he came to know intimately the desperation of having no money, of being constantly hungry, of going without, and of not having anywhere to turn for help. He had cousins and uncles and aunts, but they all gave the family a wide berth; they didn't want to know. His father often said he wanted to return home to Scotland, but the family back there didn't respond when he wrote begging for the money for a ticket. Instead, they all stayed on in Australia, living on the most meagre of rations, with few possessions, and even fewer friends.

Bobby made do the best he could, often borrowing his brother's old services overcoat to wear to school, to hide the holes in his hand-me-down pants and the fact that he rarely had socks. It was a grim, exhausting way to live, and it was an experience that would end up colouring the rest of his life. 'You did whatever you had to do to survive,' he says.

Throughout it all, however, he looked up to his long-suffering mum and saw her, as Jim did, as a saint, a model of

Christian piety, patience and forgiveness. He only wished he could be more like her. And with his brother and sisters so much older, at times too, he felt she was his only real ally. One of his happiest memories was when she took him away for a weekend, just the two of them, to a guesthouse at Daylesford, the spa town 100 kilometres north-west of Melbourne. He still has a photo of himself sitting on the side of a hill, in shorts, an old jumper and worn shoes, grinning.

'Lord knows where she found the money from for that,' he says. 'I think she was worried that I was going under in the emotional cauldron of home so she scraped together anything she could just to get me away for a few days.' Kathleen, the sister just ten years older, also tried to help. She took him to the movies a couple of times and to football games at Essendon.

As for his father, Bobby was by turn afraid of and confused by him. 'I couldn't understand why he wouldn't stop drinking, even though he could see how much his family was suffering,' he says today. 'It didn't make sense to me. I couldn't work him out at all.'

Bobby was fast becoming a bit of a loner. Looking on, others could see he was having trouble coping and took a kindly interest in him. One of those was the first parish priest of St Joseph's at Black Rock, Father John Gorry. Another was a nun, Sister Claude, from the nearby convent in Sandringham opened by the Presentation Sisters, an order that had come over from Ireland. Sister Claude had become close to Annie and considered her a wonderful Catholic woman, and agreed to keep a close eye on her youngest son at the little local church school. 'I think she also thought Mum was a saint and felt she could maybe mould Bobby into a saint as well,' says Jim. 'I was more interested in fishing and pinching eggs, but the Church got its hands on him early.'

James was eventually sacked from *The Herald* – no mean feat in those days of hard-drinking journalism – and he went back to sea, finding another job on the cargo steamer *Kowhai*, which sailed regularly between Melbourne and Tasmania. The money worries continued, however, and there were yet more times when the rent was owing and couldn't be paid, and the family would hurriedly move on to the next place. Once, they lived in two different run-down old houses on different sides of the same narrow street in Prahran, and another time in East St Kilda. Annie was frequently seen walking purposefully down to the local pawnshop in an attempt to borrow some cash to make ends meet. Sometimes, she'd be carrying something from the house, like a faded old painting in a frame, hoping the pawnbroker would be sympathetic enough to accept it and lend her five shillings.

Back then, life was always a battle, and one that helped form Bobby's attitudes, opinions and direction forever. It's not that there was even much opportunity to rail against his family's circumstances. When times got particularly tough, the last resort for his mum was always to write home to the couple's families in Scotland to ask for help. If they ever agreed to send anything, they'd send it directly to her rather than risk her husband drinking it before she saw it. Two or three times, a hundred pounds would arrive, which felt like a king's ransom to the ragged little family.

At other times, she'd simply take Bobby by the hand, and the pair of them would make the journey by tram into town to pawn her wedding ring.

Perhaps it's not so surprising that Bobby would later choose to lead a celibate life as a priest over a secular one with marriage and children, drank alcohol only sparingly and had such tremendous empathy with victims of addictions, whether that be alcohol, drugs or gambling. He'd learnt from his own childhood exactly what it was like to be a kid with little joy in his life, or hope for the future. The old Jesuit saying 'Give me the child until he is seven, and I will show you the man' has rarely ever been so true.

3

BYO and DIY

School for young Bobby Maguire offered little respite from the battles going on at home.

He started at the small Catholic primary school Our Lady of Lourdes in Armadale in January 1940, just four months after Prime Minister Robert Menzies announced Australia's entry into World War II. With troops going over to fight in Europe, North Africa and South-East Asia, the fear of a Japanese invasion at home loomed large. As a result, the school held regular drills during which the children had to race to the nearby park, where trenches had been dug for emergency shelter from air raids. Everyone had black rubber plugs to put in their mouths in the event of an attack.

'The idea was that the ground all around would shake if a

bomb hit, a bit like an earthquake,' says Bob. 'So having this in your mouth would help protect your teeth and stop you breaking your jaw. We were ready at any time for the Japanese to arrive, and we'd often play in the trenches, pretending we were fighting them.'

His best mate Brian Harman, who lived around the corner from him, remembers the hours they used to spend in those trenches with their war games, taking it in turns to play the heroic Australian soldiers and the dastardly Japanese enemy. With Brian six months younger, Bobby relished playing the captain in charge. 'He was good at giving orders, even back then,' says Brian. 'But apart from playing a bit of football and cricket in the park, we didn't really see him that much. I think he spent a lot of time at home, helping his mum. We all played out in the street a lot together, and lived in each other's houses, but I don't remember ever going to his. We didn't see so much of him. He seemed a bit of a lonely boy.'

Most of the time at school, he was still quite introverted, quiet and conscientious. 'As a boy, he was always a bit shy, but then when he was relaxed, he could be very talkative,' says his aunt Molly Langman. 'It was a question of confidence, really.' It had also become a habit to keep his head down, doing his work with the minimum of fuss, and avoiding attracting too much attention from the teachers. He'd learnt that trick at home, making sure his father didn't notice him. He wasn't particularly sociable or adventurous. 'There wasn't room for that in my life,' he says. 'I wasn't particularly interested in trying new things or changing the world. I was too busy just trying to survive.'

The school itself was a modest, newly constructed redbrick building at the back of the Gothic-style Our Lady of Lourdes

Church, finished just six years earlier with funds raised by parishioners. Next door was the presbytery, converted from an old heritage-listed mansion, Cavendish House, fronting High Street, Prahran, in its own large grounds.

Classes were big and learning was mostly by rote but Bobby, eager to learn and endlessly inquisitive, liked the lessons. There'd been no books at home, so he was thrilled to discover a whole new world in those at school. He wasn't so good at learning new words off by heart but found instead that once he knew their meaning, he'd start using them, and become familiar with them that way. He soon developed a vocabulary far more extensive and sophisticated than that of his classmates, who tended to learn words, but rarely introduce them into everyday conversation. He joined the choir too and found, to his surprise, that he was considered to have a very good singing voice. 'His father had a good voice, and Bob has too,' says his niece Peta.

At home, apart from his dutiful sister Kathleen, who continued taking him on occasional outings, no-one spent much time with him. Eileen, eleven years older, was too busy with her own life after leaving school and Jim was always out fishing and playing with his mates. Their mum tried to give Bobby attention but, at fifty-one, and still taking in work as a seamstress to make ends meet, she was always tired and a hard life had made her old before her time. And, of course, he didn't want his dad to notice him any more than he could possibly help.

With Bobby's mother a regular worshipper at the church, the new parish priest at Armadale, Father James McHugh, started taking an interest in him in his third year at the school. He was a kindly man from country Victoria, perceptive and with a good heart, who recognised that Bobby was struggling. He wasn't the easiest of mentors, however, with a tendency to be brusque and often quite curt with the small boys around him. But when Bobby turned eight, the priest invited him, together with his mate Brian, to be an altar boy. Bobby, who'd been angling for such an entree, was delighted to be given such an important role. Even better, Father McHugh lent him a traditional black cassock and white cotta, the short version of the surplice, knowing his family wouldn't be able to afford the right clothes.

'We were poor, and we should never really have been on the altar,' he says. 'How I got there, I don't know. I suppose I learnt over time to become more pushy. If you think you're on to something, you go for it. Our Maguire motto is "*Justitia et fortitudo invincibilia sunt*" – "Justice and fortitude are invincible", or "Virtue and perseverance are invincible". Our family has always been a bit like that – pushy in the cause of what's right.'

As an altar boy, he quickly found he liked the regime and the responsibilities, and relished being, for the first time, a part of a team. Being brought up a Catholic with his mum still a devout follower, he didn't think too much about the religious side of things; he absorbed the faith and its beliefs almost by osmosis. He found he enjoyed serving at the altar, though, not only as a Catholic rite but also for the mateship with his fellow altar boys, its sense of occasion and the way, for the first time in his life, it made him feel important.

Even better, Father McHugh also offered him a regular job, for five shillings a week, cleaning up the church grounds and the toilet block out the back. Bobby gratefully accepted. Never having had any money of his own, he saw it as a great chance not only to help out his mum at home, but also to buy himself occasional treats, like cakes and comics. The priest always made a point too of inviting Bobby along on outings he arranged for the altar boys, such as picnics at Ferntree Gully and the football, to watch his team Richmond, paying the cost out of his own pocket for the boy. It was excellent timing. Bobby's sister Kathleen still took him out occasionally, but she'd started courting an American serviceman stationed in Melbourne and she suddenly didn't have as much time for her little brother anymore. Bobby quietly shifted his barracking loyalties from Kathleen's Essendon to Father McHugh's Richmond.

The war finally ended in Australia twelve days before Bobby's eleventh birthday, with Japan signing an unconditional surrender. There was jubilation throughout Australia, and Melburnians flocked into the streets in displays of spontaneous celebration. It was a Sunday and Bobby and Brian had been playing in the trenches in the afternoon; they emerged to see everyone running out of their houses, with women waving their aprons and shouting, 'The war's over! The war's over!' Children were given the next day off school, and there were thanksgiving services at the church. Everyone hoped that life would be easier now. And it was, for a time. But for Bobby and his family, that time was all too short.

The year 1946 started out well. School was proving more and more enjoyable, Bobby was coming out of his shell a little more, and he was beginning to get a sense of having a life of his own. On 30 June, he had his confirmation at the church at the school, presided over by the formidable Irish-born Archbishop of Melbourne Daniel Mannix, one of the most powerful figures in Australia at the time. It was a fittingly grand occasion, which his mother and Kathleen attended. At the service, the boys' sponsor placed a hand on each candidate's shoulder, for a physical sense of support. The message was that the youngster is leaving childhood to go out into the wider world but they are not alone. It was a message Bobby treasured.

For later that same year, his world started coming crashing down around his ears. His 21-year-old sister Kathleen, already grieving that her American boyfriend had been sent away to Sydney, fell ill. She took time off from her telephony job, but steadily grew sicker and sicker. Bobby remembers her quoting from her favourite ballad, 'Danny Boy': '. . . the pipes, the pipes are calling, From glen to glen, and down the mountain side. The summer's gone, and all the flowers are dying, 'Tis you, 'tis you must go and I must bide.'

She was finally diagnosed with 'galloping consumption', a particularly virulent form of TB. The family wondered if she'd caught it from the mouthpieces of the phones on the switchboard where she worked. Only a month later, she was dead. Two days after her death, a letter arrived from her American sweetheart. He'd been diagnosed with TB in hospital, he wrote. She should get herself checked out too.

The death of his favourite sister left a massive vacuum in Bobby's life. He was devastated to lose the one person he was closest to in the world but, with the other members of his family all so consumed by their own grief, he had few places to turn. 'Kathleen was a beautiful young woman, struck down in the prime of her life,' he says. 'As a kid, she'd held my hand and taken me out, and had always looked after me. She was always there for me. When she was gone, it was a huge shock.'

Bobby rallied as best he could. He saw his mother become older and frailer almost overnight and he watched his father, always a heavy smoker, grow sick and then decline even deeper into his alcoholic haze. He could see his own future as a stark choice. On the one hand, he could give in, drop out and act up. There were plenty of temptations everywhere; lots of boys his own age, with a lot more going for them, were drifting into a life of crime. He saw he could easily become, like them, a victim of circumstance. Alternatively, he realised he could shape up and try to take charge of his own destiny as best he could, to become proactive in his life.

'I think after losing Kathleen, that's when I started to learn that I couldn't depend on other people to look after me,' he says. 'I had to learn to look out for myself, to take responsibility myself for my own life.' It was the early stirrings of his so-called 'Do-It-Yourself, Bring Your Own' philosophy that was to shape his viewpoint as he got older.

A lot of the kids he knew were becoming what were termed 'juvenile delinquents'. Many were fatherless and grandfatherless because of the war, and had little discipline left in their homes, with their mothers and siblings preoccupied with their own lives and worries. As a result, many were getting into trouble and being taken away from their families and sent to tough boys' homes in an attempt to instil some restraint and control into them. He decided that was a fate he wanted to avoid at all costs, however miserable his own home life. So having just turned twelve, he set out to make sure he and his mates stayed on the straight and narrow.

'For some reason or another, sparked by some temporary unease in postwar society, we didn't want to evolve into juvenile delinquents,' he says. 'I saw so many little kids go off like bottles of stale milk. People just didn't expect much of us. So we came to some kind of a collective awareness that we, as little boys, may well end up in trouble like other little boys who we must have been hearing about, and were determined not to end up like them. So Brian and I and a couple of others banded together to do something about it. We made a pact: we weren't going over to the darkness, we weren't going to segue into delinquency. We must have realised that you can alter the ways things are, but that you're not going to be able to do that just by wishful thinking. We had to take action, we had to take charge of our own destinies, rather than leave it to others.

'We decided if we had a place to go, a place to meet up, then we'd be able to sit and talk, play games, and have somewhere safe to gather and stay out of trouble. I think to understand a lot of my life since, you only have to go back to those two little boys in primary school.'

So with their plan in place, Bobby approached Father McHugh and asked him if they could use the parish recreational room at the back of the presbytery to gather and play games. But the priest turned them down flat. He said the adults used it to play billiards, and the rules didn't allow children. He suggested they ask the Archdiocese in Melbourne for a room instead. At first, Bobby was crushed by the knockback. Then he felt appalled that the church seemed to care more about its rules and its property than the parishioners it was supposed to serve – a criticism he was to make regularly in his later life, too. But he used the experience to steel his resolve instead, and come up with a solution himself.

Bobby thought long and hard about the quandary, and finally drew up a plan B. 'We knew we could have done better with a place where more little boys could have gone and played games or at least have a refuge, but we now knew that wasn't possible,' he says. 'So we then did a big BYO and DIY: fortunately there was another little boy whose parents said we could meet in their front room. So we met in there.'

It was surprising enough that a young lad and his mates would take such a novel lead in organising their lives, but what came next startled onlookers. Rather than just getting together a couple of times a week in the safety of that front room, they instead worked at hatching even more ambitious plans to keep themselves on the straight and narrow. Eventually, they came up with the idea of forming a football and cricket team and organising a series of social matches to keep them all occupied.

'We set up our own teams and even designed our own caps and put little metal shields on them,' says Bobby. 'Our cricket team we named the Prahran Rovers. Then we went around the pubs and arranged matches against their social clubs. We ended up playing a few matches. We were probably all eleven, twelve and thirteen, and we lost most of them, but we had a place and an identity. We enjoyed it, and it kept us out of mischief. I think the moral of our story was that everything starts with one, then to continue you need one plus one and so on. When you're kids, you also need an understanding adult to provide you with some kind of resources, like a place to meet.'

It was the youngster's first taste of organising other people, and of asking for help to get a task done, and he proved surprisingly good at it. 'I think that was really the start of my social activism,' he says. 'You can't leave it to your peer group; you have to take responsibility. You're the one who can decide whether to turn toxic and go to hell, or work out how to make life better and go well.'

The Prahran Rovers eventually pulled up stumps when Bobby grew too busy to keep organising games. As well as school, he was also doing a paper round both morning and night to earn extra cash. That might have been tough enough normally, but he didn't even own a bicycle. Instead, he'd run from house to house, to try to finish it before the school bell rang in the morning, and to get home in time for tea in the evening.

For Bobby's final year of primary school, he transferred to the primary school attached to the Christian Brothers' College (CBC) at St Kilda, a well-regarded Catholic secondary college for boys established by men of the Christian Brothers' order, who left their homes in Ireland in the nineteenth century to serve and educate the children of Irish migrants. He adjusted well but just as life seemed to be settling down, the 13-year-old faced a fresh blow.

That year, 1948, his dad James died, lung cancer finally claiming his life. It felt like another tragedy, and a release, all at the same, perplexing time. 'Daddy was no good, a drunk, poor old Jim, but a very talented man,' says Bob. 'I never could work him out, and I never understood why he carried on drinking even though it was causing his family so much hardship. I wanted to understand, but he was gone before I had a chance.'

It's a confusion that's haunted him his whole life. Says his niece Peta, 'His dad James gave everyone a tough time but both my mother and Bob really loved him. Despite everything, there must have been something about him. They both had a lot of affection for him. I suppose at the end of the day, he was still their father, whether he was a good father or bad.'

But even while Bobby was struggling to understand the loss, fate had yet another cruel hand to deal. His mentor Father McHugh had been working hard at the primary school, coaching basketball on a court he had laid for the children and planning a major expansion for the school, making moves to buy another property nearby. Throughout all his activities, however, he was always careful to make time for Bobby, to make sure he was coping with the deaths of his sister and father, and was managing in the face of his mother's poor health. But in March 1949, Father McHugh went into hospital with a minor illness. A few days later, completely unexpectedly, and in only his very early sixties, his heart gave out.

For Bobby, it seemed everyone he'd ever loved, and anyone who'd ever cared for him, was being snatched away.

At home, things were also changing fast for Bobby. His sister Eileen had married her beau Jim O'Dea and left home, and his brother Jim now did the same, with his new wife Betty. Bobby was left at the house in Prahran all alone with his mum. It could have been a good time for them both, being able to reconnect without the shadow of his father over them both. But it was too late.

His mum Annie had now turned sixty, but was a very old sixty, worn out by all the years of abuse, stress over money troubles, hard work and, of course, losing two of her children and then her husband. 'She took it very, very hard, losing Marguerite and then Kathleen,' says her niece Molly Langman. 'I think it really affected her health.' She had a stroke that left her partially paralysed down the left side of her body, unable to move her left arm and one side of her mouth, and Bobby became her carer. Legacy, the charity for dependants of former servicemen who were having a hard time, helped them out with money for school fees in the light of James's service in both the merchant navy and the Royal Navy during World War I. In addition, Jim and Betty pitched in to pay half the rent on the house. And Bobby did all he could for his mum, in between his paper rounds and moving from the primary class of CBC into the main college. But the strain began to tell on him too.

The CBC, with around 500 boys, was a much bigger school than he'd been used to and, often in classes of up to seventy, if you fell behind, it was almost impossible to catch up. In addition, many of the boys had taken extra coaching to win government scholarships to the college to help boost its funds and, without that, Bobby found himself at an immediate disadvantage. 'I'd never heard of French or Latin,' he says. 'What's more, with the maths lessons and all the algebra and geometry, and all the sciences they did, I couldn't tell what the hell they were doing. It felt like a complete mystery.'

With all the new subjects, and probably still in shock from the loss of his sister, his dad and the priest in such quick succession, he ended up failing Year 9. He was told to repeat. Luckily for him, a sympathetic lay teacher, Jack Johnston, offered him some extra tuition, free and in his own spare time, which made all the difference. 'He gave me a second chance, and I took it,'

Bob says. 'The next year, I went from boiled lollies to chocolates. I ended up dux, and in top place in English.'

He was still a very quiet boy, however, subdued and a bit of a loner. One of his teachers, Brother Leo Griffin, only twenty-nine at the time he first met the boy and known for having a scholarly, gentle manner – unlike some of the more strident brothers – kept a kindly eye on him. 'He was very quiet and very meek,' he says. 'He showed absolutely no sign of how he was to become later! But he was a bright student and tended towards the literary subjects. He was also friendly and cooperative. We used to have trouble with cleaners so we'd often give him a broom and he'd help us to sweep the school. He seemed to have a dysfunctional family and was lonely and liked hanging around after school rather than going home. He'd clean or play handball. It felt like he had little to go home to.'

As a result, Bobby tried to make the most of his schooldays. At his primary school they'd discovered he had a good voice, and now he found himself in increasing demand for the St Mary's choir. With that voice growing deeper and richer all the time, the man running the choir, Brother John Murtagh, frequently asked him to take time off his lessons to take part in practice sessions and then performances.

'All the rest of the boys had soprano voices and no bass to go with the choir,' says Brian. 'But Bob's voice was deep and so we needed him. They'd make me stand next to him to try and make my voice lower. We kept sending for him and he says these days that's why he didn't end up with such a good education; he was too busy singing for us!'

The choir became well known for its performances, and

Bobby ended up taking part in a number of eisteddfods and choral concerts around Melbourne itself. He even took part in the opera *Hansel and Gretel* at the city's iconic Princess Theatre. 'It was considered one of the best boys' choirs in Australia at the time,' says Brian. 'And Bob played an important part in it. Our "Ave Maria" would put people in tears.' It was Bobby's first taste of performing before an audience and, much to his surprise, he found he liked it very much.

Still at school, he also joined the school-based Australian Army Cadets, with its lessons in navigation and orienteering, ceremonial drill, radio communications and basic bush skills. After all those hours playing soldiers in the trenches, it felt excitingly real. He also went away to camp. 'After the war, it was a way of militarising kids,' he says now. 'You'd be hard-put to talk your way out of it, but it was considered a school honour to be in the cadets. I enjoyed it. It got me out, as I'd never really been anywhere or done much in my life, and it was always interesting to me to see boys and young men all working together as a team. I was always attracted to teamwork.'

Bobby was at last coming into his own. Previously quiet and introverted, becoming dux of his class and doing so well with the choir had given him a much-needed boost in confidence. Being expected to give orders in the cadets was also helping to sharpen his leadership skills. He started playing cricket and football at school, and was making good friends, too. As well as Brian, he'd become very friendly with Paul Garland, another boy in his year whose father was a well-known Labor politician. He'd often visit his home for tea – although always arriving late in a habit that would continue throughout his life – and listen to the political debates going on among Paul's parents and their friends. He found it all quite thrilling.

Paul was much more worldly than Bobby, and far more confident and outgoing, but the pair got on well. Brother Leo looked on approvingly at the blossoming friendship, feeling Paul would be a good influence and help prise Bobby a little further out of his shell. 'Paul was a lot more articulate and Bob was much more quiet and behind the scenes,' he says. 'I don't think Bob had been brought up with the tradition of talking – although it's hard to appreciate that now in the light of what he later became! He was also very compliant, which isn't how you'd describe him now, either. But then, Paul was the intellectual, a great scholar, and he impressed people with his intellect. Bob looked up to him, and some of that rubbed off.'

The two boys had similarly wicked senses of humour, although Paul's was, at the time, much louder than Bobby's. 'I think Bob was a bit of a late developer in a way,' says Paul. 'At school, because of his domestic situation, he didn't have much freedom to do anything and he was still trying to get his hormones together. We were very different in some ways, though. He was into the cadets while I only joined to make a mockery of them. I was the captain of the school, one year, and I'd send him to dances. I don't know if it did any good or not, but it probably made him more aware of the female of the species and helped him relate to them.' With the school being such a major influence on their lives, the two boys even started talking about becoming Christian Brothers together.

But just as life seemed to be assuming a rosier hue for Bobby, once again it all fell in a heap. His mum, who'd been poorly for some time and had gone to a convalescent home to help recover her strength, returned home even sicker. She had a congenital heart weakness – something her children were later to discover they'd all inherited too – and now also had trouble breathing and was always tired. The diagnosis was pleurisy. Sometimes it seemed to others that the only thing keeping her alive was worry over what might happen to her youngest son were she to give up the ghost.

She was well aware of his idea of perhaps becoming a Christian Brother, but wanted him to be sure he'd be doing the right thing. He'd led a pretty sheltered life, going only to Catholic schools, working in his first job for the church and being befriended by the priest and nun outside his home. His mum dearly wanted him to have some idea of life beyond the rigours of a religious vocation.

'I remember her asking me to look out for Bobby after she'd gone,' says Bob's brother Jim. 'If he did decide to become a priest, she wanted him to do something first, to work in another job for a year to get a taste of the world before the seminary. I said I'd make sure that happened.' She became sicker and sicker and, at last, towards the end of 1950, when she was just sixty-one and Bobby had turned fifteen, she died.

Bobby was absolutely heartbroken. In just a few short years, he felt he'd been robbed of everyone he'd ever loved. And now the future stretched before him, empty, uncertain and desperately lonely. 'I felt completely alone,' he says. 'It felt like everyone had left me.' He wondered whether he'd ever survive. But summoning every last vestige of his courage and stoicism, he managed to help his mother to the very end, serving as the altar boy at her funeral.

4

Behind the Eight Ball

Bobby Maguire felt himself sinking lower and lower. He was struggling to breathe; his chest was hurting with the effort. The water was closing in over his head until he was completely submerged. His eyes were stinging. He felt sure he was going to die.

He saw a religious icon appear over him. He heard a voice from somewhere far away. And he had just one thought: 'Bugger it, I was supposed to play cricket on Sunday.' Then the next thing he knew, he was being pulled roughly from the water and heaved onto the tiled floor by the pool. It was then he remembered that he'd fallen into the swimming pool, that he couldn't swim and that he'd hit his head on the side on the way down.

He was sixteen and it was yet another brush with death. 'But it just wasn't my turn,' he says bluntly. Although he was feeling utterly bereft at the loss of his loved ones, he knew it wasn't time for him to give up and fade away. 'Once your father's dead, your mother's dead and your house is gone, you can become feral. But instead, you have to start looking after yourself. I didn't have much in the way of role models. I didn't have much support. I had nothing else to run on, except my merits. I knew that I had to do everything I could for myself to make sure I came out of this.'

It was Bobby's last year at school yet he still wasn't sure what he wanted to do next. Other kids had mums and dads to guide them, to push them into jobs or advise them on careers. Despite having his sister Eileen and brother Jim, he still felt very much on his own.

When his mother died, Eileen and her husband Jim had moved back into the family home in Prahran to look after him, but it was an arrangement that was to last only three months. 'He was brought to our doorstep one day because he'd been doing something he shouldn't have,' says Betty, the wife of Bobby's brother Jim. 'He was a good kid normally but he'd been sent on an errand and he'd gone to a shop where there was a pinball machine, and he'd spent her money on that instead. Eileen wasn't impressed. She didn't have much money, and she couldn't afford money being spent like that. So Bobby's stay with them was short-lived.'

It was a rare bout of childish mischief but it had dire consequences. Bobby was suddenly homeless. As a result, he moved in with Jim and Betty instead, at their unit in South Yarra. Later, they bought a house in Glen Iris and Bobby came with them there too. 'He was very easy to get along with,' says Betty, who was just seven years older. 'He was rather quiet and a bit shy but he had a terrific sense of humour and could be a bit cynical. We didn't see too much of each other, though. I was at work all day and Jim worked and had an extra job pencilling for bookmakers, so I'd make the meal in the evening. And at weekends, he was often off playing cricket with the church, and we had a dog and Bobby used to take him for a walk. But I always felt sorry for Bobby. He was only a young lad but he'd had a hard time, and never had much fun.'

Because of the eight-year age gap between Bobby and Jim, the two brothers didn't have too much in common and Jim went away for big chunks of time with the air force as well, effectively missing out on most of his childhood. 'But he was with us for quite a time while he was doing his schooling,' Jim says. 'During that time, Betty was like a second mother to him. If it wasn't for her, I don't know what the score would have been for Bobby.'

He was now doing well at school, a conscientious student. Steered away from maths and sciences, he developed a fondness for literature, language, Latin and the classics. 'In Year 12, there was plenty to stimulate you,' he says. 'I think that's when the poor buggers who were teaching us set fire to my imagination. I'd been diverted from science as I'd been no good at it, but that last year provided me with a good education. It was enough.'

Personality-wise, Bobby was still quite reserved, with no hint of any of his later rebelliousness. He was a passable sportsman, too, playing football and cricket in his house teams. He also loved being in the Army Cadets and was turning out to be pretty good at it, attaining the rank of Cadet Lieutenant, and winning a trophy as Best Instructor of 1950. On Fridays, he'd come to school in his cadet uniform on the train, and he liked the feeling it gave him of belonging to an organisation.

His old teacher, Brother Leo Griffin, felt the brother taking the cadets, Brother William Lewis, a man with a very strong personality, was a good influence. 'He was in charge of both the cadets and sport, and he could do a lot of things and I think Bob looked up to him,' he says. 'He learned a lot from him. To Brother Lewis, nothing was ever an obstacle; he could overcome everything. That was a very good example for a boy to have. I think Bob took that lesson very much to heart, and he later managed to adopt that kind of persona too.'

Like any boy, he was also fascinated by the guns. At school, he remembers there being racks and racks of 0.22 calibre rifles, and the handball court during the day was converted into a shooting range, with a big wall of wooden cladding behind the target, backed by another wall of steel to stop bullets flying through. At Williamstown, on the other side of the bay, there was a purpose-built firing range, where teams of boys could also practise with a Vickers machine gun or Bren guns.

'The Vickers was one of my specialties; the other was the Bren gun,' he says. 'It was good fun. It was also an opportunity for an emotionally repressed boy like me to let off some steam. It helped build up your confidence, having to yell out, "Attention! *Attention!*" in public. We were all in pecking orders and I was quiet, but standing up in front of the younger ones, articulating about the weaponry and explaining how to do different things, meant you had to come out of your shell. We'd go away on camp too, which was good, and I'm sure

I can remember taking a .303 British rifle home with me.'

At school, he'd also become a prefect and was captain of his house. 'God knows how that happened,' he says now. 'We were poor, and that kind of thing didn't usually happen for people who were that poor because people tend to bully the poor, they sense a weakness and go for it. But I was being given responsibility both as an officer in the cadets and as a prefect in the classroom. I liked it. It felt good. It started giving me a sense of self-esteem, which is something I'd never really had before.'

Bobby Maguire still had no clear idea of what he wanted to do after school. He continued to toy with the idea of becoming a Christian Brother, particularly since the lack of financial support seemed an almost insurmountable obstacle for any other career choice. He'd done well enough in the cadets to be considered a good candidate for the Royal Military College in Duntroon, the Australian Army's officer-training establishment, and he dearly wanted to be a soldier, but he had no way on earth of paying his living expenses while he trained. By the same token, he'd been offered a scholarship to go to university, but again, he knew he simply didn't have the funds.

'Poverty as a boy meant I couldn't do anything or go anywhere, and it was the same story at the end of school,' he says. 'All things being equal, I think I would have gone to Duntroon, but you've got no hope because you're behind the eight ball. You've got no family, you've got no stability and you've got no dough. So even if you took the Commonwealth scholarship for your fees for university, where would you end up? Where would you have lived? How would you have paid for food? How could you buy books? It would have been impossible. And while I was all right at English, I was no good at maths and science. Uni mightn't have done me any good.'

The other option was to join a religious order. He'd been brought up by his mother, the priests who'd helped him over the years and his school to believe that a religious vocation conferred a certain amount of respectability, kudos and prestige. He'd won the school prize in religious studies and knew that path in life would be a much less costly choice. He wouldn't even need to make a vow of poverty, he thought caustically to himself; he'd been living that already his whole life. But when a recruiter from the seminary came to visit his school, at first he flat-out refused to see him. 'I made it pretty clear to the headmaster that I wasn't interested,' he says.

Slowly, however, he began to reconsider. His tough childhood had left him with a highly developed social conscience, and he liked the idea of public service. Maybe if he went into the Church, he'd be able to do some good for those who were similarly struggling.

There'd been no dramatic moment of hearing God, or experiencing a revelation about the need to follow a religious vocation. Instead, he'd simply absorbed Catholicism his whole life. 'Religion is caught, not taught, like the saying goes,' says Bob. 'It's not only biological. You inherit an ethos of Catholicism. It's not necessarily the doctrine; that has to answer to the ethos, rather than the other way around. The bishops might ask you to suspend your ethos and just admire the doctrines, but that's asking too much. You can't live off fairy floss on its own.

'Over the years, I'd caught Catholicism from my mother, from Eileen, from Kathleen. You acquire certain advisories from people. My brother was probably "a-religious"; he would have advised to beware the priests and clericalism. But the others, as well as the priests and the nuns, the Presentation Sisters, they would have had a big influence on me. I've met good people all my life. The teacher who helped me when I failed that first year, he identified something worth investing in, and that's what I've continued to do all my life. I'm made an altar boy, so I invest in that. If they make you chief altar boy, you have to invest. If they make you an Army Cadet captain, you invest. I've never believed in sinecures. If there's an opportunity, you make the most of it, and invest.'

When the religious recruiters came round a second time, he marked the box with the B, indicating an interest in becoming a Christian Brother, like his teachers at school: men whose mission was chiefly about educating the young. His mate Paul Garland, however, tried to talk him out of it. 'I thought he shouldn't go that way,' says Paul. He'd decided already that he wanted to become a priest, and Bob started to think seriously about maybe taking that step instead.

'I'd already indicated to the Christian Brothers' recruiting officer that one minute I wanted to be a Christian Brother, but the next I said, "Take my name off the list and put P down for Priest,"' he says. 'Paul was going to the seminary, and I thought I might as well go too. He was the same age as me, but he was a firebrand and a social activist. The only time I went anywhere interesting was with him to Labor Party meetings; everything else I did was pretty boring. But it wasn't just because he was going. I had this belief in DIY, and I wanted to work towards making the world a fairer place, to help people who were up against it get ahead. It was also serendipity. It meant I'd have a home, and food, for the next few years.'

Yet even if it was going to be the most economical career option, Bob still needed funds to get by. Here, his sister Eileen came up trumps. She contacted his old Black Rock mentor, Sister Claude. The nun was delighted to hear that her young protégé was thinking of entering the priesthood.

'My sister would have said, "Look, this bloke wants to go into the seminary and we can't afford it,"' Bob says. 'So Sister Claude, being an activist nun, would have said, "Don't worry, I remember you lot down at Black Rock and I remember Father John Gorry who was the parish priest had a few quid, so I'll ring him up." So she did. And Father Gorry, who was by then parish priest at St Kilda West, said he'd pay whatever fees had to be paid. I think if you were poor, you got away with half fees at the seminary, but that still left some to pay. Then of course you had all the extras, the clothes, like the cassock or soutane – the black dress thing – and incidentals like books. It was basic but it does all cost a few quid. So when he said he'd help me out, the deal was sealed, so to speak.'

But first, his brother Jim and Eileen had to think about his mum's wish that if he were ever to decide to go to the seminary, he should have a go at another job first. He shouldn't go straight from school, with no experience of any other life. It was a wish she'd repeated as she lay on her deathbed.

Bobby was surprised to hear of it, but agreed to go along with what she'd wanted. He didn't have any idea of where to look for work, but Jim quickly stepped in. Working at the wharves as a customs officer, he knew plenty of people, and organised Bobby a job as a cooper's assistant, helping make, and attach, the binding hoops that go around barrels. Bobby worked on Victoria Docks for the next three months. He quite enjoyed the physical work and the camaraderie, although he was anxious about what he should drink when the wharfies invited him to the pub after work, and asked Betty for advice.

'I told him to ask for something like lemon squash,' she says. 'So after that, he'd go into the pub with them, but he'd always order a soft drink.' Although he left after just a short time, nothing like the year his mother had hoped for, it was the start of a lifelong association with the maritime unions.

Then, in 1953, at the age of just eighteen, Bobby was driven down to Werribee, 35 kilometres south-west of Melbourne's CBD, along the road to Geelong. There, he politely thanked the parish priest of Prahran who'd given him and Paul the lift, and walked quickly across the entrance to Corpus Christi College, the Catholic seminary that would be his home for the next eight years.

5

The Cavalry Arrives

At the time Bobby entered the seminary, the Catholic Church was on the precipice of an era of momentous change.

The early 1950s was the last period of calm before the storm. Catholicism still meant mass said in Latin, the priest standing with his back to the congregation, rosary beads and hats and gloves worn to church. But the world outside was changing fast, the seeds of the coming cultural, social and religious revolution were steadily being sown and pressure was growing on Catholicism to face up to those challenges of modern life.

The war was over and a new prosperity had flowed into most of the western world, and into Australia in particular. At the same time, women were agitating for greater rights, new technologies were beginning to transform daily life and the Cold War was in full swing. The Australian Catholic Church also saw any advance in communism as a real threat, accusing the trade union movement and the Australian Labor Party of being unduly influenced by communist sympathisers. It was a charge first levelled in Melbourne and was later to lead to a bitter split between many right-wing Catholics and the party. At the same time, the Church was busy fielding the pressures of new ideas like the quests for equal rights, the peace movement, birth control and the rise of liberation theology, with its emphasis on social justice and combating poverty.

At the Werribee seminary in 1953, everyone could feel the growing tension between the old ways and the new ideas. Among some, there was enormous apprehension about what might be on its way. Among others, and for Bobby in particular, there was enormous excitement at being part of a Church in the throes of real change. He'd entered the college almost reluctantly, resigned to a life of almost last resort, a quiet and pious trainee priest. He'd even, in the light of how his father had been, signed up to the Pioneer Total Abstinence Association of the Sacred Heart, an Irish organisation for Roman Catholic teetotallers – although, hedging his bets, only until the age of twenty-five.

But the discussions now constantly taking place infected him and his friends with a passion for their faith that might previously have been considered a touch lacking. Sensing change was in the wind, he became brighter, keener, energised. 'I suppose it was then that I started to feel a part of it,' he says. 'You grow up a Catholic and it becomes an automatic part of you, but now I started really beginning to embrace it.'

Yet it still wasn't easy. For Bobby and the other newcomers, the rigid discipline and innate conservatism of the seminary was still in sharp contrast with many of the radical ideas of the time. The daily routine and teachings had changed little since the Jesuits had first drawn up their program for training priests some 300 years before. With all theology texts and study in Latin, the seminarians plodded slowly through a regime of constant prayer, Bible study, daily masses, spiritual 'direction', theology and philosophy tuition, confession, long periods of silence, and a communal hymn to end each day. 'It was boring, boring,' says Bob bluntly today, regularly referring to it as 'The Cemetery'. 'It was deathly dull. It was like a massive overdose of Catholicism. I don't even remember them ever even talking to us about celibacy. The subject just didn't come up, and it never occurred to us. That may sound strange to outsiders, but the question was never even raised. The seminary was very quiet. But it was a pretty place, you had to give them that.'

The seminary was certainly stunning. An elegant Italianate building framed by stately arches on 1000 acres, it was once the stately home of wealthy pastoralists, and the largest residence in Victoria. The Melbourne Archbishop Daniel Mannix had bought it in 1922, thinking the mansion would be perfect as a seminary, while the surrounding farmland could be worked by the students to enable it to become self-sufficient – which never quite happened. The estate eventually closed as a seminary in 1973, and is today a museum maintained by the National Trust, with one of its rooms recreated as a seminary dormitory as it would have been for the very first students in the 1920s.

But back in Bobby's time, it was still a very serious place of intense study and quiet reflection for its 131 students. There was a rule of silence during recreation time that could be broken only if absolutely necessary. And if a student had no alternative but to utter a few words, they were ordered to do so as briefly and as quietly as possible.

If they wanted to buy a newspaper or a book or to eat anywhere outside the college, they had to apply for permission, and all letters had to pass through the college post. Inside, they always had to salute ordained priests and, if they went for a walk, they had to be accompanied by at least two others. Even holiday times were regulated. When they left the college, it was a requirement to report to their local priest and when they returned, they were expected to bring with them a letter from him attesting to their good behaviour.

But the feeling of coming change in the air kept Bobby going. Archbishop Mannix had established a scholarship to send Catholic university students overseas to study, and many returned to talk at Werribee of what was happening elsewhere. Clergy from churches in other countries were also invited to lecture, and they spoke about the persecution of communist governments, new philosophies gaining ground on other continents and alternative ways of doing things.

'They had blokes coming in to the seminary all the time,' Bobby says. 'I learnt more from people coming in and talking than from the classes. We were lucky at that time; they called in people from all over the world, especially in the second half of the course. We were exposed to a breadth of thinking from all over the world, from America, the Philippines, Africa . . . everything except Roman! At the seminary, we were pretty convinced of the fundamentals, the substance, Catholicism's core business, but we would have been healthily sceptical about the cosmetics of Catholicism.'

His good friend Paul Garland was similarly cynical about some aspects of Catholicism, but excited about the changes being forecast for others. 'Personally, I think that seminary was probably the best in the world at the time, because we were all being prepared for the changes even before they happened,' he says. 'The rector at Werribee, Father Charles Mayne, was a far-seeing fellow, and he wanted us to be role-determining rather than role-determined. We had all these international speakers in who told us how the world was changing, and how religion was changing in response. We learnt about the social issues, the psychology, the scriptures. It was a time for positive renewal. Of course, some of the bishops insisted that the conservatives talk to us as well, but we learnt at the same time about alternative interpretations.'

A number of the trainee priests, Bobby and Paul among them, took to reading widely, including critics of orthodox Catholic theology alongside the recommended texts. Bobby read avidly too about Catholics who'd become well known for their social activism among the poor, homeless and hungry. Among those was devout American Catholic Dorothy Day, who was becoming increasingly well known for her social justice campaigns. She had a very orthodox and traditional sense of Catholic morality, but a progressive attitude on social and economic rights, working with another activist to set up the Catholic Worker movement, which led to a series of homes for the poor to live together communally. Another was Canadian Jean Vanier, a Catholic philosopher turned theologian, humanitarian and the founder of L'Arche, an international organisation that creates communities where people with developmental disabilities and those who assist them share life together.

Along the way, he also became a keen follower of the actions of Abbé Pierre, a French Catholic priest and hero of the World War II Resistance. He returned to the headlines in 1954 when, during an extremely cold winter, he made an impassioned plea on Radio Luxembourg, and through the pages of the newspaper *Le Figaro*, imploring citizens to come to the aid of homeless people who were freezing to death on the streets. His cry for help raised an astounding donation of 500 million francs, and the founding of the international Emmaus movement, to help the homeless, poor and refugees worldwide.

Not surprisingly, he has remained a hero of Bob's to this day.

In 1958, the changes everyone had been talking about were finally signalled to be on their way. The newly elected Pope John Paul XXIII had been intended to be a caretaker of the faith but proved instead to be an agent of massive change. He invited eighteen cardinals to attend a service in Rome at St Paul's Outside the Walls, and then called a global Church Council, putting everything up for debate: liturgy (the prayers, songs and mass); the role of the laity, with the idea of moving the congregation from being spectators to being participants; the role of the Church in the political and social world; and religious freedom and respect for other faiths.

His decision may have caught many by surprise, including

the Vatican hierarchy, but he'd felt from his own experience that it was time for the Church to take stock of its position in the world of the mid-twentieth century. He knew of the already existing movements to push the Church to modernise, and allowed them, for the first time, to be freely debated at the highest levels of the worldwide Church.

The series of councils, Vatican II, that was to end up taking place from 1962 to 1965, bringing 3000 cardinals, bishops, clergy and religious workers from around the world to Rome, was to become the most significant event of the century for the Catholic Church. The Pope was to die in June 1963, two years before the talks ended, but they continued without him. By the end, Church leaders had created a new definition of the Church, and a new way for the Church to behave in the world. The Old Testament 'People of God' became the defining image and so much changed, including the way in which priests ran mass, facing their congregation, the service no longer being held in Latin and parishioners being invited to the altar to read the Scripture. Rather than simply helping the poor, the Church debated looking at the causes of poverty instead, advocating for social and political change, encouraging inter-faith relationships, recommending religious freedoms and allowing the dress code for the clergy to be relaxed.

For progressive Catholics, Vatican II was a time of great excitement and expectation. For others, it caused immense alarm, with the loss of treasured traditions, age-old certainties and familiar, and much-loved, customs and rituals. For Bobby, it was the making of the man. 'Vatican II came and saved us,' he says. 'It was like the cavalry had arrived. I think I was wandering around in my adolescent years, all enthusiasm looking for a cause. And then, thank you Jesus, that cause presents itself. The Church enters the modern world, and you realised how undernourished you'd been. It felt like it was no more us and them, just we.'

Those Vatican II changes had a profound effect on Bobby's faith, his outlook on life and even his personality. Almost overnight he went from a quiet, shy young man, haunted by the poverty and loneliness of his youth and overshadowed by the intellect of his best friend Paul, to a trainee priest who felt the world had suddenly opened up infinite possibilities to him. He now determined to grab them with both hands and started to become much more outspoken, opinionated, loud and enterprising.

In his enthusiasm, Bobby embarked on a number of projects, writing long letters overseas to missionaries in far-flung parts of the world and circulating the replies around the class. The new skills he was learning in the classroom all the time also fed into his new leadership role. 'We started practising debating,' he says. 'We were forced to stand up and make a speech. That really helped my confidence, realising I could do that when I had to. There were a lot of us there in that priest factory and we tended to be very serious young men. They sent us down to spruikers' corner to preach,' he smiles. '"But there's no-one here," I said. "Attract them, you fool," they replied. So to survive, I turned myself into a bit of a clown. It was the only way I could compete with others who were brighter than me. And I thought if I can make others laugh, I'll get through it.'

He proved surprisingly good at it too. Vatican II, he felt, had given everyone permission to be much less reverent about the Church and its ways, and he delighted in becoming almost subversive in his attitude to its institutions. He discovered the shock value of making casual fun of previously hallowed customs and traditions. Other priests in training with him at the same time report that he'd often perform almost a stand-up comedy act in the seminary. 'He could command an audience any time,' says Father Tom Doyle, who entered the seminary behind him. 'He could be very funny. He was always a bit of a leader in the seminary. He was always a wordsmith and was funny and entertaining, and had a strong personality.'

With his new blossoming as a comedian, other outlets for tomfoolery materialised, too. The seminary had a proud tradition of the arts and the first year Bobby was there, he brought the house down when he took to the stage with a one-man comedy act in the gaps between the main show. Another year, the students put on a production of American musician Spike Jones's satirical take on the opera *Carmen*: 'Carmen Murdered'. Paul, the director, volunteered Bobby to be the star, and he ended up miming enthusiastically to the soundtrack. 'They said, "Don't put your daughter on the stage, Mrs Worthington,"' he quotes from the well-known song. 'But I went on and dressed up as Carmen Miranda, in a red dress, with fruit on my head. The Jesuits were highly intellectual, so I suppose the drama thing was a way of making my own mark.'

It was still early days, however, and testing those new freedoms sometimes caused problems. At one point, he even came close to quitting the seminary. In his third year, he was editor of its magazine and wrote a long piece debating some aspect of Catholicism. One of his teachers took angry exception to it. 'I got called in and spoken to,' he reports. 'I ended up saying that if this is as bad as you say it is, I should be told, and I'd go home. If it wasn't as bad, then it was a trivial offence, and for God's sake, stop! Don't beat it up. You don't need a sledgehammer to kill an ant.'

Secular life was changing rapidly in Australia, too. On walks outside the seminary, there were regular glimpses. 'I remember, out on one of our compulsory walks, pressing my nose to the window of the hamburger joint Greasy Joe's to see television for the first time,' Bobby says. 'They were screening the 1956 Olympics in Melbourne that were happening just down the road. It all felt so strange. Imagine: in the priest factory, I'd not read a newspaper in six years.'

Students were allowed visitors, but Bobby, without parents or many close friends, had fewer than most. His brother Jim and his wife Betty did call in every few months, however. 'We'd go and see him when we could,' Betty says. 'We felt sorry for him. He didn't have much fun in his life. But he still had a certain sense of humour, and would pull funny faces, although he was nothing like as extroverted as he became later!'

His sister Eileen, her Jim, and their children also visited, and Eileen's daughter Peta Knights remembers looking forward to those times. 'I used to love going to the seminary,' she says. 'It was a beautiful building and lovely grounds and Uncle Bob was gorgeous, and was always so funny, and he'd come in and light up the room. We'd go three or four times a year and have a picnic on the grass with blankets on the ground and just run around and kick the footie and play, or sit and chat.

'Once a year there was a big fete to raise money and I remember Uncle Bob did some carpentry lessons and made Mum a coffee table once, and another time made her a table to put her sewing machine in, so it sat flush to the surface. But it wasn't that good . . .'

Bobby kept himself busy with other physical pursuits, too. The seminary kept bees, in order to raise funds with the sale of honey, and Bobby ended up becoming the regular keeper of the thirty hives. He liked being outside with them, and drew philosophical parallels with how they lived their lives, as the ultimate collective, and how humans managed their societies. Still a great fan of teamwork – a notion that could previously have been considered subversive within the strictly hierarchical structure of the Catholic Church – he liked watching them all working together for the greater good, and wondered if mankind would ever learn from them. Yet his sympathy for the underdog was never far away. When worker bees that refused to work were driven out of the hives to die, he'd always feel a pang of sorrow. 'There are so many lessons there for humanity,' he says. 'It's all about instinct, as against our free will. And they have a mob mentality too. If it's all good, then everyone benefits but if the queen goes bad, then everyone suffers.'

Apart from the beekeeping and growing some fruit, vegetables and herbs, the land around the seminary was mostly used for sporting activities. While there, Bobby played cricket, football and handball, and also tried his hand at umpiring – with varying degrees of success. Paul Garland remembers the time he spat the dummy while refereeing a football match when everyone kept disputing his decisions. Much to the players' amazement, he blew the whistle hard, tossed it over a hedge and then stomped off the oval. 'He'd just got sick of it,' he says. 'But I think it was good for the boys. It taught them a valuable lesson!'

He was perhaps more popular on the cricket pitch. Not a particularly good player, he volunteered early on to be wicket-keeper, always the role no-one much wanted. 'I did quite well at that,' he says. 'I thought I wasn't so good at batting or bowling, so I should do something that people had a real need for instead. I think I'm good at being a niche player, and have been one, really, all my life.'

During the holidays from the seminary, Bobby always worked. Although he received generous gifts of money from his old Black Rock supporters Father Gorry and Sister Claude to enable him to continue, he had to supplement that with what he could earn in his time off. He did a huge variety of different jobs in those periods, including working back on the wharves, delivering mail for the post office and running children's playgroups. 'Today, it seems quite astonishing that people felt back then that priests, and people training for the priesthood, were the best possible people to entrust their children to,' he says. 'But at that time, no-one thought anything of it. Parents trusted us, and we looked after their children on camps as well as we possibly could. I even received notes from people thanking me for a long time afterwards. I enjoyed the work, and it was fun helping those kids have holidays. It never occurred to anyone that anything untoward would ever happen.'

At that time, Bobby even went away for his first holiday. With Paul Garland and another friend, he caught a sea ferry to Tasmania and hitchhiked around the island. It had been Paul's idea. 'For both of us it was our first time away alone,' says Paul. 'We had a good time, travelling around. I like Tasmania and have been back a number of times. But I don't know that Bob has travelled much since.' He's right. It was Bobby's first holiday, and also his last.

Physical conditions at Werribee improved after 1959, when a second campus was built at Glen Waverley to accommodate extra students, and Bobby and Paul transferred there for their last year. By then, they were both keen to get out and get on with their chosen careers. But first, of course, they had their ordinations.

Bobby's ordination on 24 July 1960 became a great family occasion. His sister Eileen sewed him his first set of vestments for his ordination. 'She put so much love into those,' says Peta. 'I think everyone knew what a tough time he'd had in childhood, and this felt like a whole new start.' One of his mum's sisters, Sadie, gave him the classic *The Book of Scotland*, bound in tartan, a keepsake he treasures to this day.

And then the 25-year-old Bobby was finally ordained at St Patrick's Cathedral, in front of his family, his friends and the faithful Father Gorry and Sister Claude, under Bishop Justin Simonds, the Coadjutor Archbishop of Melbourne, who would three years later become the first Australian-born Catholic priest to reach the rank of archbishop and would begin implementing the reforms of Vatican II. Bobby's most vivid memories of the occasion were his first-ever taste of alcohol to celebrate, now his teetotal pledge had expired – a glass of the sparkling sweet white wine Porphyry Pearl at Russell Collins Cafeteria – and how bitterly cold the day was.

'You had to throw yourself onto the floor of the cathedral and it was so cold down there,' he says. 'From the word go, you were supposed to be prostrate. But you can't do much that's creative or innovative when you're lying flat on your belly. I couldn't wait to get up and get out and start work.'

6

A Forward Scout

By the time the newly minted Father Bob Maguire emerged from the seminary in 1960, preparations for the Vatican II series of seminars were well underway and there was a mood of excitement throughout the Catholic world. It felt like something historic was about to happen, only no-one yet knew quite what.

For Father Bob and his mates, it was a time of enormous promise. They were hoping not only that Pope John XXIII would throw open the windows of the Church to let in some fresh air, as he'd promised, but also that the doors would be permanently unbolted. They felt the news that nearly everything was up for debate and that other religions had been invited to come along as observers at the Council were very good signs.

It was in this atmosphere that Father Bob made his way back into the world after spending the last eight years 'locked away'. He'd entered the seminary as a quiet, anxious boy, subdued by years of poverty, insecurity and the grief of having lost everyone close to him. He emerged as a young man a great deal more confident about his place in the world, well read and eager to explore many of the new ideas that were being tossed around. At the same time, however, he was still keen to please his superiors, and eager to make a go of his role as a 26-year-old new priest in one of the most turbulent, and dynamic, decades in the western world.

The Church hierarchy immediately saw him as someone showing enormous promise: an energetic yet faithful and obedient servant they could place almost anywhere in the Melbourne Archdiocese. And so they did. For the next thirteen years, Father Bob was posted to no fewer than seven separate parishes to serve as an assistant to the incumbent priests, with a variety of jobs. He'd spent the whole of his youth moving around from house to house as the rent fell due; this felt like simply more of the same.

His first posting was to Belgrave, 45 kilometres east of Melbourne's CBD, known as the gateway to the Dandenong Ranges. It was a quiet, pretty spot where nothing much happened, and it was a gentle easing into the kind of life he might lead in the future. He felt himself relax. 'I was always daunted by new things, and nothing came easily to me,' he says. 'Life had been a challenge from the word go and I still felt a bit lost. Being in the seminary for the last eight years meant I'd lost contact with all my friends too, but Belgrave was a very nice place to work in.'

Six months later, Father Bob's next stop, the former Olympic village of Heidelberg, north-east of the city, was much more of a struggle. For a start, his responsibilities as an assistant priest were spread over a far bigger geographical area, often well beyond the parish itself, and after spending hour after hour on a series of buses and trains, he realised he'd need a car to be able to properly fulfil his duties. That was a major hurdle. 'I'd never had money of my own and as an assistant priest, you were dependent on the parish priest to pay you,' he says. 'And if he didn't want to pay you, he didn't. It was a clerical caste system: the top clergy went from plum to plum; the others went from slum to slum. It wasn't until later that they struck a minimum wage you'd have to be paid, and there was never any talk of the maximum!'

His old mentor, Father Gorry, again came to his rescue with funds. With that money, Father Bob bought his first car, a battered old second-hand VW Beetle. It made a world of difference to his life as suddenly he was able to drive to all the far-flung places he was expected to minister to, including two hospitals, a sanatorium, a children's home and the local cemetery.

Being out in the world visiting such places proved an invaluable learning experience. The nearby Austin Hospital, previously the Austin Hospital for Incurables, was by then the largest cancer hospital in Australia, and also had a number of patients with paraplegia and TB, or battling the after-effects of strokes, as well as children who'd survived polio and car crashes. His experiences there had a major, and lasting, impact on the way he viewed the world. 'I met great sufferers at the Austin,' he says. 'I met incredible people who'd lost the use of their hands, so they'd trained themselves to paint and turn book pages with their toes, and I learnt that hospital chaplains can be a breath of fresh air from the outside, reminding people that they're not just patients, but they're people, with real lives beyond the hospital and families and hopes and dreams, but who just happen to be, at this time, in distress.' He became determined to help try to brighten their lives, and often worked hard at making them laugh. But from those who didn't make it, he learnt too. 'I developed a love for the dying, which I still have today,' he says.

Heidelberg made a lifelong impression on him in another way, too. As a kid, he'd first been a supporter of his sister Kathleen's footy team, Essendon, then of Father James McHugh's Richmond. But after so long cocooned in the seminary without TV, radio or newspapers, he'd completely lost track of the football. 'It cleansed my mind and heart of previous footy contamination,' he jokes. 'So then I was free; I could see the light.'

In Melbourne, it's considered a sin to switch team allegiances even once, but Father Bob did it now for an outrageous second time. Heidelberg back then was one of the pre-draft catchment zones from which Collingwood used to recruit players, with staff and veterans visiting schools and sports clubs to talent-spot. As a result, most of the population there were fervent Magpies supporters, inordinately proud of local boys Jack Regan, Phonse Kyne and the Twomey brothers, Bill, Mick and Pat, who'd all proved stalwarts of the team. And there was also the team's historical association with Catholicism, with its powerful patronage in the 1920s by influential businessman and prominent Australian Irish Catholic John Wren, whose life was fictionalised by writer Frank Hardy in his *Power Without Glory*. Collingwood's fans back then were mostly working-class Catholic and Irish, sharing a general sentiment of exclusion and being discriminated against. 'So I had a spiritual awakening when I went there, and emerged a Collingwood supporter,' Father Bob says, laughing.

'Football is often likened to religion; there's a ritual involved and while you go in hoping for the best, you know you're going to suffer along the way. Collingwood suits my temperament. I'm a Virgo, a drama queen, and I thrive on the agony and the ecstasy, and Collingwood always has both. Watching them is like a Greek drama: you're either on top of the world, or a long, long way below it. But it's always cathartic to go through the tragedy, blame and shame with them, and then the euphoria and the feeling that you're in heaven on earth. One moment, it's, "Oh God, Oh God, what's happening?" and then just as you're on the brink of despair and plunged into misery, they'll come good. So they then have their proudest moments while you're in the car park, having been persuaded to leave early.'

He also saw footy as a way for the Church to reach out to young people. Many of the local kids were bored and didn't have enough to do. So Father Bob, with his experience of running play centres and camps in the holidays for kids when he'd been at the seminary, appealed for footballs, cricket bats and balls and other sporting equipment and set up friendly games for all the kids to join in. 'While they were playing sport, they weren't getting into trouble,' he says. 'And you could also talk to them about things like teamwork and how they led their lives. It was a good way to connect with them.' And even if they did get into trouble, Father Bob was determined to help out there too. He volunteered to become an honorary probation officer, so he could speak up on behalf of any kids who hit difficulties, or help to supervise them if that was deemed necessary.

The priest in charge of Heidelberg, however, was a strict, old-fashioned man who didn't take kindly to an underling so different from himself in both interests and outlook, and so active in his parish. In his professional life Father Bob was keeping track of all the discussions about relaxing, modernising and reaching out with Catholicism in the run-up to Vatican II, and was fast developing his own ideas about the way to do things, and his own much more irreverent style. It wasn't long before the pair clashed. Father Bob's predecessor had left in a hurry after a row about taking a day off; now it was Father Bob's turn to feel the priest's displeasure. Relations between the pair froze to the point where the priest would communicate only via notes slid under the door of his assistant's bedroom and would lock the kitchen in the presbytery at 6 p.m., leaving milk for him in a saucepan outside. 'It was like I was the cat!' says Father Bob.

Even worse, the priest made a number of complaints about his young charge to the Archdiocese, accusing him of 'insubordination'. As a result, Father Bob was hauled in front of the auxiliary bishop Francis Fox, one of the state's most hardline conservatives, who made his name denouncing left-wing unions and the Australian Labor Party's links with communism. It was to be Father Bob's first clash with the more traditionalist elements of his Church, and the forerunner of many more to come.

After eighteen months, Father Bob was transferred to Ashburton, in Melbourne's south-east, a growing area with a large pool of postwar Housing Commission homes. It was a much happier fit. The priest presiding was a gentle man, hard-working and dedicated to his mission, despite being in poor health as a result of TB. Father Bob saw him as a tremendous role model and supported him energetically. 'We had everything a priest could wish for,' he says, nostalgically now. 'A full church, great attendance at sacraments, a strong lay leadership and hordes of teenagers and school children.' Again, he set up footy and cricket games for the kids and found they responded well to him.

In his second year there, Father Bob was put in charge when his boss was sent to the cool reaches of Mount Macedon to recuperate. Taking mass regularly, he worked hard on his own style of preaching. That curious voice and delivery – a sharp sawmill and steam-hammer tone, forged among the steel mills of Glasgow and flattened by a childhood in the suburbs of Melbourne – began to make him a distinctive presence in the pulpit, quite apart from what he actually said.

The beginning of Father Bob's stay in Ashburton coincided with the actual start of Vatican II. It had opened in October 1962, with the first session's attendees including the four men who'd later succeed Pope John XXIII as pontiffs, as Pope Paul VI, Pope John Paul I, Pope John Paul II and Pope Benedict XVI. The sessions were all packed with participants and observers from all over the world and, back in Melbourne, Father Bob read the reports from all the various sessions avidly, transfixed by much of the debate, and heartened by many of the changes being foreshadowed. He even knew some of those in Rome at the time; they included his old CBC teacher Brother Leo Griffin, who'd gone to the Vatican twelve months before on a three-year term of international study.

At the same time, many within the Ashburton congregation were alarmed by the breadth of the changes being discussed and felt keenly that both their Church and their faith were under attack. Father Bob took it upon himself to act as an emissary for the new guard, reassuring everyone that this was all for the better. He himself embraced the new order enthusiastically, seeing it as giving him licence to experiment with the way he ran masses, preached and said catechism. He took off his clerical collar, wearing it only on occasions when he felt it might 'frighten the horses' not to, and embarked on what was to become his lifelong habit of talking directly to members of his congregation from the pulpit in a much more informal, casual and, for some, shockingly unceremonious way.

But even as the Vatican II Council was drawing to a close towards the end of 1965, a movement was forming with the express aim of rewinding some of the changes. As says Father Bob's old mate Paul Garland, who was ordained at the same time, 'For us, Vatican II was a blessing; it was what we'd been hoping for. Bob was always on the side of the angels. But I can remember, even before the Council finished, one of the great men of the Vatican saying that it'd take them forty years to undo what had been done, but that they'd started on it already . . .'

Father Bob, like the other great supporters of the changes, saw one of his roles as to defend the new order, and as vigorously as he could. He drew on his cadet days as inspiration. 'We were part of the forward scouts moving among the people to educate them, and tell them that just because Mother Church had opened her windows to let in the fresh air, it didn't mean we were all going to freeze to death. On the contrary. It meant that Catholicism was going to be more open, more welcoming, and it was going to embrace change rather than fight against it. We were rallying the troops to understand that.'

Father Bob's enthusiasm for all things military wasn't confined to metaphors about his new-look Church, either. While at Ashburton, he was also invited in 1965 to be a part-time chaplain in the Army Reserve. The Vietnam War had been going for three years at that point, and conscription had been introduced in Australia following a US Government request for more support. Father Bob, sensing this was a war that wasn't going to be won any time soon, and feeling there was a great need for spiritual support and comfort among those making up the armed forces – as well as, it has to be said, needing a bit of extra cash to top up the meagre allowance he was paid as an assistant priest – immediately agreed. He'd had a soft spot for the army ever since growing up playing in the air raid trenches close by his primary school, and then his time in the army cadets. It was still with a faint pang of nostalgia that he remembered wanting a career in the armed forces. Now, finally, he was able to combine both these loves and do some good for each side. As part of his duties, he attended his unit's weekly parade, as well as its annual two-week tented training camp. It was a role he would continue to play, in his spare time, for the next four years.

Along with that post, Father Bob was also appointed chaplain to the cadet corps of his old school, the CBC. One of the boys in the cadets at the time was sixteen-year-old Frank

O'Connor, who listened, spellbound, as the priest spoke. 'There was something about the way he engaged with people that grabbed your attention,' says Frank, who was to come into contact again with his old chaplain much later. 'You felt he was focused around people, he enjoyed people. He'd only been ordained a couple of years, and he had a huge amount of energy. Listening to him, you felt energised too.'

As the Vatican II Council finally drew to a close in December 1965, so too did Father Bob's stay at Ashburton. In 1966, he was sent to the newish parish of Braybrook in the western suburbs, an area presided over by an enormously enthusiastic and energetic priest, Father Thomas Murray. 'He was a tall, flash Irishman who'd been sent out to Braybrook, a place that was poor and working class and had mud everywhere, by an HQ who wanted to cut him down to size,' says Father Bob. 'But he'd just risen to the challenge. He'd done a social audit and found the parish needed a school, so he managed to set one up.'

In fact, he'd been so determined to start a school in the area, he'd approached nearly every single order of nuns in the entire state of Victoria to ask for teachers. Eventually, in 1955, two had come forward, and they'd helped establish a temporary school in some railway huts near the station, which eventually became a fully fledged primary and secondary school, with 900 students. In 1961, however, disaster struck: the entire school was gutted by a fire set off by an electrical fault. But by the time Father Bob arrived, the school was again up and running out of a collection of portables and buildings gradually being rebuilt. It grew to become Christ the King College, and later still part of the present-day Caroline Chisholm Catholic College.

'It was quite incredible,' says Father Bob. 'After the fire, Tommy just saddles up and starts the whole thing again. But he was never quite the same. I don't think he ever properly recovered from it. We used government buildings, buses and help from state schools, and took the kids to summer schools, too. He even went over to Canada and got some Canadians to run a trade school for poor boys. It was interesting. We were becoming popular among a whole new demographic, teenagers and boys, and we set up a football team, a cricket team and basketball games to keep them busy and interested and out of trouble.' It was a great lesson in what could be done, where there was the will to do it.

This time, however, Father Bob ran foul of Father Murray's housekeeper who, he felt, was terribly over-protective of her parish priest. 'We worked well together but she complained that I was taking over,' he says today. 'It wasn't true at all, but after nine months it was then time for me to move on again . . .'

Next he was sent to the east, to East Kew, to assist a priest who gave him a very warm welcome. 'It was great to arrive; he and his parishioners said, "Thank God you're here to help!" which was wonderful,' says Father Bob. He was, again, a very different character from the priest he was there to serve, but this time they complemented each other well.

'They were chalk and cheese,' says Michael Doyle, who was around sixteen when Father Bob arrived at his parish. 'He was totally different to anything we'd seen and heard. He was like a breath of fresh air. He was so bright and so able to explain the theology that came out of Vatican II in a language that ordinary people could understand, young and old. For us kids, he was like a pied piper. He had a radical style in the way he presented himself, he could be like a stand-up comedian, holding an audience for long periods, and he had a great gift for explaining himself. At the same time, his theology was cutting-edge Vatican II theology but, while he was radical, he was never heretic. He did tend to polarise people a little bit, even back then. I think it was only a very small number of people who didn't appreciate him, though. The great mass of people, including the young and the old, and even the pretty conservative people, just loved him.'

His Vatican II ways did come as something of a shock to many, though. Robert Byrne, then a fourteen-year-old kid, still remembers the surprise of Father Bob not conducting his services right at the altar with his back to the congregation as was the old way, but turning around to face the people to say mass to them instead. 'At one point, he even came down off the step to say mass on the same level as us,' he says. 'He'd also walk around during the service and say hello to people in the pews, "Bill! How's it going?" in the middle of it. He'd also tell old ladies to put away their rosary beads because they needed to be present in the moment. "You don't need them here," he'd say. He woke people up; it was fantastic!'

He was also adamant that services shouldn't be overlong. 'He'd say an hour was enough,' Robert remembers. 'He'd say the men should go off afterwards and take their sons to football; it'd be no good coming to church if they didn't play their roles properly in the rest of their lives. They had to live the message. Or he'd say we could go now in time to see "World of Sport" on TV. That was funny as Jack O'Toole, the world champion woodchopper who often appeared on the panel of the show, was usually in church too!'

One time, Father Bob took to the pulpit talking about those who didn't like to do anything for the underprivileged as, instead of God's chosen people, God's frozen people. The congregation was hugely amused. Another time, he was given the task of reviewing the envelope collection, where he was to exhort parishioners to give a generous donation to the church to support the parish and its building programs. He talked at length about having to raise enough money to feed the hungry budgerigar back at the presbytery. The next week he was back. 'You remember the budgie I talked about last week?' he asked his assembled flock. 'Well,' he said bluntly, 'it starved to death.' That week's collection raised a great deal more cash.

At the same time, he took very seriously his duty to continue to explain Vatican II teachings, and ran a series of hour-long talks in the local school for anyone interested in coming along. 'He'd stand there with the blackboard and a piece of chalk and it would be the most entertaining hour you could imagine!' says Michael, who went on to have a long career in the Catholic education system, including working as a school principal. 'The way he spoke, with such clarity and a stunning ability to explain complex ideas of theology so simply . . . He was the absolute vanguard of the new theology in Melbourne. He was a strong influence on me.'

Father Bob also decided now was another chance to put into practice what he'd learnt at the various parishes he'd served in, and develop his expertise in helping the young people of this one. He gathered kids together from all over the area and, just as Father McHugh had once done for him, he'd cram as many of them as could fit into his increasingly battered old VW and drive them to a football match, off for a picnic or down to the river to play on the ropes strung up over the water. When that old VW blew up, he'd buy another decrepit second-hand car and work that into the ground too. 'I felt we should get the kids together as teenagers, to build a sense of community, and there we also started football and basketball games, and got them to play guitar. It worked really well.'

He started a series of youth camps for children in the holidays too, regularly taking between sixty and 150 from the parish to go camping in Cowes, the principal township of Phillip Island, and Halls Gap in the Grampians National Park. He'd raise money for them by having the kids collect golf balls from the various courses nearby and sell them back to golfers, or try to attract sponsorship. In one inspired move, he had the *Sun* newspaper write a story on the kids playing at the river, with the headline, 'Tarzans of the River', to draw attention to the need for money to give them more to do.

He was never shy about calling in favours from people he knew to help, either. One was a local electrical company, owned by a man who had a boat and water skis. Father Bob asked him to bring them down to Phillip Island and no kid that time left without a turn at water-skiing. 'It just showed the respect that everyone held him in,' says Michael. 'Most of the kids were alienated from the Church at that stage, but most of them stayed in touch with him long afterwards, asking him to marry them, baptise their children, and then marry their children and baptise their children's children.

'He was also extraordinarily generous. He'd drive up often in a different car and, when you'd ask why, it'd often turn out he'd given the last one away to someone he felt needed it more than him. He went through cars like no-one on earth. First, it was a series of old VWs, then it was early-model Toyota Corollas, utilitarian cars, nothing flash. As a result, he'd often still be paying off cars that he'd long given up. All in all, he was a very memorable stage in all our lives.'

Tony Grieve was a local teenager at the time, and also affectionately remembers Father Bob's energy and enthusiasm. 'I was in an under-seventeen football team when he arrived, and we'd lost our coach,' he says. 'So Father Bob parachuted straight in, and turned up the next week at training, dressed up in footy boots and a shirt and all the rest of it. I reckon he hadn't really played much football himself, but he volunteered to help us kids out. He ended up coaching us for three months. He didn't seem terribly well schooled in the art of footy – most of his advice was general in nature, perhaps to cover any shortcomings in experience – but he was very, very enthusiastic. He would encourage us and kept us together, telling us to be a team, and play as a team. He melded us together at a point when we might have gone our separate ways, and the team would have ceased to exist. He saved our side.

'Our football ground was a very difficult one because it had a slope. There was a definite home ground advantage. Father Bob cottoned on fast to that and made sure we always played that way. He would really let rip, and he was a great enthuser and motivator and a man for all seasons. He'd always be urging us to get in there and go for the ball. In fact, that was the greatest aspect of his coaching. We just all really appreciated him being there for us, and my affection for him has stayed ever since. We just loved him. He was the best!'

That year, 1967, Father Bob started attracting more attention elsewhere for his work. He was invited to take part in a radio broadcast for one of the first commercial radio stations in Melbourne – and one of the very first to try talkback – Radio 3DB, in its studios located in the basement of the old *Herald* building where his father had once worked. The show was the Sunday-evening 'Ask The Ministers' program, where figures representing three different faiths answered questions and discussed issues, as part of the religious broadcasting element imposed by the licence conditions. One of Father Bob's first outings was memorable for even more than his spirited arguing of his corner, often against far more conservative clerics. The show was cut short by the news that Prime Minister Harold Holt had gone missing, presumed drowned, off Cheviot Beach.

He proved such a natural on radio, however, that he continued being asked back. Producers loved that he didn't mind being outspoken, and he had a quick wit that often brought a touch of levity to the sombre religious spots that were coming under increasing pressure to attract the kinds of listeners and advertisers that their great rival pop music was routinely enjoying. And that was a gift that became even more valuable when the Australian Broadcasting Control Board in 1970 removed some of the onerous licensing conditions on radio stations to include religion. He started to appear regularly on a number of different radio stations.

After three years at East Kew, Father Bob was told it was time to move on. Many of the parishioners were broken-hearted. Robert Byrne said he'd never forget him. 'When he'd first arrived, my dog had been run over, and Father Bob rocked up one day and gave me another dog. He just saw that's what I needed, and it was what he should do. He would just do things like that. He saw a need and did what had to be done.'

From there, Father Bob was billeted to Ivanhoe, a few kilometres to the north, to help out the parish priest. There, he found a wealthy, educated bunch of parishioners who weren't slow to tell him what they thought of both his sermons and his style. He welcomed most of the feedback, and took praise and criticism equally on board to try to improve. 'It was the most affluent spot I'd ever been in, and Ivanhoe parishioners were well placed to criticise because they were, many of them, professional people – doctors, professors and musicians. They were upwardly socially mobile. They had won the right to criticise, and I was grateful.'

The resident priest wasn't quite so keen to have Father Bob try out new things from his pulpit. He complained to the Archdiocese about him, and Father Bob, after just a year, found himself moved on yet again. 'The Church would send me somewhere because there were problems, knowing they'd be putting the cat among the pigeons, but then when it caused some difficulties, they would never stand by you,' he says. 'It was all about a clash of cultures, and having no backup when it mattered. I think they ended up sending me to too many parishes too soon. But then they topped all that by sending me out into the bush. The bloody bush, for God's sake! I'd never really visited the bush before, let alone had to live there . . .'

Seymour, almost 100 kilometres north of Melbourne, is a township just off the crossing of the Hume and Goulburn Valley highways, mainly servicing the local cattle, sheep and wine industries. It was a vastly different lifestyle, and Father Bob found adapting to it tough. He tried at first, but failed miserably. While he's still remembered affectionately by many within the parish, and at least three families travelled down to South Melbourne – where he was later posted – from time to time to attend his Sunday mass and keep up their relationship with a chat afterwards and a visit to the presbytery, his memories aren't quite so fond.

'It was a whole new experience for me, and I hated it!' he says. 'At that point, I nearly had a nervous breakdown. I think I was exhausted from starting out afresh in so many new parishes over a comparatively short period of time, and working so hard in each one. And then to find myself in the bush . . . The bush? It was all too much.'

The only even faintly bright spot on the horizon was that Seymour was very close to the Australian Army's military training base of Puckapunyal.

7

Talking Underwater for Vietnam

The savagery of the war being waged overseas in Vietnam was brought starkly home to Australia with images of the bloody Tet Offensive unleashed in January 1968.

The graphic TV footage of the ferocious fighting during the series of attacks by the Viet Cong on towns and cities throughout South Vietnam, the heavy casualties and the sheer mindless desperation of the war shocked Americans, Australians and their allies, and brought the horror right into lounge rooms.

Five months later, Australian troops were sent to Bien Hoa province to intercept Viet Cong troops retreating after Tet and its subsequent campaigns and they became embroiled in the

Battle of Coral and Balmoral, which lasted twenty-five days, their longest and deadliest single engagement with enemy soldiers. As well as more than 300 Viet Cong casualties, it cost twenty-five Australians their lives.

This intensification of the Vietnam War and the realisation of how much better organised the Viet Cong and North Vietnamese Army were, certainly compared to Allied propaganda to the contrary, brought more pressure on the Australian defence forces to improve the preparation of the men they were sending into battle. As part of this, they decided to step up their 'character-training' program, a course for members of the army, navy and air force that had been founded after the Korean War. During that conflict it had been discovered that in extreme conditions of stress, in battle, in captivity or under interrogation, some American servicemen lacked the spiritual strength or emotional resilience to cope, which contributed to the high number of deserters and defectors. The Australian defence forces wanted to avoid similar problems, especially because Vietnam had the additional pressure of working with South Vietnamese soldiers, among whom it was always likely there were spies for the enemy – a factor that later became acknowledged as one of the major causes of post-traumatic stress disorder among Vietnam veterans.

So there seemed to be an urgent need to stiffen the moral fibre of the new recruits to the defence forces, by chaplains who could work well with young people. And looking around for instructors, everyone agreed: Father Bob Maguire was their man.

Living at St Mary's Church in Seymour, he was already a regular visitor to the army base at nearby Puckapunyal as a part-time army chaplain, and was delighted to receive the call. He had no hesitation in agreeing to work full time with the army character-training team, and started in 1969.

'It suited me down to the ground,' he says. 'I'd worked with the army for a while as a second string to my bow, and now the character training was perfect for me. I'd never been anywhere or done anything adventurous and they wanted me to stay safe on Australian soil, so I wasn't outside my comfort zone. I could relate equally well to religious people or secular people, and I could talk underwater . . .'

Character training was a two- or sometimes three-day course that many new recruits, both regular servicemen and conscripts, did as part of their initial training. It was designed to develop their interpersonal skills and start them thinking about what they stood for, their ethics, their respect for themselves, the importance of giving everyone a fair go and the moral conduct of war, and what they should do in the various situations they could find themselves in.

Father Bob proved a good choice as an instructor. He already had a deep affinity with the armed forces, and he knew how to talk to young people from his work with kids in the parishes he'd served in. As a consequence, he proved able to relate well to the twenty-year-old men before him, who were often leaving home for the first time to sign up for an uncertain future. He'd always had great regard for the young, feeling they were Australia's hope for the future, and this belief shone through in all his dealings with them. As a result, they tended to react well to him, as he asked them how they felt about themselves and how they saw themselves as soldiers, and talked to them about the different scenarios they might face, quizzing them on what they'd do in each circumstance. Previous instructors had merely preached at the men; Father Bob led small discussion groups of around ten soldiers each time, encouraging them to come to their own conclusions – with a little guidance from the sidelines.

'Bob was so good at asking difficult questions and starting debate about them,' says Monsignor Tony Toms, who served as an army chaplain for nineteen years, and is these days the parish priest of St Mary's at Seymour. 'He'd never give them the answers, but he'd ask them so they'd have to work them out themselves, to try and discern what they should do. His style was very confronting and his slight eccentricity was part of his teaching method but, afterwards, it turned out that out of all the instructors – Catholic, Anglican or Protestant – Bob was the one who was universally remembered!

'He'd talk and everyone would listen. He knew youth and understood the language they used and was able to bring that into the course. He never spoke for long, but he was always worth listening to. He was entertaining, and was a great facilitator of discussion. He had an expansive vision and a universal outlook on things. He could always see the big picture.'

He was always enormously entertaining too, and often in the most surprising ways. The much-decorated General Jim Barry, nowadays president of the Defence Reserves Association, remembers taking 2 Field Regiment Royal Australian Artillery jogging into the bush for a church service: one to be conducted by Father Bob, and the other by the Church of England Reverend John Leaver. When they arrived at the prearranged clearing – 'Micks to the left! Proddies to the right!' yelled General Barry – Father Bob had set up an elaborate altar, complete with cloth, cross and lit candles, on the bonnet of a Jeep. Everyone stopped dead in their tracks at the sight. 'Anyone who's not interested can come back to barracks and clean out the grease traps!' General Barry ordered. There was a rush of troops over to the priest. All went swimmingly until someone noticed that Father Bob had omitted to pull on the handbrake properly, and the Jeep rolled steadily towards the congregation. 'I can remember vividly all the howls of laughter as they all tried to get out of the way,' says the general.

'But Maguire wasn't the usual kind of God-botherer. He was an incredible person. I even did a few of his late-night radio shows on 3AW with him, where he'd answer people's phone calls. He was quite extraordinary; he could talk to anybody. He is one of a kind. He would take the micky out of his Catholic hierarchy but he didn't denigrate them at all. He'd bypass them by saying, "I have a higher authority!" by which he'd mean Jesus. He'd be good for a prime minister!'

Father Bob was in his element and enjoyed talking to the young men, and felt he was learning a lot from them. He'd had few male role models in his life to give him much guidance and he liked being able to fill that gap for others. He worked well as an instructor, bringing in training films made by the Americans and introducing role-play, a technique that would later become an important part of his teachings as a priest. He also loved the discipline of the army, the innate sense of order that contrasted strongly with his own approach to life, which often tended to verge on the hectically chaotic.

'In a funny, quirky way he loved the order and regularity of it,' says Father Hal Ranger, who worked with him on some of the courses. 'He has an innate disorder and chaos but he was very effective in that ordered environment, especially as they were able to give him the space to challenge a lot of things.' That element had already turned out, and was throughout his lifetime, to prove key to his success – or otherwise – as a priest. Within the sometimes restrictive organisation of the Catholic Church, if he was given the space to operate in his own way within an ordered structure, he and his parishioners often flourished. If the Church couldn't accommodate that, then he'd already experienced the pain and indignity of being moved on from some of the parishes in which he'd already served.

He also enjoyed the army emphasis on teamwork, one of his lifelong passions, and excelled in the art of team building. 'You can't put yourself first in the army,' he'd tell the new recruits. 'If someone needs help more than you, then they are the first to receive it. You have to work together as a team, think as a team and look after your comrades. It's about people learning practical ways of working together for a common end. In the Anzac spirit, you never leave a mate stranded. You bond with your mates and you get the job done, just like Jesus and his twelve mates did.'

He felt the teachings of Vatican II fitted in well with his new work, too: the inclusivity, the principles of debating issues rather than imposing the solutions from on high, the freedom that now allowed him to bring up formerly taboo subjects like abortion and contraception. While he found the men loved listening to parables, he tended to avoid overtly introducing religion into the debates, however. 'It was all about secular Christian humanity,' he says. 'We taught them about the first moral prerogative being to "do no harm", the guiding principle for doctors. You wanted to sow the seed of morality. You couldn't do much more. And if you did that well and it took and grew, then that good might stick. If you didn't do it well, then that seed might be lost. It was up to your temperament and talent to plant that seed as well as you could, just like with Vatican II.'

Those courses certainly had, for many of the soldiers, a lasting impact. Vietnam veteran Kevin Flemings remembers the course imparting values such as respect for women, which was to have repercussions on his life many years later. 'The course did have an effect on me,' he says. 'In 1970, I was booted out of a Toastmasters club for having the temerity to not only invite a woman to a meeting, but then propose her for membership! And it still hasn't worn off. I am a Legatee and devoted to the care of military widows.'

For Father Bob there were an extra few perks of the job, too. For the first time in his life, he started receiving a regular, reasonable wage. Never having had money before, he liked suddenly feeling much more independent, although at the start he still ended up wearing someone else's hand-me-down dress uniform because he couldn't afford to buy one of his own. He also had a fair amount of free time and he and Father Ranger were instrumental in 1971 in forming the National Council of Priests, an Australia-wide organisation of Catholic clergy for bishops, priests and deacons. Created out of the tumult of Vatican II, against the background of the Vietnam War, he served on the national executive, overseeing meetings of 300 to 400 clergy.

Rank was another bonus of life in the army that Father Bob

relished. He started off as a captain along with the other professionals coming into the army, like dentists and lawyers, and worked his way up to lieutenant-colonel as one of the chief instructors and senior lecturers. 'Although as a clergyman you allegedly had rank in the outside world, it rarely felt like it,' he says. 'In the army, it felt like you were really respected. There was lots of respect both upwards and sideways.'

After a while, he became an expert in making use of that rank, too. Father John Tinkler, who was a classmate of Father Bob's on his army chaplain's course in 1966, and who became known in the army by the nickname 'Tink', saw that firsthand. 'The idea of a chaplain is to be a friend to all ranks,' he says. 'Bob achieved that. He was respected, liked and trusted by all the soldiers, and respected by the officer ranks above him, too. Sometimes the soldiers had difficulties and needed a voice to put a point of view to a much higher rank. They told Bob their troubles and might tell him their family was having problems so could he put in a word for them to get a transfer to a base closer to home. If he felt there was a need for it, he'd then talk to someone higher up on their behalf. It was such a rigid rank structure, they really needed someone prepared to jump over other ranks on their behalf. Bob did that very well. Rank made no bloody difference to him at all. He doesn't bow and scrape – and never has since either – but he gave respect to everyone, equally.

'In the army, he really stood out. He talked in a really down-to-earth Aussie way, and talked straight, so everyone knew where they stood. If anyone started talking pompously, he'd just bring it down into ordinary language that anyone could understand. He has a superb ability with words; there's humour under nearly everything he says and he had an extraordinary ability to talk in average diggers' language, on the same level as the soldiers, so people would talk and relax around him. They'd even swear, and he wouldn't take any notice of it. Everyone liked being in his company. They'd really listen to him, and there'd always be so much laughter. He doesn't laugh so much, but everyone around him does. He was ideal for that job. He's always believed that his role in life is to help people, and he did it there superbly. He's a very fine man.'

Since his work with the young soldiers was so successful, Father Bob was also recruited as one of the three senior lecturers for the character-leadership courses run for officers and those who'd served in the forces for ten to fifteen years. This was a higher level of character training about war and the conduct of war, for twenty to twenty-five people at a time and lasting for four to five days. For this, he finally got the chance to travel, albeit only to various army bases around Australia: Kapooka, near Wagga Wagga in New South Wales; the Hampstead Barracks in Adelaide; the North Head Artillery Barracks at Manly, Sydney; the Officer Cadet School at Portsea, Victoria; and, finally, twenty-five years after he'd first dreamed of being there, the Royal Military College at Duntroon in the ACT.

Father Bob treated the officers exactly as he'd treated their troops: with respect yet without any fawning to rank. One of the things he liked so much about the Australian Army was the irreverence of the troops to authority, often working out themselves the best way to do the job without blind obedience to those above. It perfectly matched his Vatican II ideology.

To all the officers on his courses, his questions would run

along the same lines. 'Is war just?' he'd ask them. 'Or is it unjust? Are there conditions under which it could be considered just? Is war morally acceptable – or is it always immoral?' He'd bring up the possibilities of taking enemy prisoners, and how they should be treated. When you've been fighting men two minutes before, trying to kill them while they've been trying to kill you, how do you behave towards them if they surrender, or you capture them? And the big question: should they ever be executed?

At the front of everyone's minds at the time was the previous year's My Lai Massacre, where US troops had slaughtered around 450 unarmed people, mostly women, children, babies and elderly people, in a village they suspected had harboured Viet Cong soldiers. The mass execution only became public knowledge in 1969, and triggered outrage around the world. Character leadership, it was fervently hoped, would help prevent Australian troops from doing anything like that in the future. 'Australia never had a My Lai,' he now says with pride. 'And the North Vietnamese, at the end of it all, seemed to have a lot of respect for the Australians, unlike the Americans. The Americans relied on superior firepower all the time, while we would be much more like jungle fighters, like them.' As well, Australian soldiers made it their moral duty to bury the Viet Cong dead, unlike US troops who would usually leave enemy bodies to lie where they fell as a warning to others. That simple moral act won them a huge amount of regard from the enemy.

During those courses, the officers warmed to Father Bob, too. Vietnam veteran Chris Coape-Smith remembers clearly the evening the priest took a part of the course, unusually, about religion, on the doctrine of the trinity: God the Father, the Son and the Holy Spirit. 'It's something very difficult to explain,' says Chris. 'I've known priests to say, "Forget the explanation, it's too hard, just accept it". But he did explain it, and so everyone could understand. I'll never forget it. It was about 10 p.m. at night, very windy, and we were in this old building in North Head, which was pretty eerie. He started talking about God the Father and then the windows started rattling, and he said, "Yes, Father, we know you're out there!" Then they'd rattle again, and he'd say, "Yes, that's your son." Then they'd rattle a third time . . . We were all in fits of laughter by this time.

'He really had a way of talking about things in a way that was never ramming it down your throat. He was just very funny and explained things so well. His was a fantastic part of the course.'

Many of the officers were sceptical about the course before they took it, but most who came into contact with Father Bob seemed to find it tremendously helpful. Phil Davies, a captain back then, and later a brigadier, had been in the army for some time when he took the course. Father Bob won his class over from the moment he walked into the room and made a joke about having previously seen some of their number huddling in the back of the newsagent, trying to hide the fact they'd been caught looking at the girlie magazines. 'That brought the house down straightaway,' says Phil. 'From that moment on, he had everyone in the palm of his hand.

'He just understands people, whoever they are, and knows how to talk to them. His ability to engage with all denominations was an eye-opener. He's never a God-botherer who thumps and thumps and thumps his hand on the table. He's a real man of the cloth. The course was about ethical issues and how you need to be leaders of your men in some pretty serious situations, and keeping yourself and them out of harm's way. It was about giving you a better understanding of yourself, and making sure you were fit for the job. We all benefitted from his irreverent but meaningful presentations.'

Another priest who worked with him on the courses, Father Lawrence Cross, was amazed at how well he could combine humour with the serious ethical questions, all couched in exactly the same language as the tough servicemen used. 'He was marvellous and a great actor who could, like the saying of St Paul's, be "all things to all men". He was brilliant in the way he could combine the strange polarities between being a man's man, a brilliant teacher, a priest and a storyteller. He had a very novel way of presenting ideas and facts. He'd talk about Abraham in such a way that you'd think he was actually in the room! It was quite captivating.'

Father Cross even found himself the butt of one of the jokes when he drove in to a retreat one day with loud Renaissance music on his stereo, forgetting that his car windows were wound down. Father Bob, teaching a class upstairs, was startled by the sudden loud burst of heavenly music. 'Oh my God!' he exclaimed to his class. 'Jesus is here!'

But as well as giving his students a laugh, Father Bob saw his main role as making his audience think, and to challenge some of their established beliefs. From the firm foundations of his absolute faith, as a deeply traditional Catholic – despite what he could look like on the surface – he was perfectly comfortable testing out everyone else's ethics, safe within his own unshakeable convictions. Often, he'd say things deliberately to shock the officers, too. 'But when they examined what he'd said afterwards, it often wasn't as outlandish as it seemed at the time,' says Monsignor Toms. 'He had the confidence of his commanding officers and regimental sergeant-majors as well as the regular troops. He was very traditional in his theology and Church teachings, but he had a unique way about him; he was an enigma. In some ways, he could be slightly eccentric, in others he was an absolute traditionalist. Sometimes, the examples he used to illustrate his talks would come close to the knife's edge, but he always kept on the right side of the blade.'

In the army, Father Bob honed the skill of learning exactly how far he could push things. It was only later, as the Church in Australia grew more conservative post–Vatican II, that far enough was sometimes considered to be simply too far.

But back then, Father Bob continued to enjoy his work with the army until the Vietnam War ceasefire finally began in January 1973 and the new prime minister of Australia, Gough Whitlam, announced the establishment of diplomatic relations with Hanoi. At that point, only one full-time chaplain was needed with the army character-training unit.

Monsignor Gerry Cudmore had been appointed to the army two years before Father Bob, in 1963, and was the first army chaplain to actually go over to physically serve in Vietnam. As far as Father Bob was concerned, there was no contest. 'There wasn't room for the two of us and he was the real deal; I was just a chocolate soldier,' he says. 'So I stood down.'

It was then he received a letter from Cardinal James Knox, who'd taken over as the Archbishop of Melbourne from Archbishop Justin Simonds. 'By virtue of this letter I appoint you as Pastor of the Parish of St Peter and Paul in Melbourne South,' it read, 'and I commit to you the full care of souls in that Parish with all the faculties, duties, rights and privileges, according to the Code, to our Diocesan Statutes and to the approved customs . . . Would you please proceed to your new Parish on Saturday, 15 September at midday. I know that the people of your new Parish will welcome you and will receive from you the pastoral care they so richly deserve . . .'

Father Bob was delighted. 'I'd been moved around such a lot, I was tired. At last, I was about to have a permanent home. Cardinal Knox told me that when I got to South Melbourne, I could stay there. That really pleased me as it meant I could relax; I wasn't going to be moved on again.

'It was going to be the first real home I'd known. I said, "Thank you, Jesus." At last I'd be able to settle somewhere, without having that constant fear of being kicked out and having to go somewhere else. I'd be there, serving the people, for the rest of my life.'

PART 2

A HOME OF MY OWN

8

A Home at Last

Father Bob Maguire arrived at St Peter and Paul's Church in South Melbourne on 14 September 1973, the day of his thirty-ninth birthday, full of excitement for the job ahead. He had plenty of ideas and plans for the first parish he would run himself, all formed over his eight years in the seminary, tested and adapted while he assisted in other parishes, and honed by his time instructing in the army. He couldn't wait to start on them.

It took him just a week to realise that nothing was quite as he'd so fondly imagined.

The problem wasn't the church itself; he fell instantly in love with that. The first sight of it made his heart race: an imposing bluestone building designed by renowned church architect TA Kelly and constructed over three years from 1869, with an ornate rose window set into the facade, and stained-glass windows depicting the church's patrons St Peter and St Paul. 'I was grateful it was a good-looking church they'd sent me to,' says Father Bob. 'I thought to myself, "What in the name of God have I done to deserve this church?"' Inside, it was no less grand. The high altar, added in 1933, was of lightly veined white marble brought over from Italy, studded with onyx and Irish green marble and with inserts of English alabaster. To one side of the church was a large garden, with paths winding around the grassy lawns graced with magnificent native trees and benches for visitors to sit in the shade. Behind that stood the presbytery, a grand Romanesque mansion built in 1876 fitted with ornate white marble and mahogany inside, and the kind of space Father Bob didn't have a clue how he could possibly fill.

But it was the parish that came as a shock to him. While it had a long and proud history as the very first suburban parish in the Archdiocese of Melbourne, its future was beginning to look rather less certain. Originally known as Emerald Hill, in the early 1850s it became the site of Canvas Town, a tented metropolis set up by gold rush fortune-seekers, with a population of about 5000. The first priest to arrive, Capuchin monk Father John O'Connell, was appointed in 1854 and mass was celebrated in a tent on the ground where the present church now stood.

The area had flourished at first, and the two-hectare church precinct on the corner of Dorcas and Montague streets contained a number of impressive buildings housing schools, a kindergarten, convents, orphanages and hostels, with thousands of parishioners – mostly Irish or of Irish descent – regularly attending mass. By World War I, the population of the parish of South Melbourne had leapt to 48 000. At the start of World War II, however, the population had started to fall, and continued to fall, as the city sprawled outwards and private car ownership became more common, allowing people to more easily live away from the city. Yet the major decline came in the 1960s when the Housing Commission of Victoria stepped in to raze many of the traditional working-class terraced homes around the inner city and put up, in their place, a series of forty-five public housing blocks of flats.

'When I arrived, there were big hoardings up everywhere, and I said, "What's going on here?"' says Father Bob. 'They told me they were pulling all the cottages down and putting up public housing. I hadn't seen slums since the 1940s – that's a long, long gap. I'd been around the suburbs; no slums. I'd been to Braybrook; no slums. I'd been with the army; not perfect housing, but no slums. I'd seen TV reports on Vietnam and you thought, Oh dear, their houses look very poorly, but they weren't slums. And yet here, they had slums! Then the government got its beady eyes on land and space taken up by housing, and they wanted to sell it, they can't help themselves. But what they put in their place wasn't much better, and those social engineers physically demolished and socially really diminished the area.'

That housing program hit the population of South Melbourne particularly hard. They received the Housing Commission's first 'elevator flats', Emerald Hill Court, in 1962, along Dorcas Street from the church. The biggest blow, however, was the demolition of four complete streets and eighty-three buildings just one block east of St Peter and

Paul's to make room for the 31-storey Park Towers. On its completion in 1969, the precast concrete monolith was the second-tallest residential building in Australia, the third-tallest of any building in Melbourne, and the highest of its construction type in the world. It dominated the skyline and, from the church, it stood as a constant reminder of the loss of a large slice of the former congregation.

In addition, a swathe of the old weatherboard houses originally built for Irish wharf labourers in the Montague neighbourhood, north of the church, were cleared to make way for warehouses and car showrooms, effectively turning that area into a ghost town and cutting back the number of locals even more. In the ensuing couple of years, the population slumped to just under 27 000. Many of those left were busy rallying together to have the clearances stopped, while the planned building of the nearby Westgate Freeway cost even more homes before its start in 1975.

'Those planners ripped the heart out of South Melbourne,' says Father Bob. 'The slums were pulled down, and the neighbourhood was decimated. So many people had left the community, there was hardly any congregation left. The ones remaining were suffering social dislocation, they were shell-shocked, they were battle-scarred. They were still fighting and at the same time, they were grieving their loss. Massive surgery had been done to their region. The oldies woke up in the morning and it was almost unrecognisable. Whole swathes of it were just flattened. They were, "What the hell's happened to our town?"'

One local from that time, Carol Leahy, says they were very dark days. 'When I was a young girl in South Melbourne, we had a very big church congregation,' she says. 'In the church, there were pews up to the back doors, and every section would be taken, with people standing at the back. There'd be 2000 people at mass.

'But then in the '60s, they started to build Park Towers. Around there the houses were lean-tos, they were slums, and there were as many rats as were people. But what happened as a result was that people started leaving. The girls I went to school with all moved out to Noble Park and beyond. So throughout the '60s and early '70s, they moved to the outer suburbs. That left just the older people, which is another reason it went from a big community to a small one.'

Those who remained had mostly lived through both the Depression and the war and, as a result, they tended to be quite traditional, conventional and wary of change. Their previous priest, Father Lou Heriot, had been a dynamic 'people person' who'd been at the parish for just four years before moving on. His predecessor, the Irish-born Monsignor Thomas Power, had served for a remarkable twenty-seven years from 1942 up until his death at the age of eighty-five. Little wonder, then, that Father Bob, with some of his more iconoclastic views, was seen by some parishioners as rather like a bull barging his way through a china shop. 'The distress flare had already gone up for what had happened to the town, and now here I'd blown into a culture that had been there for 150 years,' he says. 'The church had become a little like an old cardigan for the locals. Snatch their grandmother's cardigan from them and you'll have trouble. And that's what happened.'

His first curate, Father Kevin Burke, now the priest at Eltham, says it was a complete contrast in style. 'Lou was quite progressive but more traditional than Bob, although everyone looks a lot more traditional alongside Bob! Bob was a colourful, charismatic type, like a prophet from the Old Testament who challenges people. He had a strange way of talking too, and of presenting things.'

Local man Kevin Lee attended his first mass and was astonished by the new priest. 'I thought, what the hell has the archbishop done to us?' he recalls. 'He seemed gruff and angry, and wanted us to do more for the poor. After that, I saw some people dodging his masses to go to one of his assistant priest's. He got stuck into people, said we weren't doing enough. So it was easier for some people just to go to a different mass and hear sweet things. But after a while, I got used to him, and liked what he was saying and doing.'

Father Bob's outbursts could sometimes be pretty intemperate. 'He'd say that we should be solving other people's problems, especially those of us better equipped to help,' says Frank O'Connor, who'd first met him as the cadet chaplain at CBC and had started attending his church after being intrigued by a sign on the side of the church bearing a quotation from Che Guevara about struggle being a part of life. 'It was very challenging stuff he would throw at people and occasionally, in typical Bob fashion, he would go over the top. You'd feel harangued about doing something about those less well-off, and that used to turn a few people off.'

Carol Leahy felt much the same. 'He was very, very different to anyone we'd ever known,' she says. 'He came in with his own ideas, and just went for it. He was so confronting with his thoughts, and he rattled a lot of people's cages. It could be hard sitting there, with him yelling at you sometimes from the pulpit! Some people left, and never came back. Some people left, but then came back later, over time, while some new people came in too. At the beginning, I really didn't like his ways and how he handled things. But then, all of a sudden, one day I understood what he was saying and how he was applying it to everyday life, and it all started to make sense to me.

'A lot of people used to come out of church on a Sunday after the service and say he'd made them rethink a lot of things and how they'd agreed to do one thing that week they'd never done before, like go out of their way to help someone, smile and say hello to someone or look carefully at their attitudes to others, try to listen to people with a different point of view and share their ideas. Then you'd find out that person wasn't that different to yourself. He always made us think.'

There were other aspects of the parish that made it a less-cohesive community, too. The underworld war for control of Melbourne's waterside was in full swing at that point and, just a month after Father Bob's arrival, the feared Federated Ship Painters and Dockers Union top dog Pat Shannon was gunned down in a South Melbourne pub, the Druids Hotel. With Australia's most corrupt union pretty much a criminal subculture, a network of gangsters later featured in the 'Underbelly' TV franchise whose crimes included murder, standover rackets, theft, extortion, drug dealing and prostitution, locals lived in fear that the fighting, as well as the incipient drug wars, would spread. 'I wasn't used to things like that,' says Father Bob. 'It didn't fuss me, but South Melbourne hadn't been terribly welcoming in the first place . . . But one of the assistant priests went off to give a comment to the media, and I started thinking that maybe we should set up a room in the house as a radio studio . . .'

Some parts of South Melbourne, particularly around the new estates, were also plagued by many of the same problems that the planners had hoped to solve. A number of the new tenants were unemployed, living in poverty and suffering poor health, conditions made worse in the early '70s by economic stagflation (caused by the dramatic rise in oil prices as a result of the Organisation of Arab Petroleum Exporting Countries' embargo), and the increasing rate of divorce and family breakdown.

After World War II, South Melbourne had received a large number of migrants too, many of whom were refugees and displaced persons still suffering the trauma of leaving their homelands. With the increase in Housing Commission homes available in the 1960s, the number of migrants to the area rose steadily, from 5.7 per cent of the population before 1960 to 8.9 per cent up to 1970. The newcomers were usually on lower-than-average incomes, forced to work in unskilled jobs, and they routinely suffered the kind of discrimination common before the abolition of the White Australia Policy in 1973. In short, many were getting a pretty raw deal.

And it was often their children, torn between their parents' culture and the desire to fit in with their peers at school, who were struggling the most. 'I found many of the kids were really alienated,' says Father Bob. 'They didn't know which way to go, which culture to be a part of. They were under terrible pressures. Some of them had left home, looking for somewhere to stay, while others were still at home, but they were alienated at home. I decided we should really try to help these young people, we should do a lot of social justice work, we should be looking outwards to help others. We should remodel ourselves as a missionary church, a parish with a mission.

'Our patron saints, Peter and Paul, two giants of Christian strength, made it easier for me to find a focus for South Melbourne pastoral and missionary strategies. Ordained for the old Church, but destined to work in the new, I was already inclined towards ambivalence: orthodox and unconventional is the style I personally adopt. To do the Church's thing in one's own way is the best combination I can propose. In a nutshell, Peter kept the faith, he was the orthodox one, while Paul was orthopractical: he got things done and made sure the faith was shared around, especially among people previously thought ineligible. Peter was blessed with a rock-solid conviction that Jesus had conquered sin and death. Paul couldn't rest until everyone everywhere had heard the Name and been shown the Way.

'The name of the church suits me. Both have to exist together. You can't have one without the other, and that's the problem with the clerics in the Church today. They say the faith is more important, whereas I believe what you do with it is the most important thing. The faith had been preserved in South Melbourne by staunch and loyal Catholics, but each generation has to find its own expression of Catholicism.'

At first, Father Bob used all his old tried and true methods. He organised football games, he opened up a nearby tennis court, he turned an old vacant block behind the church into a basketball court and he started a gym for youngsters to learn how to box at the back of the presbytery. In 1975, the new

Labor government launched a disadvantaged schools program to provide additional financial assistance for more than 1000 schools whose students suffered special socioeconomic difficulties. 'Someone rung us up and told us we were a disadvantaged area, and asked what our primary school on the property needed to make a difference,' says Father Bob. 'I told them we'd like a PE teacher because we'd never had one and I thought that would really help the kids. So they eventually said we could have the money for that.'

The trouble was, some of the young people Father Bob was trying to help had much more serious problems. Heroin and substance abuse was just becoming a part of their lives, and much more dramatic action was needed. 'The place was awash with drugs at that time,' he says. 'I didn't know anything about those. In the suburban parishes I'd been in, we'd have a game of footy or basketball and have a chat, and everything would be all right. It was all so simple. This was a completely different world. These kids were in inner-city Melbourne in an area that had been decimated by social engineering, their lives were tough and it was pretty hard for them to play basketball, and both impossible and dangerous for them to box, if they were drunk or out of it on drugs . . .'

But if all those people weren't coming to the church to receive help, Father Bob made a monumental decision: he would take the church to them.

9

Greater Fools Than Me

Father Bob Maguire knew reaching out to a bunch of young people who weren't regular churchgoers, with many never having been to his church – or perhaps any church – in their lives, would be a tough call. But he was determined to try. It would just take a bit more creativity to find ways of making contact and then taking the church, and its resources, to them. He could use the church buildings and grounds to give them a safe place of refuge, as well things to do with all the sporting areas he'd started, while he could work beyond the church as well to find new ways of making sure they could survive and thrive. So immediately he set out to visit those kids in the places they liked to go, where they felt comfortable, on street corners, in parks, in coffee lounges and outside hotels.

'We'd go to wherever they gathered to connect,' he says. 'As a result, we ended up making contact with a lot of young people in the district. It didn't come naturally to us because a lot of the people needing our help were migrants, and they were Greek Orthodox, Muslims, Catholics – but not Roman Catholics – Kurds and so on. It was fascinating to interface with them, but we had to work out what we could do, what we had to offer them. As part of that, I also did more work as an honorary probation and parole officer so I could be on hand if anyone got into trouble. We were never there to proselytise; we wanted to offer them good, practical help.

'While there were homeless kids around, many of the kids in the neighbourhood were still at home, but they were alienated at home. Their parents were from one culture, and they were growing up in another and they were having to work through a big clash of those cultures, and it was often very difficult for them. But one thing we did have was a back room behind the presbytery. We thought we could open it up and offer them that as a safe place to go. These days, I know the last place a kid goes to look for safety is with a Roman Catholic priest, but in those days it was the only safe place.'

Slowly but surely, the neighbourhood kids responded and started dropping by for a chat, or a coffee, or to meet up with other young people in the presbytery. Father Bob, as a young boy, may have been denied a church meeting place by his old priest, but he sure as hell was going to make sure these kids had a safe space of their own.

Then, one day, he had a call from Social Services. They'd found a young man from Sydney wandering the streets on his own, sleeping rough. Could Father Bob extend his help to him?

He was only seventeen, yet he had the haunted, world-weary look Father Bob had seen so often in the eyes of men returning from fighting in Vietnam.

But Brian Rudd's battles, the priest soon learned, had been of a completely different kind. And they'd started at the age of just three months when the authorities took him and his four brothers away from their parents, both chronic alcoholics.

From that point on, Brian's life as a ward of the state became even tougher. He was sent to a boys' home in Ballarat, 110 kilometres north-west of Melbourne, where the regime was hard and disciplined, and if any one child overstepped the mark or played up, everyone was punished. Brian still felt luckier than most, however. Often his older brothers would try to protect him, and the five little boys made an earnest vow to each other: to always stick together and look out for one another.

But at seven years old, Brian's world again came crashing down around his ears. The brothers were summoned and told they were being moved on – and each to a different children's home. 'I think they thought if they split us up, we'd be easier to control,' says Brian. 'It's harder to push you around if you're a tight-knit little group. There were 170 boys in that home, and they saw us as a threat! So the easiest thing for them to do was eliminate the threat. I was sent off to a boys' home in Surrey Hills, Melbourne, and I never saw my brothers again.'

Five years later, he was moved again to another home and, at the age of twelve, he tried to take his own life. He survived – just – and was later transferred to yet another home. Three of these homes were to become notorious as places where cruelty to children was routinely practised, as described in the

2004 report of the Senate inquiry Forgotten Australians. In one, youngsters were locked in isolation in cupboards, dark rooms, attics and cellars for long periods as punishment for minor misdemeanours; in another, a common punishment was forcing children to scrub toilets and corridors with toothbrushes.

'It felt I spent my whole childhood locked up,' says Brian. 'Every so often, it seemed I was being re-arrested and being sent somewhere worse.' At fifteen, he finally escaped, and went to work in a brickyard. Then he decided that he desperately wanted to see his family again, and set out for South Melbourne, where he'd been born, to look for them. The news he could glean about his brothers wasn't good. One, he learnt, had hanged himself. The suspicion was that he'd been sexually abused in his children's home. Another brother had jumped off a bridge and ended up breaking his back.

Undeterred, Brian continued searching for his mother. It took him a long time to trace her but, when he finally knocked on her front door, there was nothing like the warm welcome he'd so fondly imagined all those years. 'She didn't want to know me,' he says bluntly. 'It was horrendous. It was extremely hard to realise even my mother didn't want me. She wasn't even sorry that she'd been made to give me up . . .'

Devastated, Brian wandered the streets until someone noticed him and reported him to the social welfare department, which contacted Father Bob for help. Brian was more than willing to meet up with the priest. 'I'd heard Father Bob was a good bloke, and I had nowhere to stay,' he says. 'So he said I could stay there for a couple of nights. But I was wary because in the homes I'd been in, priests sometimes abused children. So I refused to come in, but slept out in the garden.

Then I started to realise that he wasn't like that. And he became a very good friend to me. If he hadn't looked after me back then, I wouldn't have survived.'

By then, in 1975, the forty-year-old Father Bob was steadily winning back the local parishioners who'd found him too different and had either avoided his services, or gone off to another church. Many were now drifting back, persuaded by stories from the regulars that, while his ways were pretty unconventional, his beliefs were extremely orthodox. 'You know,' someone was heard to remark one day, 'he's a funny bloke and he does go overboard at times, but there's no doubt that he really is the genuine article. He's the full bottle with the gospel!' A woman even approached him one day to say he was dangerous. 'You're an orthodox posing as a revolutionary,' she told him. 'That makes you doubly dangerous . . .'

Father Bob was known to play up to their doubts, too. One Sunday, he thundered from the pulpit, 'I know what you're thinking! I know what you're thinking! You're thinking you've seen greater fools than me come and go!' Another time, frustrated by the way people tended to cluster in the back pews, he moved the altar to the entrance of the church so they'd be, in fact, in the front row.

He'd also regularly jest in his services about his 'wife', waiting in the wings for him, by the name of Grace. On other occasions, he told the congregation that they were listening to 'the ravings of an idiot' but interspersed this with socioeconomic issues allied with faith. 'Religion; forget religion,' he was fond of saying. 'It's full of mumbo jumbo. It's always a question of faith and The Truth.'

One day he even managed to scandalise nearly everyone by turning up after the death of Pope John Paul I in 1978, just before his successor was named, carrying a rolled-up newspaper, and declaring, 'I've got the form guide!' But, slowly and surely, he managed to charm the locals with his passion for his cause, his firm faith, the way in which he made the gospel so accessible and engaging, and his eagerness to take his ministry to the people, rather than wait for them to come to him.

In that, he was also extraordinarily inclusive. The hymn 'Glory to God in the Highest', the words the angels were said to have sung when Jesus's birth was announced to the shepherds, he loved instead to paraphrase as 'Glory to God in the Lowest'. He made it his duty to call on sex workers in the area, responding to any critics that they were just as much his parishioners as any regular churchgoer. Occasionally, he'd take along visiting seminarians, established clergy and even the odd nun working with him too. 'But they'd generally only last about twenty minutes,' he chuckles. At one point, he received a male truckie into the church who'd undergone a sex change to become a woman, and performed a baptism for her new self.

He turned out to have a great way with children, too. He talked to them in a remarkably egalitarian way, as if he were taking them into his confidence, never talking down to them. If, when he was taking mass or giving a talk to a school, he spotted a child who had anything wrong with them, or were perhaps in a wheelchair, he always made reference to them, to try to make them feel special, and included. His old curate Father Kevin Burke remembers him taking his first communion at a South Melbourne school when a father pushed his son in, lying on what looked like a hospital trolley. Father Bob immediately snapped to attention. 'Park over here!' he yelled, pointing to a spot near the front. 'There's no meter here!' And when he felt the service had gone on too long, he asked Father Burke if they could leave out a part of it, then went back to the microphone to say, 'Look, we've had a committee meeting here, and we've decided that's enough . . .'

His experiments weren't always successful, though. One of his early group of kids, John Cindric, remembers how the priest built a ramp for them to use with skateboards and rollerskates. 'He was always helping us, and we loved that!' he says. 'It was just great hanging out with him and catching these snippets of thought balloons that came from his head. But two weeks later, some of the mums came down and beat the shit out of it. They thought the kids could get hurt.'

Father Bob would also regularly go down to the wharves to see members of the Painters and Dockers Union, against the advice of many people worried about his safety. But the army had prepared him well for facing tough people who frequently used strong language. In fact, he was never averse to using similarly colourful language himself where he felt the occasion warranted.

'He did a lot of work with people who were un-churched, unhappy, dysfunctional and might be considered by others to be outcasts,' says former army Major John Guy, who first met Father Bob at a character-leadership course and, inspired by his example, went on to devote his life to helping kids in trouble through his own Southern Cross Leadership Program. 'In that, he was a true priest. He didn't require people to come to where he was; he would go to where the people went. Some people might find that side of life ugly, and rough and difficult, but he saw the beauty in people whatever they were up to. I saw him as imitating Christ in that work.

'He was operating on the fringes of the Church even back then. A lot of officials of the Church didn't like what he was doing but that's what Christ experienced as well with Judaism. The God "experts" didn't recognise him, but the poor people did. Father Bob is about the ministry of Christ, of the miracles of love and healing rather than about the institutions of the Church. He was never judgemental, either. He just had this great joie de vivre, with a lovely humour. Listening to him was like listening to Alfred Hitchcock. He looked like him, he told a great story, and he had this wonderful dry humour. As well, he was totally unaffected. It didn't matter to him who he was talking to; he was always himself. He'd talk to a room full of generals and majors and captains of the army, and he'd still say, "Now, darlings, let's talk about such and such . . ." And then he'd speak in such a good, earthy way, everyone would listen.'

In his determination to make his church all-embracing, he wasn't prepared to toe anyone else's line. Well-known Labor Party senator and official Pat Kennelly, a South Melbourne local, had been banned by his own church in the bitterness over the 1950s Labor 'split' in which he'd battled hard against the influence of the right-wing Catholic movement on the party. Father Bob instead invited him along to services at St Peter and Paul's. He even offered an apology from the Catholic Church for their treatment of him. And after the discovery of the body of Jack 'Putty Nose' Nicholls, the man who'd followed murdered Pat Shannon to become the secretary of the notorious Painters and Dockers and was infamous for uttering the immortal line about the union turf war, 'We catch and kill our own', Father Bob volunteered to perform the funeral.

On the day of the service, union members brandishing their banners marched in a long funeral procession along Dorcas Street to the church and then stood outside. Father Bob immediately shouted out, 'Tell them Dockers, if they're not going to come in, we'll have to come out!' They all obediently filed in.

Damian Coleridge had moved to South Melbourne for a job teaching art history at the Victorian College of the Arts the same year that Brian Rudd first knocked on Father Bob's door. Damian's brother Mark, later to become the Archbishop of Brisbane, suggested he go along and listen to this most unusual priest. He did, and was startled by the figure at the pulpit.

'I'd never been a regular churchgoer and, when I sat half-way down the church listening to him, I thought he must be nuts!' says Damian. 'He was just so different. Then someone there asked me to come to a liturgy meeting, so I did. I was just intrigued by what Father Bob was all about. And one thing led to another . . .'

As a result of that first meeting, Damian ended up staying on at the church to organise parish liturgies and become almost Father Bob's right-hand man. As a volunteer, he tried to put into practice many of the priest's ideas, schemes and pet projects aimed at involving his congregation in helping those less fortunate. Their relationship fell into a steady pattern. Father Bob would go off early in the morning for his daily bicycle ride in the neighbourhood, around South Melbourne, Albert Park and Middle Park, cheerfully hailing everyone he met along the way. On his return, he'd call Damian aside to tell him he'd had yet another idea.

'Whatever needed to be done, I'd do it,' says Damian. 'Bob's always been a great entrepreneur, full of ideas, some more ambitious than others. One day, he rode his bike past a place opposite South Melbourne market and saw a For Rent sign in the window. He said, 'That's an interesting spot! We should try to get hold of it!' Then I'd go and look at it and think, How could we make use of it? Eventually, that place became The Produce Store, involving eighty of our parishioners.'

Damian helped rally everyone to renovate the old store, paint it, furnish it and then run it for local people. It became a tea, coffee and scones shop and a popular meeting place. One visiting German sailor went there and declared it his favourite coffee house because of the friendliness of all the staff and other customers. It helped make money for Father Bob's other projects too. After all the running costs, and the voluntary work of parishioners – aged from just ten years old to eighty-three –who cleaned, cooked, sewed, washed the tablecloths and served customers, it was making a profit of two hundred dollars a month. But even after it was up and running, Father Bob didn't stop planning. He immediately went on to work out what could happen in its next phase: possibly young people opening it for other young people on Sundays.

For Father Bob, it was all about bringing his Vatican II philosophy to the parish. He wanted to empower parishioners to start and run projects, for them to take the initiative, for his church very much to be 'the people's church'. 'Youse blokes I expect to personify the Jesus of the twentieth century in this neck of the woods,' he explained. He was simply, as he was becoming so fond of saying in a flashback to his army days, merely the commander-in-chief. 'Or think of me just as the conductor of the orchestra,' he'd tell the congregation. 'You are the ones playing the instruments, you are the ones making the music. I'm not a one-man band.'

Local Frank O'Connor says Father Bob didn't want even liturgy to be a spectator sport; he wanted it to be interactive and to be the people's liturgy. 'He didn't want the Scriptures just to be read,' Frank says. 'He wanted them to be dissected, the meaning for today, here and now, understood and implemented, with people really living the gospel message. He felt that the Vatican II message was to "flatten the model", that the Church couldn't remain dominated from the top by the Pope and bishops, but that it belonged to the people, the parishioners. They were part of his constant message to encourage us to take responsibility for our parish, with our liturgical celebrations designed by and for local people, and where people have an idea or the passion to do something he would support them to the hilt and give them the authority.'

As a result, members of the congregation started playing an active part in services, taking over the readings and coming up with different ways of celebrating religious occasions. To begin with, this different way of doing things baffled some people but gradually they became used to it, and many began to relish being more involved. 'Instead of just preaching to us about religion, he let us live religion,' says parishioner Carol Leahy. 'At first, a lot of things flew over our heads. But then he made us use our brains and delve a bit deeper. My spirituality and faith grew. It became an everyday faith instead of just once a week.'

A number of projects around St Peter and Paul's were also

taking off and flourishing. Even the basketball had grown to the point where four male teams and one female team had been formed, with locals helping to coach and run the teams, as well as entering them into various tournaments. Two men had also come forward to run the boxing gym, as different from each other as chalk and cheese: Bob, who'd migrated to Australia from Burma in 1964 and was an amateur who'd won seventy-five of his seventy-eight fights, and went on to train Olympic boxers; and Charlie, an Italian and a professional boxer with eleven fights behind him.

There were also plays put on at a local hotel, film nights, parish dinner-dances and tea and coffee served at get-togethers after the Sunday mass. Although attendances were still dwindling from the huge masses of the 1930s and 1940s, and the church had been reconfigured to seat 225, between 700 and 900 people would still attend services at Easter and Christmas. At Easter there was also an Easter parade, and on Shrove Tuesday a procession through South Melbourne complete with a Scottish pipe band, clowns, banners and streamers, followed by pancakes at the town hall. At Christmas, one of the parishioners would craft a Christmas tree into a cross and a group would go carolling to raise funds. At Pentecost, to symbolise the flame of the Holy Spirit coming down to the apostles, the tree would be burned.

A young mothers' prayer group was set up, a children's liturgy group and kids' camps of the kind Father Bob had run in his younger days as a seminarian. Talks were held with the great Sydney-based humanitarian Reverend Ted Noffs about starting up adult education centres, and a weekly newsletter, the 'Southerly Buster' – that's continued to this day – was launched. Meanwhile, the parish council was revitalised, and encouraged to become more flexible, open and engaged with the local community. The house at the back of the presbytery was turned into a meeting place and a venue for young people to gather, and sometimes sleep overnight, and was dubbed the Outback House.

It wasn't always smooth sailing, however. Some of the young people were quite volatile, particularly if they'd been drinking or taking drugs, and incidents weren't uncommon. One helper once had a knife held to his throat, the police were called and everyone was pulled out and lined up against a wall until the police accepted that the situation had been brought under control. Also, some of Father Bob's ideas were so audacious, no-one could even begin to imagine how they might be acted on successfully or ever work in the way he outlined. Others foundered on a shortage of funds. The priest also sometimes clashed with his parishioners over what some saw as his haranguing them to help those less well-off.

Father Bob saw it a little differently. 'You'd throw the cat among the pigeons, and the pigeons would flap their wings and run around until they all eventually settled down,' he says. 'And if it hadn't all eventually settled down, of course, then I'd have been forced to move on. I wouldn't have stayed.'

But stay he did, and he embarked on more and more far-reaching changes. One of the most important was opening up the presbytery to become a house in which everyone was welcome. Father Bob had said early on that it wasn't the church's role to lock its doors against such a sea of misfortune. Now, on any single day, its occupants might include someone helping him out in the house, a youngster who'd needed somewhere to stay for a night, an outreach worker, local volunteers having a meeting about an event or project, one of the basketball coaches, a visiting priest from another area, a pastoral worker, a parish group having a meeting, or someone preparing a dinner for another bunch of parishioners. 'More and more, the presbytery has become the parish house, a meeting place, a home for the heart and open to all,' says Father Bob. 'Inch by inch, the door has been opened. Even at times if it's a little like a madhouse, still everyone is welcome.'

Damian, along with Father Bob and the priest's newly acquired dog, a standard poodle called Rocky, was often at the centre of all the activity. 'My main interest was involving other parishioners in the life of the parish,' he says. 'And that's where I discovered the body of Christ. His body isn't dead and buried; it was with that motley mob in South Melbourne, an incredibly motley bunch of people, marvellously motley. Someone once said that it's easy to experience God in your world, you just have to open the door. And that door was opened in South Melbourne back then.'

Damian now had a job as a teacher's aide in a local high school to help support himself while continuing his voluntary work for Father Bob and the church, including involvement in Sunday masses. 'There were some people who were wary of Bob and his ways, but once they'd got to know him, they liked him,' he says. 'Not many people dropped out. People in South Melbourne were generally very faithful. Bob was someone who'd found a home in South Melbourne and fallen in love with the people, especially the outsiders and the ones who didn't have homes themselves. So while the locals might have gone over a bit of a speed hump at first, once they'd adjusted, they really liked him. You might have strong disagreements with him but the bottom line is that he speaks from the heart of Christian matter, he lives the gospel of Jesus Christ full-on. I don't think anyone who came through that place didn't leave the better for it. No-one felt short-changed.'

Father Bob was, more and more, being dubbed the local 'people whisperer', as someone you could go to with problems and, although he couldn't always solve them, he would still make you feel so much better about yourself. And even when he occasionally downright refused to help the odd visitor, no-one complained.

One homeless man, Robert, came by one day to eat breakfast out the back. Afterwards, he called up to Father Bob to ask for some cash. The priest came out on to the balcony and shook his head. 'I know you've got a bottle of whiskey in your coat pocket,' Father Bob shouted down to him. 'And a bottle of pills in your backpack. So no! Get out of here!' At that, the man laughed uproariously. 'Good on you, Father,' he yelled back. 'See you next time!'

Brian Rudd's visit to St Peter and Paul's changed both the lives of Father Bob and his parish in other ways, too. The next year, Brian, by now a regular visitor, called by to tell Father Bob about another young man having terrible problems in the neighbourhood. 'He's even worse off than me!' he exclaimed. His name was Costas and he was, in turn, to have a massive impact on everyone he came into contact with. And for Father Bob, he was to end up, years later, causing more heartache than anyone could ever have thought possible.

10

Talking the Talk and Walking the Walk

Costas Vasiliou was a wild kid, the likes of which Father Bob Maguire had never before encountered. He'd first come across him at the age of fifteen, after a social worker called to see if the priest would be prepared to mentor the boy. Costas wasn't a bad kid, but he desperately needed a kindly guiding hand, she'd said. He needed a personal mentor, someone who could spend quality time with him on his own. Could Father Bob help? Would he?

Father Bob was reluctant to get involved with such a young child. 'No, no, no,' he insisted. 'A Catholic priest and a fifteen-year-old boy? Can you imagine how that would look to the outside world? I'm not the right person for this.' Of course, the priest had helped many boys and young men before, but either they were always together with their friends, or there were plenty of other people around them all the time. That way, he felt both he and his charges were protected from anyone thinking there was anything untoward happening from either side.

'Some of the kids we helped were precocious, and they'd insinuate themselves into the kitchen of the presbytery to get a feed,' Father Bob says. 'If you saw that now, kids in a Catholic presbytery, you'd jump to the conclusion that the priest was a paedophile. But those kids always travelled in groups, thank God, so that made it all so much easier. You wouldn't be alone with them. You wouldn't even give anyone the chance to think anything bad was happening. But now they were suggesting I mentor a fifteen-year-old boy, and I knew that could be a recipe for disaster.'

The social worker, however, was just as determined. 'But you have a great reputation for helping kids, and you've been a probation officer for years,' she replied. 'You could make a huge difference to his life.'

The priest sighed. 'Well, why don't you get him put on probation then?' he asked finally. 'Then I can be his probation officer, and I'll help him that way.'

Then, in a totally unrelated approach, Brian Rudd also came along, suggesting he give Costas a hand. Father Bob, by then forty-one, suddenly felt he had no choice but to meet the boy, and see what he could do for him. It was a decision that would have repercussions for decades to come.

For Costas, Father Bob soon discovered, had real psychological problems. Many could be traced directly back to his family, who'd migrated to Australia from Cyprus in the late 1950s. Back home, his father had been a member of the Ethniki Organosis Kyprion Agoniston, a Greek Cypriot paramilitary group fighting a violent campaign for an end to British rule in Cyprus, and had been imprisoned for a time, possibly tortured. As if that wasn't bad enough, when they arrived in Melbourne they were all put to work by the member of their extended family who'd sponsored them to come. 'I think the father was already mad by the time he got here, and then the indignity of discovering his family was being put to work by better-off members of the family finished him off,' says Father Bob. 'He never got over that. He had a strong sense of justice, and that felt unjust. He felt he'd suffered a grave dishonour. Here he was, a man and his wife and their seven sons and one daughter installed above a fish and chip shop having to work long, long hours, with very little freedom . . .'

He and his wife were already traumatised, and found it extremely hard to look after such a large family. As a result, they put each of the boys, from time to time, into boys' homes to be looked after. They imagined they'd be better cared for there, but sadly, some of the boys emerged even worse, having suffered physical or sexual abuse. Two died young.

Costas, the middle son, was so eager to avoid being put into care that he'd race home from school every lunchtime to wash the breakfast dishes, and then run back at the end of the day to tidy the house ready for his mum to come back from the factory where she worked to earn extra money. He'd hoped she'd never make him leave home but when he too was put into residential care, he was devastated. 'The mother just couldn't handle her kids,' says Father Bob. 'But Costas was always angry about that. He felt so betrayed. He resented that all his life. He'd been the one who looked after his mum and the other children. He'd come home from school to clean and polish and be the good, reliable son. He couldn't believe what she'd done to him. He too ended up with a great sense of injustice, just like his father.'

By the age of fifteen, he'd already become a regular drug user and had a criminal record. 'He was sad first, then mad, then bad. Costas went from one home to another to another, but he would never talk about his times there. He felt abused, mostly emotional abuse from his family, but then the persistent post-trauma stress of having been a ward of state. At one place, he had weekend leave and one of his brothers was meant to pick him up and take him home, but he'd often be left at the gate, waiting, waiting, and no-one would come. Imagine that! You're looking forward to two days away and then it would get darker and darker and you're still standing waiting, always at the risk of the manager coming out and saying, "You've got to come back now." He'd then hide, just in case his brother would still come. And if his brother did come, he'd immediately put Costas down, saying he was only a drug addict. Whether that convinced him he might as well carry on like a lunatic, I don't know . . .'

Father Bob tried hard to get Costas professional help, to have him put into rehab, a health unit, a halfway house. But no solution ever stuck, or seemed to work out. Costas would reappear from time to time to sleep in the back room, the Outback House and sometimes in the presbytery itself. At other times, he'd just disappear, roaming around the neighbourhood.

He never took drugs in front of Father Bob, but the priest often had reason to suspect he was still using heroin. There were times when Father Bob dearly wished he hadn't taken on Costas but, then again, he knew the boy had nowhere else to turn and, because of his own life, he knew that feeling well. He saw himself as having an inescapable duty to help, especially since no-one else would. 'We were very protective of Costas but, in hindsight, we should never have got involved,' he says. 'We thought he'd thrive with opportunities and the chance for redemption but redemption was never on the cards, really. We had no idea that the care would last so long . . .'

Costas's plight had also helped alert Father Bob to a fast-growing problem in Melbourne: youth homelessness. Costas had nowhere to go, neither did Brian, and more and more young people were turning up at the church also looking for somewhere safe to sleep.

Back in the mid-1970s, youth homelessness wasn't recognised as a significant social problem; it was seen merely as a predicament affecting a few isolated individuals. But throughout the decade, it was emerging more and more clearly as a major crisis in society brought about by changing economic, social and political conditions. A shortage of affordable housing, rising unemployment, the breakdown of families, an increase in domestic violence and the availability of hard drugs all played a part. Two influential reports, the Report of the Working Party on Homeless Men and Women, in 1973, and Homeless People and the Law, in 1976, both revealed youth homelessness to be a growing problem, with estimates that there were between 3000 and 4000 people homeless each night in Melbourne alone. Ten years later, in the mid-1980s, the accounting firm Coopers and Lybrand put the national figure at close to 40 000.

Father Bob was now seeing with his own eyes a growing number of young homeless people arriving at his door, often traipsing down to South Melbourne from St Kilda and Fitzroy along a route he nicknamed the Ho Chi Minh Trail. Always touched by their stories of difficulties and desperation, and having never had a secure, stable home himself as a kid, he empathised hugely with their plight, and wondered what he could do.

Finally, after talking it through with everyone around him, he decided to set up a halfway house in a two-storey terrace on nearby Cecil Street to provide emergency accommodation for some of the young people. It was to be staffed by volunteer parishioners and, in time, hopefully, qualified youth workers. The decision was made that the philosophy of the project should be 'to encourage the local community to fulfil its Christian obligation in providing emergency accommodation and counselling to needy youths without counting the cost'. While the Victorian Government provided a grant for its setup, most of the funds from that point on were raised by locals. 'A fantastic amount of work was put in on a voluntary basis,' says Father Bob. 'It ranged from volunteer live-in workers to cooks and cleaners and local businesses donating goods and services. Also, a local businessmen's group was formed to raise funds and encourage donations. It showed that with genuine effort on the part of ordinary people, great things can be achieved.'

One of the people pledging a huge amount of time to the project was Henry Nissen. A former Commonwealth boxing champion, he'd just retired from his fighting career and was running a clothing business with his family, working as a volunteer with disadvantaged youth at Pentridge Prison and doing welfare work in a children's home in Burwood, when he met the priest. 'I was doing well, and felt it was about time I gave something back to the community,' he says. 'The next thing I knew, I was doing street work and helping run Cecil House and doing . . . well. . . whatever Bob wanted me to do.'

In Henry, Father Bob had found a great asset. He too had endured a difficult childhood, so he was naturally empathetic with kids going through tough times. He and his twin brother Leon had been born to a Jewish family in 1948 in a refugee centre in what had been the Nazi concentration camp at Belsen. Their father, a tailor, had fled Poland for Russia and served in the army, marrying a Ukrainian girl. The couple, their son and their twin boys migrated to Australia when Henry was one, with his mum immediately suffering a nervous breakdown. His dad was working so hard to keep their heads above water that Henry and his brothers were in and out of children's homes until the age of ten.

A little kid and a natural target, Henry was beaten up by a school bully and decided to learn how to fight. Leon soon joined him and the pair won numerous boxing titles throughout their careers, appearing as regulars on the television show 'Golden Gloves'. Henry represented Australia in the Commonwealth Games, won the Australian and the Commonwealth flyweight titles and was, in the early 1970s, the number-three contender for the World Title. His nickname as a boxer was 'Hammering Henry, the Hustling Hebrew'. Now he invested a lot of that hustling into raising funds for Cecil House, and much of his passion into helping kids. As well as working for a tailor during the day, he ended up one of the most regular locals at the halfway house, donating money to help with its upkeep as well as fundraising, running it day-to-day, cooking meals there in the evenings, and sleeping over. 'Boxing was good training in becoming a youth worker,' he says. 'You need a lot of discipline in boxing, and that spills over into keeping your life in order and trying to help others manage their lives better too.'

He was extremely well equipped for his work in other ways, too. Many of the young people staying at the house were drinking heavily or taking drugs and were sometimes violent. Henry could defend himself seemingly effortlessly and was the perfect person to wade into a fight and stop it stone dead.

Father Bob often found such behaviour terribly disheartening. It was obvious some of the young people had given up all hope of ever living a normal life, and he was regularly taken aback by the degree of desperation.

'They were only young but some of them seemed twice their age,' says Father Bob. 'I'd tell them, "If you keep on going like this, you'll die." I didn't realise they didn't give a rat's arse if they lived or died. But I just wanted us to get through to them. They had so much talent; they were full of it. I tried normal things, like basketball and cricket and football, but they couldn't do anything as they were so often under the influence of drugs. Some of them were crazy kids. They could no longer do normal things. Sometimes we wondered what was wrong with these kids. They were drinking cough mixture, sniffing glue, injecting themselves. But at least they weren't on the streets; they had somewhere safe to sleep.'

Henry, Damian, other helpers and later the authorities themselves saw Father Bob as becoming the pioneer for this kind of work in Australia. He was even more unusual in that he began regularly talking to the press about the problems of youth homelessness, one of the first people with a public profile and in any position of authority to do so. When he sensed that some people just didn't believe that such poverty existed on the streets of Melbourne, he even persuaded a TV station to send a camera crew out with him. The story they came back with caused a sensation when it was aired.

Henry enjoyed Father Bob's approach, liked the work, got on well with the kids and proved an expert at encouraging other volunteers to come and lend a hand. One of them, Liz, a teacher at St Peter and Paul's Primary School and a volunteer cook at Cecil House on a Monday night, he even ended up marrying – with Father Bob officiating on the steps of St Peter and Paul's, since Henry, not being a Catholic, could hardly be married inside. 'It wasn't a terribly romantic way to meet,' says Liz, who at the time of writing had just celebrated their thirtieth wedding anniversary. 'But the halfway house was a very worthwhile project. Father Bob was very open all the time to trying new things to make a difference.'

After three years of Cecil House, Father Bob realised this experiment couldn't go on for too much longer. He needed more people with expertise, he needed more money and he needed a proper structure in which to run a youth refuge for street kids. He still had local young neighbourhood people staying in the presbytery from time to time and in the Outback

House, but for these street kids from all over, he felt he needed to offer them a lot more help.

And it was then that he came across Brother Alex McDonald.

Reading the newspaper one morning, Father Bob saw a story about a Jesuit brother in St Kilda working with young homeless people. He called him and arranged a meeting.

'I thought I'd better get some expert advice on this, call in the specialists,' Father Bob says. 'No-one seemed to know much about this. No-one was doing much about it in those days. It was all so new. You can't stand back and ask, "Who will come and help us?" You have to get out there and bloody do it yourself.'

Brother Alex McDonald was a tall, thin, gangly young man, with a scruffy beard and an earnest expression, who looked much older than his twenty-eight years. But he had, it turned out, plenty of experience of homelessness – both professionally and personally. As a child in Scotland, he'd been put in an orphanage as a baby. A nun told him both his parents were dead. He still remembers vividly the day when, at six years of age, all the children were gathered together and a nun called out, 'Hands up all those of you who would like to go to Australia!' Obviously, none of the youngsters had a clue what Australia was. They imagined it might be a nice place for a day out. Everyone's hand shot up.

As a result, in 1953 Alex was one of around 50000 children shipped to Australia after World War II under the British child migration scheme, an arrangement that was later to spark massive controversy with the youngsters at its heart dubbed 'the lost children of the empire'. Many suffered physical, psychological and sexual abuse, and many, it turned out, had parents back in Britain who'd left their children in temporary care as they sorted out personal crises, only to discover they'd been shipped to the other side of the world, with no hope of contacting them.

Alex ended up in a Christian Brothers' orphanage in Western Australia, where the six year old was raped, and endured regular beatings. At twelve, he was put to work on a farm, managed to escape, was caught and sent back to the orphanage, and escaped again and went on the run. Now homeless, and all alone, he slept in parks, ate leftovers from rubbish bins, broke into houses for money to survive, joined a bikie gang and ended up in a reform centre. Eventually, a kindly couple took pity on him and took him in, allowing him to continue his education at night school.

In his late teens, however, he was shocked to be approached one day by a man who introduced himself as his brother. He, it turned out, had been shipped to Australia a few years earlier and had seen his social welfare file when he was enlisted to fight in Vietnam, discovering letters sent from their mother, and the name of his brother, Alex. The pair spent one very happy day together, vowing to stay in touch. But Alex's brother never returned from the war. He was killed in action.

Alex continued studying and eventually trained, and qualified, as a youth worker. In 1971, he joined the Jesuits in Melbourne and began his work with street kids, running the Manresa People's Centre in Hawthorn and the Mother Teresa Centre in Greenvale. Just like Father Bob, his own childhood had been tough, and he wanted to help others having difficulties, who felt they had nowhere to go and no-one to turn to.

The two men found they had similar ideologies, and the same burning desire to help kids. Brother Alex told the priest of the increasing numbers of children he'd met on the streets of Melbourne who were sleeping rough. Nearly all tended to be there through home circumstances: some had been thrown out after disagreements with parents or because their parents could no longer afford to keep them; some had run away to escape violent or alcoholic fathers; and some, usually preschool-aged children, had been dumped in parks, on the streets or even in public toilets. Many were getting involved in crime and were now taking hard drugs to blot out the pain, and pushing drugs to others to feed their own addiction. A number, both boys and girls, were turning to prostitution to earn enough money to keep going. For those streets were a hard place to live. Brother Alex himself had been slashed with a knife when he went to help a young boy he saw being cut with razor blades by gang members.

'So at that meeting with Alex, we agreed to form an alliance,' Father Bob says. 'We needed someone with experience of working on the streets, and he needed backup. So we almost reinvented the parish of South Melbourne as the parish with a real mission. You just did things like that yourself, and the top of the town [the Archbishop's office] would say, "Thank God someone's doing something! Take our blessing." And off you'd go . . .'

As a result of that meeting, the fledgling body Open Family was formed in 1978. 'We called it Open Family because if you don't have a family, you'll be lost,' says Father Bob, doubtless recalling the hard times of his own youth, when he could so easily have gone to the dark side himself. 'So we decided we'd be a kind of family to anyone who needed one instead.' Open Family immediately started gathering food, blankets and clothing for street kids and opening youth hostels in both St Kilda and South Melbourne, in Park Street, near Montague Street. Henry went along to help Brother Alex, going out into the streets at night to look for homeless kids and try to persuade them to come back to one of the refuges. Father Bob spent a lot of his time raising more funds, talking at business meetings about the urgent need for such a venture, rallying parishioners to support it, and having meetings with government bodies.

'It was all about helping people on the streets and befriending them,' says Henry. 'We were all talking to them, winning their trust, and often taking them back to the youth hostel where they could sleep the night. Some of them were on the run from the police, or had run away from home because they'd had an argument; there were times I would take the kids home on the train. Other days, I might go to court and speak up for them, talk on their behalf. I'd encourage them to go to school to get educated and try to help them in every way possible.'

His past as a boxer came in handy in a number of ways. Sometimes a street kid would become aggressive towards him, and Henry would gently mention his boxing, and then invite the kid to take the first swing. 'They always backed down then!' he laughs. 'Also, through my boxing, I became a member of the Variety Club of Australia and asked them if they would give Bob a bus. So they did, and we converted the bus to a mobile home from which we could cook and help people in need as we drove around. Providing food was a good way of connecting with people.'

TV star Tony Barber, the host of the long-running show 'Sale of the Century', as well as 'Family Feud' and 'The Great Temptation', was heavily involved with the Variety Club at the time and, in helping organise that bus for Father Bob, met up with the priest. He was instantly won over to his cause. 'He was very impressive and I found his whole approach refreshing,' says Tony, who had two teenage daughters of his own. 'It was quite remarkable to see what this guy was doing. He'd formed a good partnership with Alex for the Foundation, and the way he'd got his church to work in a social welfare capacity was much more like a Latin American church in some ways.

'His operation at that stage was pretty hand-to-mouth and I spent a lot of time in the office, helping. Bob was running the whole show, but he's less of an executive organiser and more of a street person himself! He was always so good with young people. He'd get angry with kids for taking drugs, but he'd never condemn them. He was never judgemental. I came to see him as a guy who really talks the talk, and walks the walk.'

He was also someone who never missed an opportunity to push the story of street kids and what needed to be done to an ever-broader section of the population. And very soon the chance came to bring their plight, and to propel what he and his organisation were doing, to a whole new, national audience.

11

Nothing to Live for

A dark night in St Kilda. A young girl, barefoot and in jeans, steps off a train, climbs over the high railings of the platform, crosses the road and then slumps on the ground, her back to a concrete post. Her shoulders are hunched, her face is crumpled, she looks lost to the world. She can be no more than fifteen years old.

'I don't have anything to live for, really,' she says. 'I really don't care what happens to me now. I don't know why. I just want to die.'

Further up the street, police officers talk about finding kids already dead in public toilets with needles still in their arms. 'You see girls, reasonably clean-looking kids, who don't appear to have any ties,' one says. 'You see them over a two-year period gradually destroy themselves with speed, alcohol and prostitution . . .' And another: 'This becomes so much more than a job. It could be your younger sister, slumped in the corner of a railway station or prostate in a toilet somewhere . . .'

These were scenes from the streets of Melbourne in 1982, when a documentary called *Street Kids*, made by two filmmakers who moved into a notoriously sleazy boarding house in St Kilda and befriended a number of youngsters forced by circumstance to live on the streets, shocked the world. In Australia, it premiered at the 1983 Melbourne Film Festival, provoking horror and outrage among its audience. In the US, it was reviewed by the *New York Times*, which said, 'Although this documentary is set in a small section of Melbourne, it could benefit anyone wanting to know more about the plight of homeless teens in general.'

This was the grim milieu in which Father Bob Maguire, Brother Alex McDonald and Henry Nissen now found themselves working. Brother Alex, who helped produce the documentary, also made an appearance on screen. He talked about how, by 3 a.m. or 4 a.m. in the morning patrolling the streets of Melbourne for Open Family – which in 1981 had become incorporated as the Open Family Foundation – he might have seen twenty to thirty young people between the ages of ten and eighteen wandering around and sleeping rough, gradually drifting into a life of crime, drugs and sex work to survive. 'You can't get a job without somewhere to live,' says one fifteen year old. 'And you can't get a place to live without money from a job. You're in a hole and there's no way to get out.'

For Father Bob, it was a situation completely beyond his experience and expertise. 'Back then, you didn't know what to do, you'd never come across this before,' says the then forty-seven year old. 'Some of these kids even then were too far gone to help. You didn't know what the social prognosis was for them. In those days, there was no social prognosis. It was something completely new. All people were doing was juggling them, warehousing them and recycling them through the courts. We knew we had to do something. Once you go on the streets and become involved, you always run the risk of exacerbating the alienation, but offering them a safe place to sleep was the first step.

'It was hard work, though. Alex was the one who went in and tried to sort out most of the dramas. I don't mind causing drama, but I'm not a great lover of reacting to drama. And, like Costas, a lot of them were very difficult. They were unloved and unloving, and they'd lost the art of being nice or hadn't had the chance of developing any niceness. Some people used to talk about the "deserving poor" and the "undeserving poor". The distinction was ridiculous, and it was good to have the clout of the Catholic Church to help them. But it wasn't always easy.'

Studies were beginning to delve into some of the reasons for youth homelessness and coming up with explanations such as physical, sexual and emotional abuse by parents, step parents and/or siblings, the breakdown of families, neglect, separation from the birth family, time in state care and witnessing violent acts, particularly in the home. The result was often childhood trauma, which would then make it difficult for young people to form and sustain relationships with others, sometimes for the rest of their lives. This, in turn, could lead to mental illness or substance abuse, with drugs or alcohol, in an attempt to blot out the pain. Being homeless for any period seemed to increase the trauma, with the constant risk of assault on the streets, and desperation likely to lead to crime or prostitution, for both boys and girls, to earn money.

In that same year, publicity around the Open Family Foundation and its work, the documentary and the increasing amount of research on street kids led to the 1982 Senate Standing Committee Report on Youth Homelessness. It was the first sign that the Federal Government was starting to recognise the issue as a growing social problem. While they had few concrete facts on its scale, parliamentarians also began talking about trying to put some money into helping with emergency accommodation.

For Father Bob, it was all too little too late. With the Foundation's hostels in St Kilda and his own Cecil House full of young people, Costas more often than not at the presbytery, and Brian still sometimes dropping by, he realised he and his parishioners were now playing a vital role in keeping these youngsters alive. And, more and more, those parishioners were signalling their willingness to become involved.

The parishioners themselves were still a disparate mix of long-term South Melbourne residents, Italians who'd arrived in the 1960s, residents from the public housing developments, overseas migrants and the children of those migrants, and middle-class newcomers just beginning to move into the area. 'Many people began to feel at home in this diverse parish community because, under Bob's leadership, it opened itself up and invited a great range of people to come into the parish house, the schools, the church, the basketball court out the back, and the other facilities,' says Damian Coleridge.

'Among them were homeless people, young people wanting to get off the streets, local young people often from immigrant families, people looking for a word of encouragement from someone, and many, many others. Many different people began to feel accepted and at home there and, as parishioners, we began to understand more and more that in the end we belonged to one another; that a local church had to do what Jesus did and be a home for people who had nowhere else to go. Experiencing this ourselves, with Bob enabling it to happen and giving it direction and meaning, we wanted to share it with others. It became the mission of the South Melbourne church and, in doing this, we found ourselves living out the gospels. It was real and it was wonderful. And Bob was a key figure through it all, a prophetic figure, leading by word and example.'

Costas, loud and rambunctious, could always be a challenge, especially if he'd been taking drugs, but Father Bob insisted the parish had a duty to look after him. There were a few who disagreed, but it was usually much easier to go along with what the priest wanted than argue against him. As a compromise, at one stage Damian swapped homes with Costas, so Costas moved into his rented house and he moved into the presbytery to give everyone a break.

TV news and current affairs journalist Geraldine Doogue, later to host the ABC religious affairs program 'Compass', encountered Father Bob when she was writing a documentary in 1986 about the Catholic Church, 'A Shifting Heart', and also met Costas. 'He was a gorgeous-looking boy, but he was really feral,' she says. 'He was seriously deranged. He was right on the edge. For Bob, there were tremendous ethical dilemmas. He could cope with the boy stealing from him, but when he realised he was being violent towards a girl, he told him he would be out if he laid a finger on her again. Bob was working with some seriously damaged people, for whom there might not be any redemption, and I really admired him for his open-eyed compassion.'

The first child to die hit Father Bob particularly hard.

He was a teenager who'd been living on the streets and who'd been rapidly sliding into alcoholism. Everyone had tried to help him but had been unable to get through. He seemed a child completely lost to the world around him. Not long after his sixteenth birthday, he died of acute alcohol poisoning.

Father Bob was distraught. 'He died on our watch,' he says. 'He should never have died. A young boy like that . . . it was a terrible thing. But you'd talk to these young people, and ask them how long they think they'd live. They'd say, "Till our twenties." That was shocking to me that they didn't care about life at all. But I wanted to keep them alive, they all had so much promise. All men and women are born equal, but they don't get equal access to the world's rewards. It's important to give a leg up to the people at the bottom of the ladder, because they're just as talented as those at the top; they just don't get the same opportunities. I wanted to keep these young people alive, I wanted them to fulfil their potential. But we failed with him.'

That was only a taste of the grief that was to come, too. These youngsters were incredibly vulnerable to exploitation and, without hope that things would ever get better for them, and without much guidance, often made bad choices. One eighteen year old from a Greek family had become mixed up with a gang working the streets of Melbourne. The Foundation had given him somewhere to stay, and was helping him find a job and get his life back together when gang members managed to hunt him down. He was executed on the streets. 'He got involved with some nasty underworld characters,' says Father Bob. 'A lot were dying on the southern front. I'd had no idea that kids would die or be forced into such nasty business.'

As the number of child deaths climbed, the tragedies attracted increasing publicity and local concern, and gradually the police began to become more and more involved. At a meeting with senior Victorian police officials in 1982, Father Bob and Brother Alex pressed them to crack down on the people trying to exploit the homeless youngsters, particularly sexually. At first, the police were wary of conceding the extent of the problems but finally agreed to set up a 'child abuse' unit, the Delta Task Force, to try to counter child molestation, child prostitution and the paedophile rings known to be preying on the vulnerable youngsters. It was the first time the police had tried to infiltrate such rings, and set out specifically to help prevent kids being exploited.

There were certainly some successes: the news of the formation of the crack squad was known to have deterred some people from taking advantage of youngsters, and the street kids themselves, often via Brother Alex, Father Bob or their growing band of street workers and parish volunteers, started providing information about activity on the streets. 'It worked extremely well at first,' says Father Bob. 'The young people could tell us if people were bothering them, or new drug-pushers were arriving on the scene, and we could inform the police. The police then would take action. It was always difficult, though, gathering enough evidence to actually prosecute. But it was a good lesson in the importance of forming strategic alliances and with the police involved, the public were keener to see street kids as victims rather than offenders.'

Their involvement and cooperation also gave the Foundation more credibility. Brother Alex was often invited to meetings of business leaders and charity groups to talk about its work, and often ended up leaving his audience in tears at his heartrending stories – and with sizeable sums of money in donations. 'He was extremely good at that,' says Father Bob. 'People sensed, somehow, that he was the real deal.' Delta was finally wound up in 1986 after infiltrating a paedophile support group and its attempt to set up in Melbourne, with the Victorian Police Child Exploitation Unit later set up in its place to continue its work.

Meanwhile, at home in South Melbourne, parishioners continued to become more and more involved in looking after kids, and in raising funds to allow the work to continue. Some volunteers would traipse around the platforms of railway stations, looking for homeless kids to divert to the refuges, while some prepared food to serve them and others helped staff the hostels. Still more helped out at all the sporting facilities Father Bob had made available around the place. As well as the produce store, locals also participated in Nightwatch, where they minded the presbytery on weekday evenings to keep an eye on the kids there, and were often rostered on overnight to answer the phone and door, give out food and vouchers and provide 24/7 support to people who needed it.

Parishioners started an op shop to raise money for the work with the kids, ran English classes for migrants, conducted a clinic opposite the church in Montague Street with a doctor, naturopath and masseur, and put on civic masses, debates and lectures. They also put on a number of plays, one written by Damian, with hundreds attending each production.

Building a fresh sense of community in the area, with the church at its base, also helped when they protested unwelcome changes happening in the neighbourhood, such as new massage parlours applying for planning permission – which locals feared might merely turn out to be brothels – and, even more urgently, the idea of relocating the historic South Melbourne VFL club from its home on the lake oval to Sydney. Since the population of the area had fallen to half its postwar figure, support for the club had slumped with it and it hadn't won a premiership since 1933. Now it had the chance to be reborn as Sydney's first Australian Rules team, the Sydney Swans. But since the club had been an intrinsic part of the local landscape since 1874, Father Bob joined in arguing against the move north wholeheartedly.

'So it wasn't enough to rip the guts out of South Melbourne by bulldozing the homes; now they wanted to break its heart,' he says. 'Everyone knew I was a Collingwood supporter, but I didn't want us to lose our team. Feelings ran very high about that.' In the end, however, that was one battle he didn't win.

Money was always tight at the parish because of the vast array of activities going on, yet the church and the precinct's building were in desperate need of repair and money to be spent on their upkeep. Father Bob asked the Archdiocese for a loan to fix up the church and the almost-derelict Emerald Hall, but the answer came back immediately: No, not possible. 'We were caught in a cleft stick,' he explains. 'Usually you'd have the parishioners to pay for such things but we no longer had the population we'd once had. The church was poor, too. We discovered in the presbytery a suitcase full of coins left when Monsignor Tom Power died. We also found a few unpresented cheques used as bookmarks over the years. But apart from those, we had nothing like the kind of money we needed for the buildings.

'I'd been used to being poor and I didn't mind scrounging money from parishioners. I'd been begging for money all my life, and am still begging. But we had a bit of a skeleton crew so that wasn't a real possibility for the kind of cash we needed to keep the place going.'

Instead, Father Bob took a long, hard look at the state of all the buildings and realised, with the dwindling congregation, many were hardly being used at all. Together with parishioner Frank O'Connor, he started to draw up long-term plans to make the parish self-financing. The first stage in 1978 was to sell the convent at St Vincent Place, with the proceeds going into a complete renovation of St Peter and Paul's. 'I ran the idea of selling the convent building past head office, and they agreed. We had a number of disposable assets that we really needed to dispose of, in order to keep going, and they seemed perfectly happy instead for us to sell some of those assets. That's what disposable assets are for, after all, isn't it? Disposal!'

The number of curates at the church and presbytery was also falling, down from its previous peak of four to just Father Bob. After ten years working in the parish, Damian had also left, and later took up a job with the St Vincent de Paul Society in Victoria. 'But my time with Father Bob was the formative experience of my life,' he says. 'Discovering Christ in the company of all those people . . . It changed my life forever.'

Luckily, the parish was becoming well known for its work and a number of seminarians-in-training would arrive for pastoral experience to help out. Missionaries just back from overseas would also come to stay for short spells. 'The missionaries in particular fitted in very nicely,' says Father Bob. 'They'd worked in the barrios. They understood what we were trying to do.' Other working priests would regularly drop by too, to offer their services.

Among these was a priest by the name of Father Vincent Kiss. He was a member of the Diocese of Wagga Wagga, New South Wales' largest inland city, midway between Melbourne and Sydney, but had been seconded in 1983 to work as manager for ANZ Trustees, distributing funds between various charities. He'd just bought a house up the road in Cecil Street, South Melbourne, and was now wondering if Father Bob ever needed any help conducting masses.

Father Bob was delighted. The tall, silver-haired Father Kiss came with impeccable credentials. The son of a housekeeper to the local parish priest in Randwick, Sydney, he first became a fundraiser for a missionary group, then entered the seminary in New South Wales' Blue Mountains to study for the priesthood, being ordained four years after Father Bob in 1964. He served as a curate in North Albury, then as a priest in Wagga and finally as a missionary in Vanuatu. After two years, he returned to Wagga, and took up a position as the Catholic director of youth, helping with youth camps – the kind of experience very close to Father Bob's own heart – and in 1979 he was appointed the executive director of the Youth Affairs Council of Victoria. The next year he was seconded by the Diocese of Wagga to become manager of charitable trusts for Trustee Executors. When that company crashed in 1983, its assets were taken over by ANZ Trustees, and Father Kiss was appointed manager, with the discretion to distribute up to $100 000 to good causes. What's more, Father Kiss, now fifty-one, said that the Open Family Foundation might be eligible to receive some cash from the Trust. Father Bob should just apply and he'd see what could be done.

For Father Bob, this all felt like manna from heaven. It was pretty much his first experience of philanthropy from a large corporation but, ever cautious where his beloved Foundation was concerned, and with that old army discipline deeply ingrained, he decided to double-check on the priest just to make absolutely sure all was as he'd said. He called the diocesan office at Wagga to speak to the bishop. Bishop Francis Carroll, however, had left to become Archbishop of Canberra and Goulburn and a successor hadn't yet been appointed. So instead, Father Bob spoke to a senior official who confirmed Father Kiss was a priest in good standing with the Diocese. Reassured, Father Bob then checked with the Melbourne Diocesan Office that it would be all right to make use of his offer to help, and it agreed. As a result, Father Bob suggested that Father Kiss take a number of masses at St Peter and Paul's, and happily filled in an application for funds.

Over the next year, Father Kiss proved a popular addition to the church and its work. Parishioners warmed to the elegant, charismatic priest, and enjoyed his carefully thought-out and meticulously presented services. With the funds, he proved as good as his word too. Father Bob applied, and the money did indeed come through. Father Kiss also had his own charitable foundation, sponsoring kids to come over from Vanuatu to Australia to learn computer skills they could then put to good use back home. 'I thought, "Good on him!"' says Father Bob. 'He explained that, for tax reasons, it really helped to channel funds for that charity through Australian charities so we also agreed, along with a number of other charities, to let the funds pass through the Foundation. He showed us letters from the Vanuatu Government about this.'

Father Kiss held masses at St Peter and Paul's for about a year and a half before he became too busy with his other work to continue. In the interim, he'd become a regular fixture on the Melbourne social circuit, endearing himself to all the most fashionable socialites, and philanthropists. He appeared often on the arms of Lillian Frank, Jeanne Pratt and Lady Primrose Potter as their escorts to functions, and they were always effusive in their praise of him. Jeanne described Father Kiss as 'like Jesus Christ. He is not priestly, he is saintly.' Another society matron, Sheila Scotter, said he was 'an utterly charming man' who would always support fundraising for cultural causes like the Victorian State Opera. Apart from the Open Family Foundation, other major recipients of his largesse included Lions International, International Social Services and the Fitzroy Community Youth Centre. And no-one, least of all Father Bob, suspected that he was anything but genuine.

The Open Family Foundation was, in the meantime, thriving. More and more street kids had heard of the organisation and, receiving only good reports of the work of Father Bob and Brother Alex, were coming forward to ask for help. A number of new youth workers had been taken on to expand the Foundation's services, and South Melbourne parishioners continued to put in long hours as volunteers to help keep everything going.

Henry Nissen seemed to be working all hours to help. 'We had the hostels and the food bus and we were driving around the streets, helping young people in need,' he says. 'We'd help them in any way we could, even involving them in football teams, cricket, athletics, boxing . . . everything to try to give these people a better chance in life.'

The Foundation seemed to be so incredibly busy all the time, no-one really noticed a tiny news item buried on page sixteen of the Melbourne *Age*. The article on 30 November 1987 was about a middle-aged man dying after being stabbed at a boarding house in Newport, 7 kilometres south-west of the CBD. It seemed the man had gone into his room in the early evening with two women, thought to be sex workers. An hour later, neighbours noticed the two women run out of the room, jump into his car and speed off. They found the man staggering to the front porch where he collapsed and died at the scene. The women, a pair of sisters, were later both caught and charged with murder. But thirteen days after the fatal stabbing came the bombshell. A man was now being charged with being an accessory after the fact of murder, and that man was no less than Brother Alex.

Everyone was left reeling with shock. The police were

alleging Brother Alex had provided money for the two sisters to leave Victoria, so they might manage to evade capture. He let it be known through his solicitor that he'd be contesting the charge. The Jesuit had often sailed close to the wind, everyone had to admit, but something like this was completely unexpected.

'Alex had a very troubled life and I think he often identified closely with some of the most desperate people on the streets,' says Father Bob. 'You tread a very fine line as a street worker, and sometimes that could be hard. You do get some people who get so close to the street kids, they actually become one of them. They become part of their lives . . .'

But as the months went by and Brother Alex's committal for trial was set down for November 1988, Father Bob despaired that his work with street kids, and his treasured Foundation, might all come to an untimely, and ugly, end.

12

A Day in Court

The wait for Brother Alex McDonald's court case was proving excruciating. Everyone was bewildered about what had happened and, with the Jesuit having such a high profile with the Open Family Foundation, Father Bob worried about what the fallout might be.

The parish seemed to take this latest setback in their stride, however, and rallied round to take up the slack. Reinforcements also arrived in the form of two young men Father Bob had helped a few years before, and who had never forgotten what a difference he'd made to their lives.

Chris Apostolidis had been only fourteen when he'd first met the priest in 1981, and was an angry kid. Born in Greece, but migrating to Australia with his family at the age of three, he'd had his childhood in Melbourne but then returned to Greece at the age of ten. A year later, he was brought back to Australia again. 'I was confused,' he says. 'Apart from the disruption of moving between the two countries each time, I was caught between two worlds: having a Greek background and speaking the language because that was all my parents spoke, then going out into a society that was a whole different culture. What made it even harder was, when we came here the second time, my parents bought a milk bar. But because they couldn't speak English, I had to be there, literally all day. I could only occasionally go to school; they just couldn't run it without me helping them.'

At just eleven years old, Chris had to mind the counter almost single-handedly and had a little fold-out bed underneath to sleep on when the shop was empty. Angry at having to be there such long hours, and resentful he was missing out on school and his friends, he'd take pleasure in hiding from customers, then jumping up at the last minute to take them by surprise. 'I wanted to shock people,' he says. 'I'd then stand and just look at them. I was inviting them to do something. I was this crazy kid and the anger was building up and up in me, it was suffocating me. Anyone said the wrong thing to me, I'd jump on them. I was violent. I got to the point where I knew I had to get out of that state, and I took off.'

He wandered around, sleeping at friends' houses and then, at the age of twelve, he discovered nightclubs. He'd always loved music and, looking much older than his age, he'd get into clubs and stay there all night, dancing. He started entering dance competitions and, mastering the new hip-hop dance craze out of the US, he soon began winning. In between, he'd go along to St Peter and Paul's where he let out some of his anger, boxing at the gym around the back. There he met another boy the same age, Mem River, who was also going through tough times. Some days, the pair might box or play basketball there, or join in a game of soccer. Father Bob was helping Mem at that stage, and so would occasionally have a chat with Chris, too.

'Father Bob took a real interest in my dancing, asking me about it and encouraging me,' Chris says. 'He suggested I try a bigger variety of arts instead of just the street dancing and helped me experiment. He'd take me here and there and to other schools to introduce me to other styles.' At the same time, Father Bob was also giving Mem a hand, often taking him along to charity functions and fundraisers. 'It was like he was providing a one-on-one finishing school!' says Mem. 'He'd talk to me about how to behave in public, how to speak, what fork to use for the meal. He was teaching me how to fit in.'

The priest's help felt, to both boys, absolutely invaluable. 'He constantly influenced us,' says Chris. 'The environment he'd created for us was so important. We were all touched by his influence, his goodwill, the good intent that comes from the heart. It helped far more people than he personally could, one on one. Just knowing he was there, and was supporting us, absolutely made a difference. That helps you organise yourself, it gives you some kind of purpose. And my love of dancing was greater than any other desire. It made me feel liberated, it gave me power, it was phenomenal.'

Mem had also suffered, like Chris, from a culture clash between his daily life in modern-day Australia and his home life, but his family was doing it even tougher. His parents had been members of the Kurdish aristocracy but had their land taken from them and had set up home with their five children in a single room in a Kurdish ghetto in Turkey. When they had the chance to come to Australia, they grabbed it, settling in Melbourne. But Mem's father found it extremely hard to adjust to their new life and the family suffered.

By the time Mem, the youngest of the children, had hit seventeen, he'd already been on the streets and in and out of boys' homes for five years, and had been locked up in Melbourne, Sydney, Brisbane and Adelaide for a variety of offences, including assault and robbery. 'I was a bad boy, very bad,' he says. 'I'd done a lot of drugs, heroin and everything else available, I'd been involved in prostitution myself and pimped myself as well as girls, my brothers were gangsters and I was involved with organised crime gangs. I had so much anger. But I didn't want to be part of that world anymore. It was all too brutal. I wanted to do something with my life. I wanted to study. It wasn't in my nature to be involved in the kind of things they were doing.'

A social worker eventually advised him to go to Father Bob's boxing gym to try to get rid of some of his energy in a safe environment. Over the weeks, the boxing coach there couldn't understand why sometimes he'd box well, and other times, not at all. When Mem explained that it probably depended on whether he'd had somewhere to sleep the night before and food to eat, the coach took him to meet Father Bob.

'He sat down with me at the kitchen table, and talked,' says Mem. 'Then he offered me a room and took me to see it. I was really suss and I thought, "If this old guy, if he fucking tries to touch me or anything, I'm just going to punch him in the face, knock him out, probably rob him and leave." I didn't trust anyone. Growing up on the streets, if anyone wants to give you anything, they usually wanted a lot more back from you. But while I was getting ready to deck him, he goes to a picture of the Madonna and Jesus, and a crucifix, at the top of the bed and takes them off the wall, saying, "You're not a Christian, you're a Muslim, you shouldn't have to look at these all the time." I thought, "That's different!"

'The more I stayed there, the more I began to trust him. I knew lots of the other guys trusted him, and they would have told me if anything wasn't right as we'd been on the streets together and were pretty open about that kind of thing. Then Father Bob asked me what I wanted to do and, because I hadn't been at school since the age of twelve, I said I can't read everything in the newspaper, only half a sentence of things, so he got me tutors who came in to teach me to read and write properly. Then he enrolled me in night school.'

Mem had only one real hiccup, when his brothers came looking for him and threatened Father Bob, demanding he return their 'asset'. The priest was cool and calm, and didn't budge an inch. 'I may have looked calm, but I was frightened,' he says now. 'I thought we were going to be done to death!' As soon as they'd left, he contacted an old Turkish friend who knew one of the brothers, and asked him to smooth everything over. The brothers then finally, reluctantly, retreated. Mem stayed on, carried on working at his lessons and continued at the boxing gym, where he met Chris and practised break-dancing with him, eventually entering competitions and doing appearances all over Melbourne and interstate.

Chris was also dancing with another five-person crew and

they eventually won the Australian Break Dance Competition held by the TV show 'Countdown', and were offered a tour of Australia. On the success of that, they were sent on a twenty-day tour of Asia. Chris loved the experience so much, he returned soon after and persuaded Mem to go with him this time. The pair formed a dance duo and, particularly after Mem hooked up with a big Indonesian pop star, were feted wherever they went, dancing, appearing as her support act, featuring in a couple of films, being flown around the country and being written about in magazines and newspapers. Finally, Chris and Mem split up and they both, separately, stayed on in Indonesia. Chris spent time with a family he'd got to know and became very close to them, relishing learning about a culture in which Christians, Buddhists and Muslims seemed so happy to live and work together. After a year, he returned to Melbourne, ready to start a new life back home. Mem, still with the singer, became embroiled in an underground political movement. When things turned nasty, and he was told to get out of the country as quickly as he could, he called Father Bob for help. The priest immediately sent him a ticket.

It was now 1987. Brother Alex was still awaiting trial and Costas was still causing havoc wherever he went. Mem asked Father Bob, now fifty-two, what he could do to help. The priest asked him if he could take over the old World Vision warehouse five blocks east of the church for the Open Family Foundation. He did, and started to get a range of activities going in the space, including basketball, cricket, another boxing gym and karate. When Chris had returned to Australia, he'd rented a tiny office on top of a convenience store, so Mem now asked him if he'd like to rent some space in the warehouse.

Chris happily agreed and, when Mem left to study full-time at Melbourne University, Chris worked hard to renovate the building, and to transform it into a useful, and valuable, asset for the Foundation, even starting a deli-cafeteria on the site with his brother.

Father Bob watched them with interest, taking great pleasure in how well they were both doing. 'Since the death of the first boy we'd helped, that sixteen year old, some of the other people we'd been helping had died. It was heartbreaking. Some had committed suicide; others had been killed in fights or in drug overdoses. It was so very hard each time anyone fell.

'So to see these boys coming good, it was very rewarding. I'd look at them and thank Jesus they survived, and were doing all right.'

Brother Alex finally had his day in the Melbourne Magistrate's Court on 2 November 1988, and pleaded not guilty to the charge of being an accessory to murder. The police argued that he provided cash to the two sisters who'd been arrested for the alleged murder of the man in the boarding house; Brother Alex denied the charge. After hearing from both sides, magistrate Kevin Mason finally found insufficient evidence to send him to trial, although he rebuked the Jesuit for having been 'far from frank' with police.

So while Brother Alex had been cleared, his position with the Open Family Foundation was untenable. Father Bob's old mate Frank O'Connor was given the task of telling him his role was over. It was a tough call to make, but everyone felt sure now that the Foundation would manage to survive without him.

At that, Brother Alex promptly vanished from Melbourne. It later turned out he'd returned to Perth and, many years later, was tracked down by another of his brothers. He'd also discovered their mother was still alive and had been searching for her lost children all her life. Alex made the trek to Scotland for an emotional reunion, during which she presented him with a wad of letters, written to him over the years but returned unopened by the Christian Brothers. He then came back to Melbourne, left the Jesuits, married and changed his name. He is now working in the areas of counselling and youth suicide, but he and Father Bob are no longer in contact. 'It's all past history now,' says Alex today of his involvement with the Open Family Foundation and Father Bob. 'He's a very generous man but I don't want to look back. I've nothing to add.'

Yet despite all the problems, it seemed vital that the Foundation continue its work with homeless kids. In 1989, following a two-year inquiry by the Human Rights Commissioner Brian Burdekin, his report 'Our Homeless Children' was released, revealing that between 20 000 and 25 000 Australian children, some as young as twelve, were homeless. The findings shocked the nation. Many of those children had left their family homes to escape from adults who were abusing them physically, sexually and emotionally and were living on the streets, in shopping centres, in squats, under bridges, in the bush and in clothing bins. The report, and the public outcry it caused, only served to harden Father Bob's resolve to keep on helping.

'We were always punching above our weight, especially where children had been sexually abused,' says Father Bob.

'A lot of the children were very difficult to help. But we always tried, we always offered. Sometimes kids refused our help but that didn't matter. They knew we'd be there if they changed their minds.'

It wasn't only teens and young men and women Father Bob helped, either. One day, he opened the door of the presbytery to see a basket sitting on the front step, with a soft mewing coming from inside. He bent down to pick up the basket and found a handwritten note attached to a blanket. 'Please, Father Bob,' it read, 'look after my baby.' The priest gently took the basket and its contents inside, and called the police. 'In the old days, we would have called a local woman to look after a baby like that,' he says. 'But now, you have to call the police, have the baby "arrested", and they either find the mother or a suitable home.' Many years later, the adoptive father of baby Virginia would write to Father Bob, asking for a meeting. He then turned up at the presbytery with his daughter on his arm, so they could both say, 'Thank you'.

Having successfully survived the loss of Brother Alex, an even more pressing problem for the Foundation presented itself: money. By now, the Foundation had street kids staying in the hostels, out the back of the presbytery in the Outback House and, as the number of children in need grew, even upstairs. Lots of projects were started up for them, some of which worked, and some of which most definitely didn't.

One experiment was a sandwich shop in St Kilda, which Father Bob imagined as a social enterprise where street kids could be employed, learn new skills and earn their own living. It was a good idea, and a brave move, but it never really took off. 'When it comes to the detail around some of those things,

Bob's not very patient,' says Frank O'Connor. 'So sometimes these things used to happen without anybody knowing. He'd meet an estate agent who'd perhaps say, "I've got this shop for you," and Bob would say, "OK!" He'd then commit to it without perhaps enough due diligence. That shop absorbed a massive amount of money and it became a bit of a centre for a while where street kids would hang out, but it never really developed into a social enterprise where young people were actually learning enough skills to become self-sufficient and be able to get jobs elsewhere.'

Another expensive move was a grander version of the half-way house on Cecil Street, a much bigger house by the beach at Elwood. The kids loved it, but it never worked out quite as well as was hoped. That house was closed down after about a year.

A third venture that had its ups and downs was the purchase of a farm near Ballarat. The idea was a sound one: Father Bob saw it as a great place to move youngsters away from the streets, out of their familiar inner-city environment and away from its temptations to enable them to make a fresh start. In this, he was a forerunner of successful enterprises like the New South Wales–based Youth Off the Streets, run by Father Chris Riley. But just like Father Chris's first farm, set up five years later, where two kids ended up having a baby together and others burned down a neighbour's shearing shed, it was a tumultuous ride. Things went well at first, with the farm providing a wonderful place for kids to go for short holidays, and to serve as a healthy refuge. The young people who went to stay loved it. One of the groups presented Father Bob with a photograph album of them helping out at the farm, having meals at the big old wooden table in the dining room, and clowning around afterwards, together with a pile of letters of thanks.

Some were short and to the point. 'To Father Bob, Thank you, Love Vicki,' and 'To Bob, Thanks for the trip, Dave.' Others were a little longer. 'Thanks, Bob,' another read. 'Thanks for having this trip and giving me the chance to get away to clear my head and to get away from everyone. Thanks, Stephen.' Jim felt much the same. 'Bob, This is to say Thanks for what you have done for us and this has woken me up about life. So thanks again, Jim.' A trio got together to write a joint covering letter for the album. 'Dear Father Bob, This album is given to you in gratitude for the wonderful time we all had. When we got there everyone was so nice. They all tryed [sic] to make us feel welcome. I feel we all benifeted [sic] in our own way, for me Flinders St steps are now in the past. I found that people can be nice with out wanting anything in return. I think trips like this can benifit [sic] a lot of other kids who like some of us have never been away. We are all deeply grateful for this opportunity. Thank you very much. All our love, Karen, Phil and David.'

But Father Bob simply didn't have the funds to keep the farm running smoothly, especially since it needed around $15 000 worth of work. With Brother Alex's departure, donations dropping because of the financial squeeze and so many other projects vying for the available cash, it started to prove simply too expensive to continue. In 1988, the live-in husband-and-wife team running the farm were told that their contracts were to be terminated. And at that, all hell broke loose.

The pair came to stay at the presbytery for a while, along with the kids already billeted there, then laid a complaint to the Melbourne Archdiocese, alleging the kids were getting up to all sorts of trouble, and that there were financial irregularities in the way both the farm and the Foundation as a whole were being run. They said too that they'd uncovered evidence of the misappropriation of funds by the Open Family Foundation, Father Bob or others. The priest was shocked to his core. 'The place up in the bush was a good one, but I just couldn't keep it running,' he says. 'Then the girl who managed the farm, she turned. It was totally unexpected.'

But worse was to come. The pair had also passed on their claims to a high-profile media figure who was to prove a very vocal, and powerful, enemy.

13

Making a Powerful Enemy

It caught Father Bob Maguire completely by surprise. Ever on the hunt for more funds for the Open Family Foundation and now in dire financial straits with Brother Alex gone and so many projects needing money, in late 1988 he'd come up with the idea of a radiothon to raise money.

Since the 53-year-old priest was still regularly appearing on radio, particularly with his weekly shows variously on 3AK and 3AW, more and more on TV, and with a regular column in 'The Catholic Advocate', he was becoming a well-known personality, not only in Melbourne but nationally. He hoped an appeal for funds on the radio, talking about the Foundation and its good works, would help attract donations. The parish had been raising as much as it could – a walkathon had just raised a few thousand dollars and Father Kiss's donations from the ANZ Trustees were proving useful – but there still wasn't enough to fund everything Father Bob wanted to achieve.

To publicise the radiothon, Father Bob went on a number of radio and TV shows to talk about what they were doing. He was a welcome guest on most; he was rapidly becoming known as someone both worthy and amusing, with a great turn of phrase and interesting way of looking at things. On the surface, he could appear grumpy and gruff but, underneath, many people perceived him as soft-hearted with his causes, yet with the hard edge of someone absolutely determined to get things done.

So when Derryn Hinch invited him for an interview on 3AW, Father Bob was delighted to go on. Hinch was a very powerful figure in the media at the time, with the top-rating morning show, a series as host of the TV show 'Beauty and the Beast' under his belt, and the TV current affairs show on the Seven Network, 'Hinch'.

What happened next was something he had no idea was coming. Hinch welcomed him on, then said, 'I have here some affidavits . . .' The priest was puzzled. He had no idea what an affidavit was but, from the tone of Hinch's voice, it didn't sound like a good thing. Hinch went on to say he had details of unsavoury goings-on among kids staying in the St Peter and Paul's presbytery, and claims of financial mismanagement and misappropriation. Father Bob was, for almost the first time in his life, dumbstruck. He'd had no idea the claims were being treated seriously.

'We were in a bit of strife at the time, as the Open Family Foundation had shrunk since Alex left, and we'd gone down from ten street workers to one to look after all the kids who still needed looking after,' he says. 'I was trying to handle nearly everything myself. There were some kids upstairs in the presbytery, and apparently some of the affidavits made allegations about what they might have been doing up there. Well, most of them weren't angels – they were kids who'd been fighting for their survival on the streets and many of them were very damaged – but at least they were in a safe place. Hinch seemed to be suggesting I was responsible for everything about them, which would have been absolutely impossible!'

Father Bob stumbled through the rest of the interview, at one stage asking listeners if they could be absolutely sure where their own children were, and what they were doing, every minute of the day. When he came off air, he contacted the police, and invited them to come into the presbytery and investigate the claims. 'I was innocent, but I needed to be cleared publicly,' he says. While the skirmish helped give the radiothon even more publicity and turn it into a healthy fundraiser, he feared it might hurt his reputation in the long term. 'I felt these kind of allegations, even though I believed them to be totally unfounded, could really damage the Foundation and the work we were doing.'

Hinch was already on record as having disapproved of some of Father Bob's methods. He'd received a phone call once from someone who said he'd seen a young man knocking on the priest's door and asking for money. Father Bob opened the door, the caller said, listened to what he had to say and gave him twenty dollars. The young man, Hinch then alleged, had later used that money to help pay for drugs.

If true, that would highlight a fundamental difference between the two men's ideologies. Hinch believed Father Bob should have given him a food voucher, or set up an account at a local supermarket where he could have bought food. Father Bob, on the other hand, felt he had an unassailable duty to help young people, especially with guidance and support to make decisions of their own. If they asked for money and sometimes made a bad decision to spend that money on drugs, well, there was always the chance that maybe next time they came to him, they might talk to him more and end up making a better choice. He sometimes even answered the door wearing a hard hat. When the caller would ask why, he'd reply, 'In case you hit me on me head!' It would always raise a smile and sometimes be just the start of a connection Father Bob could work on.

'I wouldn't give someone knocking on the door any more than twenty dollars because there might be a possibility of them spending the money on drugs,' says Father Bob now. 'At the back of my head would be the thought that a hit of heroin back in those days would cost fifty dollars – that was before the price fell dramatically – so twenty dollars would be neither here nor there. It's meant simply as a response to an immediate need; the fiscal cliff varies with each individual. You can't have a committee meeting with experts every time someone rings your bell and says they're hungry. It's a gesture, and it's a sign of respect not to question the person asking. It's shades of grey, like that Lazyboy hip-hop song ['Underwear Goes Inside the Pants'] where the singer talks about a homeless guy asking him for money, but he refuses, saying he might use it on drugs and alcohol, then realises that's exactly what he's going to use it on himself.'

Besides, Father Bob had grown up with a tradition of begging. His mother had had to beg from Legacy for help because she had no money, then from the pawnshops, while he'd begged first from Father McGorry in order to make it through the seminary, and later for his various charities. He knew what it was like to have to cringingly plead for cash, and he didn't want others to feel the same shame or to go without.

Others too could see the sense of those twenty-dollar handouts. One of the regular parish volunteers, Colleen Miller, says Father Bob certainly wouldn't give money to just anyone who asked, though. 'Those early street kids he came across first, like Brian and Costas and the others, he felt he should always be there for them,' she says. 'They'd had such hard lives, he desperately wanted to make things better for them. And if any of those early ones spent the money on drugs, he'd think, at the end of the day, that it was better he gave them twenty dollars than they go off to rob someone for it, or burgle a house. People who want drugs are often desperate and they'll do anything to get money, and their victims can be traumatised for a long, long time. If Father Bob could avoid that, he'd reason that was a wise thing to do.'

But wise or not, in Hinch Father Bob had made himself a powerful and resolute enemy, and one who would soon return to the attack.

While Father Bob was still helping support so many kids, some of them were still falling by the wayside. Without a good start in life, he discovered they never managed to develop the emotional resilience necessary to keep facing hurdles and clambering over them each time. He'd support some through enormous difficulties, only to hear a few days, weeks, months or even years later the terrible news he always dreaded: that another one had died by their own hand. Taking a heroin overdose, alcoholic binge-drinking, swallowing a lethal cocktail of prescription pills, being involved in a suspicious car crash or hanging themselves . . . It all happened far too often, and claimed way too many young lives.

'A lot of people look at these kids on the streets and say they're no-hopers,' he says. 'I see kids who are someone's son or daughter, someone's sister or brother. They may be in a bad way now, but most have a very sad story behind why they're there, and why they're the way they now are. Kids have today become the innocent victims of thirty years of one-upmanship by adults who just don't care, but pay more attention to being independent and getting ahead. This is a parish at war. If you lose the battle for kids, then you can say goodbye to the future. There's nothing left. I never lose hope. I may lose my marbles, but never my hope.'

The toll of kids who'd died was mounting all the time and, by the end of the 1980s, it had hit twenty. Every death touched him deeply. 'It was terrible,' says Colleen. 'He felt responsible for all those young people. Protecting them he saw as a duty that he took very seriously. It was very sad to see the number of young people whose lives were destroyed by the situation they were in. One died who was a father to a couple of children. That was a horrible shock. Another one was the friend of someone who died and spoke at his funeral, saying he was going to try to make a difference, so that wouldn't happen to anyone else in the future. A couple of years later, he died, too. Father Bob always took it very hard.'

Others ended up in jail, and Father Bob made it a point of honour to stay in touch. He might one day receive a letter from one asking for the money for new razor blades, or from another asking him to remember a girlfriend's birthday. 'These are often kids without hope, who've had no families, been wards of the state, or have suffered violence and abuse throughout their young lives,' the priest says. 'They need us to be good friends to them. They are thought of as nobodies. They're the forgotten generation. They're fighting for their lives.

'It's not just the poor, working-class kids, either. Other kids are now joining them, from middle-class families. Their parents are often too busy with their own lives to give them the attention they need. We're seeing more of those on drugs like Harry the Horse [heroin] now, and more of those with mental illnesses.

'Yet they constantly amaze me. One kid said to me one day that he didn't have much hope himself – his father was a drunk, his grandfather was a drunk, and now he was a drunk. But at least he recognised that, which was the first step to doing something about it. These kids now are so wise compared to previous generations. And while we may think some of these characters are bad, and they certainly do bad things, the amount of good in them always staggers me. It often comes from left field when you least expect it. It might be in the way they care for each other, or do someone else a good turn.

While he still saw an enormous need for the Open Family

Foundation, there was another problem now arising. Many of the people approaching him for help, including his first street kids, were now older than the eighteen-year-old cut-off point for clients of the Foundation's work. Yet they obviously still needed a helping hand. 'And I'm not bloody well going to abandon them now!' he vowed.

To solve the problem, he set up an alternative project in 1989, The Emerald Hill Mission, expressly for older people in the neighbourhood. With a group of local businesspeople volunteering to raise funds, and Henry Nissen happy to move from the Foundation to the Mission, he launched this new initiative.

Henry, in particular, was delighted. 'I was always getting into trouble for helping the older people who were over-age but who'd been our younger clients originally,' he says. 'They still needed the support. Unfortunately, you don't always know when a person is going to be able to help themselves. All we can do is guide them, encourage them, help them and support them where we can along the way. Sometimes people will respond, and sometimes they won't. We can't teach them the skills of life if they don't have the ability to learn!'

Father Bob, however, had immense confidence in his band of troops helping him realise his vision and, as the 'commander-in-chief', he watched everything that was happening like a hawk. Everyone became used to him dropping by to check up on things, and to have a chat with the 'associates' – he refused to call the people they were helping the traditional term 'clients' – to make sure all was well. Everyone, 'associates', workers, volunteers and the general public, regarded him with growing admiration.

That same year came a concrete expression of that appreciation. Father Bob was summoned to Government House to receive a Medal of the Order of Australia. When he was interviewed, he joked about it. 'Don't know why they're giving it to me,' he said gruffly. 'I'm only the commander-in-chief. I'm not the one doing the bloody work.'

But secretly, he was pleased, very pleased. Not for himself, but because he knew the honour would give his various projects even more standing and profile, and, hopefully, most importantly of all, help boost the coffers.

The financial situation by now was becoming quite perilous. Father Bob made numerous appeals for more money and even applied to the state government, for the first time, for public funds – something he'd always avoided as he said he hated the red tape and rigid rules that invariably went along with it. The request was turned down; officials said they'd received the forms for emergency funding past the cut-off date.

Father Bob went on the attack through the media, saying he was in dire need of $30 000 to keep operating, otherwise he'd have to start shutting down projects. At one point, with an unerring instinct for what makes news, he threatened to return his OAM to Governor-General Bill Hayden as a symbol of his disgust at the government refusing to help. But then his old charge Chris Apostolidis, who'd been running his dance school in the old warehouse up the road, heard about the need for cash, and offered to help. The warehouse was being sold by its owners World Vision, and Father Bob had offered him a place at the old run-down Emerald Hall after it had failed to sell to bring in more capital and a report he'd commissioned on it came back to say it needed $600 000 worth of work to make it habitable. As a result, a long-term lease sounded the best option, especially as Chris had signalled his willingness to undertake a complete restoration to provide a new home for his Dance World, with Father Bob as its patron. But now Chris decided to take some time out to help his old mentor.

'The Open Family Foundation was going through a rough patch,' he says. 'It was a dark period when they were in a bit of debt, I think to the tune of about $200 000. My girlfriend at the time – who became my wife – was a bookkeeper and she helped him do all the books, and I decided to try to help him raise money. Father Bob always wants to help people, and he'd really helped me, and I felt this was a chance for me to give back.'

Chris had an inspired idea. In 1989, the British singer, songwriter and Genesis frontman Phil Collins had produced his most successful album yet, *. . . But Seriously,* featuring the anti-homelessness anthem 'Another Day in Paradise'. The song highlighted the issue of homelessness existing side-by-side with great wealth amid complete government apathy, and peaked at number one in the US, number two in the UK and was an immediate hit in Australia, too. As a result, Collins embarked on a world tour with the album in 1990, setting four dates for concerts in Melbourne in March.

Chris contacted the Australian promoter with the suggestion that Collins sing 'Another Day in Paradise' at the finale of each concert, and volunteers from the Open Family Foundation would come along with buckets to collect money at the end of each performance. He had a call back a few weeks later, to be told: Phil likes it. He'll do it. At the end of each concert, he announced from the stage that there'd be a collection for the homeless outside. They ended up collecting over $200 000.

'It was great to see it all work out so well,' says Chris. 'Father Bob always wants to help people in need so it was good to be able to help him. He's helped me shape my point of view on so many topics, and I implement all the things I've learnt in my life, and ultimately they become morals, your way of being. He's had the biggest impact on me.'

The success of Chris's first fundraising effort inspired others to join in too. A local businessman came up with the proposal that the Foundation should be nominated as a charity recipient of some of the profits from the lucky envelope machines being installed in pubs and clubs around Melbourne. A kind of poker machine dispensing bingo tickets with certain letters, numbers or symbols that have to be matched to the ones showing on the screen, they started to provide a real injection of cash.

At that point, more help arrived for the Foundation. One was Father Bob's old mate from his army and National Council of Priests days, Father Hal Ranger. He'd gone to work at the nearby Sacred Heart Mission in St Kilda and Father Bob offered him a place to stay at the presbytery. He was always happy to lend a hand around the place in his spare time and proved a helpful sounding board for some of Father Bob's ideas.

'He's always been such a generous guy and it was pretty much open house at his place,' says Father Ranger, now the associate pastor at St Patrick's Cathedral in Toowoomba,

Queensland. 'Everyone was welcomed in a fairly eccentric way, even if it often meant being yelled at from the top veranda, "Who's there?"

'Others might avoid the kind of people he was helping. They were broken and hurting and often took refuge in grog or the needle. For many people it would have salved their conscience just to put some money in an envelope but he went into their world, and opened his heart, his arms and usually his pockets to help. People responded so well to him. They sensed his own pain from a difficult past, his great strength and the free spirit within.'

Also coming along to help in a more formal way with the Open Family Foundation was former Christian Brother teacher Nathan Stirling. In the early 1980s, he'd wanted to set up some kind of project to help street kids in Canberra and, seeing Father Bob and Brother Alex McDonald as the Australian pioneers for that kind of work, he'd met the priest back then to talk about what they were doing. Their street work in particular impressed him and, as a result, he'd set up Open Family ACT. Now, the two men started talking about merging the two enterprises and in 1992, it became Open Family Australia. Nathan was appointed CEO, running the organisation from Canberra, with the idea of making it truly national.

There still seemed to be a need for someone to take charge in Melbourne itself, however. TV star and volunteer Tony Barber saw that clearly. 'From doing some work in their office, I could see it was pretty much rough and tumble,' he says. 'My advice to Bob was that he needed a full-time organiser in Melbourne. It was about that time that a lot of charities were doing that: having an organiser on their books instead of just different volunteers coming and going. Bob's at his best in a hands-on role, when he's fundraising, or begging as he calls it, with someone else keeping the records to make sure everything is shipshape.'

He meant it quite literally too, recommending a former high-ranking naval officer, retired Commodore Jim Dickson, for the position of executive director. Jim willingly took it on, but found it a baptism of fire. 'I had only recently come out of the military and nothing could have been a bigger contrast after a long service career than going into an organisation like that!' he says. 'There was very little organisation, in fact. It was more a collection of well-intentioned and very sympathetic people of diverse backgrounds who wanted to support Bob's desire to give street kids a better chance in life. It was a wake-up call for me. But I did manage to put a degree of organisation and administrative sense into the running of the place, and try to have a reasonable spread of responsibilities between those people already there, some of whom were very strong-minded individuals, and getting them to work collectively.

'I have a high regard for Bob's compassionate heart and his genuine desire to do good for the poor and the struggling. He has a wonderful empathy with them and talks to them in a way they understand and appreciate. But while he had an understanding of the military from his time there, regrettably the military's way of doing things by the book hadn't rubbed off on him. I have to say, his organisation's administrative and financial processes weren't ones that I had a lot of respect for. I did make some changes, but didn't achieve everything I would have like to have achieved for Open Family in my time there.'

Jim stayed just over a year, and then Nathan moved to

Melbourne. His energy, experience and organisational skills, adding to the structures Jim had started to put into a project that had previously just grown organically, were perfect foils for the way in which Father Bob worked.

'The Foundation was more like a movement than an organisation, with parishioners and businesspeople and an outreach worker and lots of kids,' says Nathan. 'My aim was to put it on a more stable footing and to regrow the organisation. I'd always found Bob an inspiring figure. There's something about the way he's able to communicate around social justice issues that does connect with people.

'He's a real character. He can be quite gruff and come across as quite grumpy, and he might say "No" to some things, but then he can change his mind. He's also a very funny guy with a dry humour, who puts interesting spins on things when you're not expecting it. My role was to keep the work focused on core business. Bob would be inclined to consider flights of fancy – but they weren't necessarily fanciful, they were real things, but we were always just constrained by resources.'

There was still a need for more money but, with Nathan now on board and Father Ranger around to help, Father Bob started to relax, and to look forward to a period of sustained growth. It was then that Derryn Hinch made another potentially devastating move.

Father Vincent Kiss, who'd become well known in South Melbourne for the masses he'd conducted when he first arrived and was still providing the Open Family Foundation, among many other charities, with funds from the ANZ

Trustees, was rarely out of the news. His stature was growing nationally. He was on the board of the Elizabethan Theatre Trust, the Victorian State Opera and the Emergency Services Foundation, as well as being a member of the Guardianship and Administration Board and the Intellectual Disability Review Panel, and an advisor to the Victorian Minister of Housing. In 1989, he was appointed President of Philanthropy Australia, the national peak body for charity patronage. It was a real indication of the general esteem in which he was held. With its figureheads Patricia Feilman, the founding Executive Secretary of The Ian Potter Foundation, and Meriel Wilmot, Executive Officer of The Myer Foundation, it was seen as the ultimate mark of respect.

The following year, Father Kiss grabbed world headlines after he flew to Italy to officiate at the wedding of Primrose 'Pitty Pat' Dunlop and airline steward Lorenzo Montesini, aka Prince Giustiniani, Count of the Phanaar, Knight of St Sophia, Baron Alexandroff, in Venice's majestic Basilica di San Pietro. When it was called off amid lurid allegations that Montesini had gone off with his best man, it was the priest who fronted the international press.

But in 1992, Father Kiss's meteoric rise turned into a sudden, steep fall: police charged him with stealing $1.8 million from the ANZ Bank's charitable trust. That had been how he'd managed to fund such an opulent lifestyle, which included large donations to charity himself, buying no fewer than three homes in Melbourne in addition to a sumptuous villa in the Philippines, eating in all the best restaurants and enjoying seventeen overseas trips in five years.

For Father Bob, and all the other charity heads who'd been

duped by the priest, the revelation was a bombshell. 'We'd obviously had no idea,' he says. 'We'd all been told the money was going to his charity in Vanuatu, and he'd shown us all the right papers and had all the right credentials. Vincent Kiss was a highly respected member of society, lauded by the media, and everything came on ANZ letterhead. He was involved in a number of high-profile charities, who all seemed to trust him too. We even received letters from the Vanuatu Government, thanking us for our help. But we were babes in the woods. We had no idea it would turn out to be a slush fund for himself.'

Derryn Hinch had been harbouring suspicions for years about the society priest and his entourage of 'ladies who lunch' and he leapt on Father Kiss's arrest with alacrity, saying he'd effectively been laundering money through the various charities he was supposedly supporting. Kiss would give them a large cheque, they would bank 10 per cent of it for themselves and then write him another cheque for his own charity, the Vanuatu Development Project, which turned out to be merely a private bank account operated by Father Kiss.

Hinch then returned to the attack on Father Bob, which he'd begun with the affidavits from the former workers at his farm. He accused him of making 'a pact with the devil'. Hinch alleged, 'For a fee for his charity, he let Kiss use him as a money-laundering service. He should have been asking questions. If someone comes along and says, "Here is $100 000 but I want $90 000 back", alarm bells should be ringing.'

Father Bob was indignant. 'The implication was either that I was a dill or, worse still, an accomplice,' he says. 'But I'd checked up on Kiss when he turned up in my church. My first reaction was to check this bloke out. I pestered Wagga to find out if he was in good standing, and they said, "Yes." Then Kiss was okayed by HQ [the Melbourne Archdiocese]. The local Christians loved him because he was nice and he was flamboyant and he smiled a lot. He had a lot to do with other charities too, including the Lions and Philanthropy Australia. He conned far cleverer people than me. But then he was arrested and the police phoned me, saying he'd funded a number of charities and they were asking for the books. So I took them all in.'

He was undergoing his second major police investigation in just three years and, while he hoped for the best, he feared the worst.

14

The Murky Stuff of Human Lives

The Vincent Kiss scandal and the allegations contained in the farm workers' affidavits weighed heavily on Father Bob Maguire while the police fraud squad and the ANZ Bank carried out all their investigations. Publicly, he put a brave face on what was happening. Privately, he worried that his own growing profile might make him and his projects a desirable target.

He'd always been good at winning friends, and inspiring supporters and admirers; now he started to realise he was also pretty good at making enemies.

But then again, he rarely pulled his punches, even when he was aiming at some of the most powerful in the land. In 1990, for example, billionaire businessman Kerry Packer had suffered a heart attack while playing polo in Sydney and had been clinically dead for six minutes. In a press conference after a successful bypass operation, he said of his temporary 'death', 'I've been to the other side and let me tell you, son, there's fucking nothing there . . . there's no-one waiting there for you, there's no-one to judge you so you can do what you bloody well like!'

When that was put to Father Bob, he didn't hesitate for a second. 'I think that says a lot more about God's judgement on Kerry Packer,' he said, 'than about what really awaits us on the other side.'

Controversy and criticism for someone as out there as Father Bob was pretty much to be expected in his line of work anyway, believes Father Hal Ranger, who stayed on at his priest friend's presbytery until 1996. 'Once you kind of get into the murky stuff of human lives, you are bound to get a bit of mud on you,' he says. 'That's all right. That's where the action is. What happens in many suburban parishes is pretty artificial at times, and not necessarily about engaging with the nitty gritty of life. The truth of the matter is that most people are only really open to the extraordinary faithfulness of God when everything else they've depended upon has fallen away.'

In 1993, however, Father Bob was to get some relief from the mire. Kiss was sent to jail for seven years for theft and fraud, and all the investigations cleared Father Bob of any wrongdoing. Detective Chief Inspector Robert Michell of the Major Fraud Group of the Victorian Police, a man later to be appointed chief investigator of the Police Integrity Commission, wrote Archbishop Frank Little a letter saying all the allegations 'have been investigated and found to be entirely without substance'.

It was the complete exoneration Father Bob had hoped for, but he wondered whether that would be enough to stop Derryn Hinch's attacks. He suspected it might not.

It was another era of great change in Father Bob's parish. The nature of the suburb, now united with St Kilda and Port Melbourne to form Port Phillip city – a merger Father Bob had fought unsuccessfully against side-by-side with the locals – was undergoing a steady transformation. The number of children enrolled in the four local Catholic schools had been dropping steadily, so Father Bob masterminded the amalgamation of the four unviable schools in the parishes of South Melbourne, Port Melbourne, Middle Park and West St Kilda into one regional primary school, Galilee, on the site of the former St Peter and Paul's School. 'That was a big achievement,' says Father Ernie Smith, in neighbouring St Kilda. Father Smith had established the enormously successful Sacred Heart Mission, looking after people in need, but leaving the street kids to Open Family. 'There'd been lots of regional secondary schools, but no regional primary. It was a big step forward for Catholic education.' Father Bob was also put in charge of bringing together the different parishes in the region, including Fitzroy, Collingwood, East Melbourne, Richmond and South Yarra, as one 'deanery' to help in the sharing of resources.

Towards the end of the 1980s, South Melbourne had experienced one of the city's biggest waves of gentrification and that trend was gaining momentum all the time. Newcomers to the area were renovating a lot of the older houses and real estate prices were rising exponentially. South Melbourne, with its market and growing number of cafes and restaurants, as well as its proximity to the CBD, was now considered a much more desirable place to live. 'It became a tale of two cities, the poor living side-by-side with the rich,' says Father Bob. But the influx of new people, often with money, time and a willingness to lend a hand to those less fortunate, gave Father Bob fresh impetus to introduce new programs, and expand the ones he had. Under Nathan Stirling, Open Family Australia was thriving, it was more organised and had even started applying for government grants, with the priest having fans on all sides of politics.

Brian Loughnane, a South Melbourne local and now the federal director of the Liberal Party of Australia, was back then the chief of staff to the Victorian Minister for Youth Affairs Vin Heffernan, who'd been awarded an Order of Australia for his work helping disadvantaged and homeless children. 'Vin was great mates with Bob and he had a great empathy with the very practical and outcomes-focused work Bob was doing,' he says. 'There was a lot of resistance to Open Family within parts of the government bureaucracy, but we saw the value in what he was doing and were able to help and be supportive financially with grants and things like that.'

That kind of assistance helped Open Family recruit more outreach workers to look after street kids over a wider swathe of Melbourne, and now there was also a growing band of volunteers at the ready, both new hands and old. 'There were now two sides to South Melbourne,' says Sister Catherine Flynn, one of the Faithful Companions of Jesus congregation, who approached Father Bob asking if they could help him in 1994. 'There were the poor, but also a lot of the volunteers were fairly well-heeled people who wanted to give, people of money and influence. Father Bob attracted those kinds of people as well as the down-and-outs.'

Mem River was meanwhile proving a huge asset to Father Bob's work with kids on the streets. While he'd managed to forge a good career for himself as a film-maker, producing and directing documentaries, as well as recording soundtracks, he was also keen to help others in need. Just as Father Bob had helped him years before, he was determined to pass on the favour and took on an old Christian Brothers house and converted it into a refuge, with a big games zone and youngsters attending the school next door.

One of his toughest residents was a young deaf boy who'd been placed there as a last resort by the courts. He started off angry and violent, throwing things off the balcony and kicking over the TV. 'But I tried to communicate with him and learnt sign language,' says Mem. 'Then I could interpret for him with others too. I think when he realised we cared, he was fine. He moved on finally and is now working as a youth councillor for deaf people. He was a real success story.'

Two other new projects, the Parish Open House and the Parish House of Hospitality, offered assistance to underprivileged residents. Local pensioner Maureen Johnston was a mainstay of both. A battler herself, with four children, several grandchildren and a sixteen-year-old grandson she'd been the primary carer of for the past six years, she'd been a recipient of Father Bob's generosity in the past, and wanted to do something for others. She started off on the food bus with Henry Nissen as it drove around Port Melbourne, St Kilda and the Flinders Street Station areas, preparing and handing out sandwiches and hot coffee. She proved a natural at interacting with those who came for a bite of food and to see a friendly face.

She wanted to do more, however. She turned up another day with six hotdogs and four cheese sandwiches – all she could afford to make – and, together with another volunteer, Henri Ser, took a second bus on another beat to a public housing area of Port Melbourne. 'It started slowly but we went out the next week and there were more people,' says Henri. 'Then there were more, so we started to get more money, thanks to Bob, and we bought more food, and that food van service has grown ever since.'

Yet Maureen still wasn't satisfied with that and, in 1994, volunteered four days a week to provide food for people from the back of the church. It began with unpacking and handing out food from Foodbank Victoria, a newly formed charity gathering food donations, including end-of-line, mislabelled and overrun stock, and redistributing it to people experiencing hardship. Visitors could also ask advice on where to find help on housing, clothing, travel tickets and all their general welfare needs over coffee with friendly volunteers. But in Maureen's conversations with recipients, she realised that many were also in need of a regular, healthy cooked meal. So she then embarked on a program of providing free evening meals two days a week, and breakfasts on a third day. Very soon, up to eighty people were turning up at each mealtime.

Her dedication was astonishing. Even though she was a

pensioner, was terribly stooped and had chronic health problems, she'd insist on walking to the supermarket herself every day to pick up supplies in her trolley. 'The success of the project relied entirely on Maureen's confidence, unselfish dedication and genuine care for the South Melbourne marginalised,' says Father Bob, who later pressed for her to receive a Medal of the Order of Australia. When he wasn't successful, he presented her with an award of his own creation, the 'order of St Peter and St Paul' honours system. 'Maureen not only provided people with food and an opportunity to interact with others, but she encouraged them to participate in the preparation, cooking and cleaning up, enhancing their self-esteem and providing them with a sense of purpose, belonging and pride. She had a passion for helping people get their lives back in order with encouragement and without judgement.'

But back in the day, one of the most dedicated supporters of the program was Sister Catherine. She'd begun helping in the school, but then went to the back of the church to assist with the food. She found many of the recipients had tragic stories, family problems and psychological issues. 'Many would have been brilliant people but their brains had been affected by their past, or alcohol, or the way they were living,' she says. 'Some were almost ashamed to have to come and ask for help, but others were shameless. Bob had such vision with many of those initiatives. He'd give you a lot of liberty and things could go wrong and some people often wanted more structure, but he had so many great ideas, like food programs and providing scholarships for those in trouble. He could often be cranky but he'd drop by and could talk to every Tom, Dick and Harry, but also those much higher up the line. That's a real talent. Although he didn't fit with the establishment, I really believe in him.'

Many were feeling much the same way. They saw Father Bob as a real honest-to-goodness knockabout bloke, the kind of old-fashioned ideal of a priest who could be a best mate to everyone and anyone. He was known for giving away his jacket to anyone who said they were cold, and once famously turned up at the presbytery without his shoes after going out for a walk and handing them over to a boy who was going for a job and needed to look smart for the interview. A group once had a collection to raise the money for his fare back to Scotland to see his family; he ended up giving the money to 'a few people who needed it more than me'. His cousins back there were sad that he never came over to visit, but they understood. 'We would have loved to have seen our hero, and he's never had a holiday, but he gave away the money to more deserving causes,' says Frank Maguire. 'He's a gentle man who cares.'

Another time, he appeared in a rather fine leather coat, donated that morning to the presbytery by the widow of a man who'd just died. Yet he also had a sharp brain and a fiendish intellect, and read constantly to improve his mind. As well as reading his Bible every day – 'pretty much an occupational hazard,' he shrugs – he'd usually spend his evenings alone with a book, about theology, history, philosophy, sociology, or even a mainstream bestseller, just so he could keep in touch with the social mores. His schooling hadn't been the best, but he set about educating himself instead on the kinds of subjects he felt mattered.

'Whenever you're in doubt, go back to history,' he'd often advise. 'History has so many of the answers.' He was admired both within Catholic circles and beyond. After speaking at the 2000 national Catholic Education Conference, for instance, he received a letter with the feedback, 'Father Bob Maguire, brilliant, a man of incredible enthusiasm and deep love of the people he helps, serves and washes the feet of. Very practical and different with much food for thought . . . Can you get enough of this man's spirituality? He is articulate, well read and makes you know you can do it.'

He was also praised as a social entrepreneur, although some of his followers despaired at some of his more outlandish ideas. 'I've seen some doozies over time,' says Frank O'Connor. 'But they all arose because of that fierce desire he has to ensure that the disadvantaged, the disenfranchised and those whom society would rather discard and forget, all have the opportunity to say, "Well at least somebody has been willing to try and help me."'

He was tireless in supporting local activities, too. Just as he'd protested fourteen years before about the loss of South Melbourne's VFL team and then the council amalgamation, he now joined in the series of protests about plans to shift the Australian Grand Prix from Adelaide to a street circuit in Albert Park. Like other locals, he saw it as unfair to turn a public park into a private playground for one week a year, and believed the huge amount of money it would cost to stage it each year could be much better spent elsewhere. But, as with the other two campaigns, this was another lost cause, and the first Grand Prix was held in Melbourne in 1996. 'Bob has always been the unelected, de facto mayor of South Melbourne,' says Brian Loughnane. 'He's part of the heartbeat of South Melbourne.'

Yet the 55-year-old Father Bob could also be a chameleon in the way he connected with both rich and poor, and even changed the way he spoke in accordance with the circumstances – and what he could get out of them to help his flock. Many people saw him as an old leftie, good mates with all the unions, but he also had strong links with members of the Liberal Party and big business. 'He's always been able to get on with people, and he's never been party political,' says Brian. 'At the end of the day, he does good work and that's what attracts people.'

He often puzzled everyone, however, with his use of language, and the metaphors he conjured up, often without bothering to explain them. He'd regularly go off on his own tangents and loved playing with words, either deliberately mispronouncing them or using the wrong ones: 'I'll put it in the dairy!' he'd constantly declare, leaving callers wondering if some future engagement would ever actually end up in his big black appointments book.

'Sometimes the gap between him and them would be too wide and people might think he was crazy, mad and rambling,' says Father Ranger. 'But there was always real meaning behind the riddles he spoke in, although it would take a while to understand it . . . and he doesn't waste time explaining.'

In addition, Father Bob's strong anti-authoritarian streak attracted some, but could alarm the more conservative of his congregation. 'His shtick was this vagabond outlaw priest,' says Tony Barber, 'and he plays it for all it's worth. He could be a nightmare for a large organisation; he just does his own thing, and is determined to do his own thing. But as well as being a rough diamond on top, he also has the deep compassion of his priestly vocation. I had some personal problems at one stage, and he was tremendous and I was able to get some very, very good direction.'

In public, Father Bob could be very much the man for all seasons. In church, he swept many away with his powerful, flowing oratory, usually speaking without any notes at all, and could hold an audience spellbound. 'Sometimes, he'd speak just like a westie but other times he'd use unbelievably beautiful language,' says Mavis Keighery, a long-time local supporter who worked for eighteen years for the Emerald Hill Mission and associated ventures. 'And out of this man would come such wisdom.' Most mornings, he'd still go for his bike ride around the area, stopping to chat to people on the way, and at other times, he'd walk his dog, Rocky, greeting most people he passed by name, and asking them how they were. Once, a motorist pulled up to ask for directions. Father Bob lent into the open window, asking, 'Are you lost?' The driver recognised him immediately. 'No, Father, we're found,' he replied. Some evenings the priest would host big dinners around the magnificent carved dining table of the presbytery, with the intellectuals of the parish and the heads of various other religious denominations. He'd often be away too, speaking at conferences, seminars and functions, attending dinners and meeting business and political leaders to talk about his work, while he continued to have weekly spots on radio stations 3AK, 3AW and 3RRR, appeared often on TV current affairs shows, and wrote a regular column in the Catholic journal *Kairos*.

But in private, he tended to be a surprisingly solitary man, preferring to spend evenings alone with Rocky, a good book, or in front of the TV – and often talking to it, too. Sometimes, he'd watch it with Costas, or seek him out for a chat, but more often he preferred his own company. Once, he was even heard to declare in church, 'Hell may be a never-ending dinner party!'

Frank O'Connor thinks he knows the priest's secret. 'Having got to know him very well over the years, you start to recognise he is really very shy,' he says. 'Of course, on a Myers-Briggs personality type test, he'd be off the scale as an outgoing extrovert, but I think his natural shyness is one of the reasons he puts on such a performance. He likes playing the role of the mad priest because it can mask over his insecurity.'

His first curate in his early days in South Melbourne, Father Kevin Burke, always suspected that. Father Bob would often disappear after having lunch with people for some quiet time alone. 'You'd organise dinner with him, and he'd always be late too, complaining that someone had forgotten to put it in the diary. He can be hard to contact too. Deep down, I think he's quite a shy man, but always a fascinating character . . .'

As a sign of that shyness, back in the presbytery Father Bob didn't often really like to eat with other people. 'He's never really been a social man, even though that would surprise many,' says Mavis Keighery. 'Father Ranger once told me that Bob never ate with him. He'd take his meal upstairs and read or watch TV while he was eating instead. He's a bit of a loner. He's also a shocking cook. He used to buy fillet steak and, if he was going out all day, he'd pre-cook it in a skillet in the morning then leave it to heat up when he got back in. What a way to have steak! And while he eats apples and bananas, I've never seen him prepare a vegetable.'

The healthiest thing about him, said some of those who weren't such great fans, was always his ego. An old seminarian colleague of his, now retired, once branded him a narcissist. Others are quick to his defence, however. 'He was called that a couple of times, but that wouldn't be my emphasis,' says Damian Coleridge. 'People respond to Bob and he's able to reach out to them in a way certainly no other priest in the Diocese is able to do. He's become a legend for that.'

The first time Father Bob heard the description, he thought he was being accused of being an arsonist. When he understood it was actually a narcissist, he denied the claim. He admits there have been times when he's had tickets on himself, but refutes that it's egotism. 'I don't believe that to be true,' he says. 'I don't personally enjoy public appearances. I do like others, however, to enjoy those appearances. Awareness-raising is part of a Catholic priest's work, among Catholic worshippers or secondary-school students at Catholic colleges or spirituality at the pub gatherings. I don't do any of these things for self-promotion except as a self-appointed representative of "gonzo" Catholicism. I suppose I have become a bit of an "infotainment" priest, but it's all about covert evangelism. It was never "Look at me!" It was always about the faith.'

The priest who coined the description these days declines to comment further on Father Bob, but it wasn't the last time anyone attributed Father Bob with a healthy ego.

But then again, he'd always give you a choice, says one of his critics, drily. He can be good like that. It's either his way or the highway.

15

Keeping Hope Alive

Costas was still causing havoc for everyone around him. He was a big man with a loud voice and while sometimes he could be gentle and sweet, generally he was strident and irrational and could be aggressive.

Father Bob tried every avenue he could think of to help. He'd place him in rental accommodation and pay the rent in advance, but Costas would invariably be asked to leave as his behaviour would upset the neighbours. He'd sign him up for adult education courses but Costas would then drop out, or be kicked out, within weeks. He constantly asked social services, the health department, the federal MP, the local council, the police, for assistance for him, but it always seemed just too hard; they didn't know what they could do. Instead, it was left to the priest, as almost the last resort, to stop him slipping through the cracks in the system, to try to keep Costas going as best he could.

'At first, I couldn't understand why he shouted all the time,' Father Bob says. 'He'd shriek and scream and it would be terrible. Then I met some of his family and they all did that. That's the volume at which they conducted their lives. But he'd be a liability in the neighbourhood. He was almost beyond our ability to help.' But while Costas at fifteen had been a handful, he very soon became much worse. 'Bloody heroin took over from the age of eighteen. His drug use was covert. He'd never do it in front of me. I tried to help him, even though it was expensive creating a financial biosphere around him, but the main thing became just keeping him alive, and making sure he wasn't being taken advantage of, in the hope he'd improve. But even worse was speed amphetamines. I think that drove him mad over the years. It was acquired madness syndrome. They were very dark, torrid times.'

Costas was often in trouble, and Father Bob would always come to his aid, asking favours from his network of friends and supporters of his work. His good mate, lawyer Tony Joyce, was one. Tony first encountered Costas when Father Bob asked him to help find a barrister to represent the young man in court. Tony arranged for his friend, legendary criminal barrister Brian Bourke, to appear for him, and for no fee. 'Costas didn't even turn up,' says Tony. 'He was a real pain in the arse. I have the greatest respect for Bob, but Costas became a millstone around his neck, one of his great problems. And he was never able to say to him, "Off you go!" He didn't have that kind of hard love.'

There were constantly dramas around Costas. He broke a window at the presbytery once, and threatened Father Bob. He menaced Father Hal Ranger with a knife. Another time, he overdosed and had to be rushed to hospital. But in 1990, things took a distinct turn for the worse. Costas was driving a car that aquaplaned in torrential rain along the tram tracks in St Kilda and into another car. The two passengers in the second car, the parents of the driver, were taken to hospital and later died. Costas, then twenty-eight, ended up spending a year in prison, first at the old HM Pentridge Prison and then at HM Ararat Prison, just over 200 kilometres north-west of Melbourne, for culpable driving.

'That buggered him,' says Father Bob. 'It was too early in his life. Things changed in his head after that. His behaviour became more bizarre. I wanted the authorities to intervene as they had the power, but they'd always say, "Thank you for your letter but . . ." It was hopeless. But when he was in Pentridge, I remember him saying once in the remand yard, he'd pray to God that someone would stick by him for life. He didn't have anyone else. I felt as if I had no choice.'

Soon after Costas's imprisonment, Father Bob had his own personal brush with the law. He'd been late for a Collingwood match, and arrived to find the car park was full. As was the habit of many of the team's followers, he parked on a nearby street in a 'No Parking' area. He'd just climbed out of his car, however, when the police arrived and told him to move his car. The priest argued that he didn't have to. The police officer said he did, and he'd be arrested if he refused to do so. Father Bob stuck to his guns, insisting loftily that a recent paper by Mr Barry Beach, QC had reported that citizens had a right to discuss with public servants whatever they were being told to do.

'I was indulging myself in an intellectual exercise,' he now admits, sheepishly. 'The constable arresting me had the name of Huckoff – fancy being arrested by someone of that name! – and I ended up being marched by four officers to the secretary's room until the police van arrived and I was tossed into that and taken to Richmond police station. I think I'd just been elected to the Chair of the national priests' senate and I had tickets on myself.'

Father Bob was eventually freed in time to race back to the ground and watch the last quarter of the match. He was charged with refusing to obey a legitimate instruction but was then advised by a friend in the force to apologise and, as it was a first offence, he might not have to go to court. So he did, and he didn't end up in court. 'That's the most exciting thing that's ever happened to me!' he says today. 'But I do feel embarrassed by it now.'

In those days, he always seemed to have boundless energy for everything, and was never short on ideas for keeping his parishioners engaged, challenged and, usually at the same time, dazed and amused. He'd regularly open his masses by reassuring the congregation he wouldn't go over an hour, and he'd stop in time for a sporting event, a sports TV program or for the children to get home to watch a cartoon show.

At other services, he could also behave in quite unexpected ways. Once, at a funeral, he leant down to the coffin and rapped on it sharply with his knuckles, calling out, 'Is there anybody there?' As the service halted in stunned silence, he smiled. 'See!' he said. 'There's no-one there!' As a lesson in explaining how the soul had departed the body, and illustrating how 'the man is still with us, but in a new way', it was startlingly effective. There were a few nervous laughs, until everyone finally joined in.

He was also asked to conduct a funeral service for the brother-in-law of an old friend, General Jim Barry from his army days. The bereaved was a jazz musician and Father Bob conducted a lively service full of jazz music and jazz talk, which had parishioners also flocking into the church to join in. 'Don't worry about those old folk on your right,' Father Bob instructed the mourners. 'They're only my parishioners!' Those parishioners shrugged and smiled back at him.

Another time at a funeral, he berated everyone for looking so solemn and sad. 'Cheer up!' he ordered. 'I don't know why you're crying – he's the one who's dead, not you! You should be happy and celebrate his life and remember him as he was!' Through their tears, everyone smiled. Afterwards, some of the mourners said it was the most upbeat, and best, funeral they'd ever had the misfortune to attend.

By contrast, many of the clients of the Emerald Hill Mission were being kept very much alive. They now had access to an ever-growing range of services, not only the 150 meals cooked each week, the forty food parcels given out and the barbecues that were later added, but also family mediation; counselling for drug, alcohol, problem gambling and mental health issues;

assistance with job seeking; and a full program of sports and recreational outings. In addition, voluntary outreach workers provided financial support, furniture and accommodation to families, and there were school scholarships available. Another program even helped women who worked or had worked in the sex industry, set up opposite a brothel and called – ironically – Mary's Wayside Chapel, with the idea of Mother Mary keeping a reassuring eye on the welfare of the women, and as a respectful nod to Ted Knoff's Wayside Chapel in Sydney.

When General Barry called in at the presbytery a few days after his late brother-in-law's funeral service to drop off his clothes for Father Bob to distribute, he was startled by the people he met there. 'The place was full of derelicts and drop-outs that he was feeding and looking after,' he says. 'But I sat down with a few of them and had a cup of tea. They thought Bob was God, and I could understand why!'

The vast majority would tend to stay a few days when they were at their lowest, pick themselves up again with Father Bob's help, then get back out on their way again. The only ones Father Bob kept a closer eye on were the drug addicts, understanding he couldn't trust them while they were in the grip of their addictions. The others all respected him and his few possessions, and would protect him with their lives.

'I think a lot of people liked the feeling that they had Father Bob's support,' says Colleen Miller, one of the new breed of volunteers, a woman who'd just moved into the area with her family and, with time on her hands, had been looking for some charity work. She'd ended up helping with the Friday barbecues and the Mondays handing out food parcels. 'On Fridays, around twenty to thirty people would sit down with us every week and, after a while, they learned to trust you and some would pour their hearts out. We'd just sit around and drink coffee and some would smoke and some would talk and a few would whinge. Father Bob would often call by to see how things were going. He could be warm and sometimes a bit aloof, but he always gave you good advice. Sometimes he'd tell you to back off and be a bit careful with some of the people, and not be too naive. But he'd always be there for you. He really does care, even though he often doesn't show it, and never in a warm, loving, fuzzy way. He's much more gruff.'

When fellow newcomer Henri Ser first met Father Bob in 1993, he also found him extremely brusque. He'd gone along to an orientation evening for Open Family volunteers and at about 8.25 p.m. the priest appeared in a blue Hawaiian shirt and made a short speech about how important it was to help people. 'Then he just stopped!' says Henri. 'He looked at his watch and said, "Shit! I've got to go. 'Law and Order' starts in two minutes." Then he just walked out. It was, What the hell was that?'

Henri had nearly lost his daughter to cancer when she was young, and had made a pact with God to give back in some way. A private investigator with defence solicitors, he volunteered to help with the food bus in 1993 and started working for Father Bob full time in 1999. 'We argue all the time, we have a lot of disagreements, but always make up,' he says. 'I think he likes my Jewishness. The head of the Jewish Burial Society asked to meet Bob one day and they started talking about the price of burying people. When Bob heard it only cost about $1200 to bury Jewish people, he said, "What! Can you sneak me in?"'

Over the years, they've got to know many of the people they've helped extremely well. One man lived on the streets for thirty-eight years and loved the lifestyle. Father Bob would give Henri a food parcel every day to drop off to him. Another man was once the vice-president of a big bank but when his marriage began to break down, he started drinking heavily. He lost everything and ended up sleeping in boarding houses, and then on the streets. One young man was shunned by his family after getting a job; his parents had never worked, and disapproved of him for doing so. Father Bob supported him for years. Still another lost his business, a pizza shop, when his marriage also failed, and he slept for an astonishing three years in his car. 'Father Bob paid for him to do graphic arts at TAFE and he passed,' says Henri. 'Then we helped get him an apartment but for the first three weeks he was too scared to go inside, and he slept still in his car. But now he stays in the apartment, is doing a bit of graphic arts work and runs bush-walking trips for the homeless.

'You get all sorts of people on the streets, from ex-killers who've been institutionalised by their time in jail and go back to jail to a man who was living in America but didn't renew his green card and was dumped back here with nothing. Unfortunately a lot of the people we feed, and who I see on a day-to-day basis, have mental health problems, and the mental health system is crap. They often start to self-medicate and they get a bit crazy. I call it ill-at-ease. They can be drug addicts or alcoholics . . . The average would be about ten deaths a year. A lot of them commit suicide in their forties. I think maybe they've had enough and they can't keep going and it all gets too much for them.'

There was still a critical need for more money for Open Family and throughout the 1990s, there were a number of appeals for funds. These took many forms, from the Irish folk group The Fureys on St Patrick's Day suggesting everyone forego a Guinness and give the cash instead to Open Family, to Australian rocker Angry Anderson urging everyone to 'chuck a buck' to Father Bob for National Homeless Week. Melbourne's eight radio stations combined forces to launch one appeal, and a direct mail campaign to 500 000 Victorian households was undertaken, while Father Bob himself implored companies to donate the money they would have paid to government under the new Training Levy Guarantee Fund legislation to him instead. 'Getting kids off the street, out of their sick environments, is often their last chance,' he said. 'The cost to society of these kids ending up on the scrapheap in the long term is far greater than the 1 per cent levy!'

Sometimes, shock tactics were used. In 1993, a TV commercial 'Roo Cull' featured vigilante death squads hunting street kids; it was banned by the main TV networks and criticised by the Federal Government. In 1994, another showing wolves chasing terrified street kids down laneways – said to symbolise the problems threatening the youngsters like homelessness, violence, drugs and prostitution – was banished until later than 9 p.m. Father Bob was outraged. 'We show the horrors of the massacres in Rwanda on our prime-time news and this is only a parable, it isn't even realism,' he protested. 'If you were seeing adults prowling the public lavatories in Victoria looking for kids for sex, then we might talk about restricting the material to mature audiences only.'

Open Family's national profile was rising sharply, and the organisation was given an even greater boost with the United Nations naming it as operating the most advanced management system of street kids in the world. In 1992, the UN had held a World Summit for Children, with the largest group of world leaders ever convened to discuss their responsibilities to children and their future, ending up making their landmark World Declaration on the Survival, Development and Protection of Children. Open Family's work was studied and praised.

But still Father Bob saw keeping public attention on the needs of homeless young people as crucial. He had a side of a church building painted with a colourful mural by an artist who'd been helped by Open Family when he was in trouble for spraying graffiti, and spoke at every event he could on the discovery of a number of street kids who'd been buried in unmarked graves at a cemetery in northern Melbourne. He was particularly concerned too that more and more middle-class kids were joining those already on the streets or sleeping at friends' homes and squatting at overcrowded flats. Among Melbourne's estimated 1500 homeless teenagers, he'd seen kids as young as ten running away from home, being lured into drinking and using drugs, sniffing paint, glue and butane, and ending up being preyed on by paedophiles and involved in vandalism, theft and robberies. He also put a photo on his 'children's altar' of smiling two-year-old Daniel Valerio, the child who was battered to death by his mother's boyfriend in 1990, to remind everyone of what can happen when good people do nothing.

The appeals were successful to some extent. A hospital in

Albert Park donated a large house to be used to provide crisis accommodation and Visy chairman Richard Pratt, whose wife Jeanne had once been such a big fan of Father Vincent Kiss, gave $50 000 and urged other businesses to help too. TV personality Geraldine Doogue also came to interview him again when she started at 'Compass' in 1998. 'He was just remarkable,' she says. 'I thought he had a deep faith and I think he's an entrepreneur of religion, a backbone of the Australian Catholic Church. I thought his values were right; there was depth to them. He's as sharp as a tack. He made quite an impact on me, as he does on a lot of people. I've never been fond of people who tilt at absurd windmills and keep tilting, but he's not one of them. There's a lot of rebel in him, and I wouldn't like dealing with him in the hierarchy, but he's pragmatic. I know two people on the crew said he was a living saint.'

All in all, the late 1990s was a time of great blessings – and curses. When Father Bob publicly blessed the new $1.8 billion Crown casino complex, sprinkling holy water in its direction, he was slammed by Baptist Minister the Reverend Tim Costello, the head of the Interchurch Gambling Taskforce. 'The God of Jesus would have nothing to do with that,' thundered the Reverend Costello. 'Whatever tribal god Bob is using is the god of greed, the god of monopoly . . . Most certainly it should not be blessed. The glitz and glamour is to hide the fact it is built upon shattered hopes and greed.'

Father Bob, never one to shy away from a scrap, defended his corner with just as much passion. 'It's a special place in Melbourne and a lot of people are working and coming through here,' he said. 'They handed over a bus to our parish.

They've been good to us. And just because we bless soldiers, it doesn't mean we're endorsing destruction.'

Also receiving a blessing was St Peter and Paul's church itself, when George Pell, then the Archbishop of Melbourne, visited to bless the building at the end of the renovations Father Bob had overseen. Afterwards, he met parishioners, with Father Bob, over supper. It was the third time the two men had met. The Archbishop had served for a short time on the board of Open Family, and had even been out on the food bus. At the blessing, they greeted each other like old friends. It was a cordiality, however, that wasn't to last.

The afterglow of the blessing was soon clouded, in any case, by the curse of Father Vincent Kiss. The jailing of the priest for fraud had offered only temporary relief from both the scandal itself, and Derryn Hinch. While Kiss was in jail, a man came forward to accuse the priest of indecently assaulting him in 1965 when he was a thirteen-year-old boy and Kiss was thirty-four. He'd been a member of the Young Christian Students Association, during Kiss's tenure as the Director of Youth for Wagga Wagga.

More boys then came forward to press similar claims. Kiss had plied the boys with alcohol, they said, taken them off on holidays in fast cars, and had sexually abused them. He'd assaulted others, they alleged, during their training as altar boys and after athletics training in a steam room.

In 1999, as Kiss was released from HM Ararat Prison, having served his seven-year sentence for fraud, he was immediately re-arrested and charged with child sex crimes. His name was also linked with an alleged network of paedophiles operating out of an area of the Philippines 90 kilometres south of the capital, Manila. Hinch, who'd been investigating Kiss on suspicion of such activity for years, was triumphant. Father Bob was appalled. This latest turn of events was deeply shocking to him, and he steeled himself for the maelstrom of criticism that was surely headed his way.

PART 3

THE TROUBLES

16

The Worst of Times

If Father Bob Maguire could ever have imagined having an *annus horribilis*, the year 2002 was it.

Most people's difficulties in life generally come down to two things: money and sex. Father Bob's troubles were similar, but with a priestly twist. The number-one issue was money – both that there was never enough of it, and Father Bob's handling of what there was. The second involved accusations of sexual abuse levelled at fellow priests, and going right to the top.

On the money front, things weren't travelling well. The work of both Open Family Australia and the Emerald Hill Mission had expanded so widely and so quickly, it was perhaps inevitable there would be problems.

In 2002 alone, for instance, Open Family's outreach workers were to see 626 kids from the age of twelve to eighteen from around thirty different ethnic backgrounds in Melbourne, Canberra and now Sydney, too. The intervention work included helping the youngsters make contact with their families, providing family mediation and support, organising visits to GPs and community health workers, and giving them access to drug and alcohol programs. Of the kids being seen, follow-up contact found that the lives of 317 had since improved, while 147 experienced a stabilisation in their conditions. Around a quarter continued on a downward slope.

Street kid Erica was perhaps typical of a number of the young people on Open Family's books. She'd run away from home at eleven, after suffering years of sexual and emotional abuse. When a street outreach worker first encountered her, she was sixteen and a hopeless heroin addict, working as a prostitute to maintain both her habit and that of her boyfriend. 'She was a tough little veteran of street life,' said Open Family's Carmel Barber. 'We made life plans and appointments which Erica endorsed enthusiastically, but which she never attempted to carry out.'

The young girl then disappeared until turning up two years later on the streets of Frankston. Carmel gave her a business card. Erica phoned her that night, saying she needed help. She was three months pregnant, her boyfriend was violent towards her and she was sleeping on the beach. Open Family swung into action, arranging for her to stay in a caravan park, giving her some emergency funds and then putting her on a methadone plan to get off heroin. She was later housed in a two-bedroom unit. 'Erica now has a beautiful baby boy and is making a valiant effort to be a fantastic mum to her son,' Carmel reported. 'She is determined that he will have a better life than she had.'

It was young people like Erica that kept Father Bob, by then sixty-seven, pressing so hard for his organisations to help more kids, and continue assistance to the adults many had become. 'When a young person is finally ready to ask for help, we have to be there to give them that help,' he says. 'So many of them are trying to run on their own merits but just need a helping hand from someone at a critical time. If that's not forthcoming, then they may be lost forever.'

He knew that from the thirty-one young people he'd already lost among the street kids and neighbourhood youngsters he'd been trying to help from the beginning. Many had killed themselves out of desperation; others had been killed by their pushers, drugs, alcohol, gang members or enemies; one died in jail; another in a fight. In 2001, he decided to honour their memory and, on the back of a memorial to local babies who'd died that had previously been established in the church garden by parishioners, he had a slab of granite placed, with the first names and first letter of the surname of each of the dead inscribed into it. 'Forgive us our sins. We have already forgiven you yours,' he had written. 'We died on your watch during the 70s, 80s, and 90s urban drug wars. We were only 20-somethings. Lest We Forget.'

'Anzac Day commemorates those who died in the war but this goes further,' says Father Bob. 'Here we're talking about the destruction of major parts of a whole new young generation. Here, they can rest peacefully at last. They may have sinned, but they're still worthy of remembrance. And I put they'd forgiven us our sin – of neglecting them, of not caring enough about them.' Having the memorial constructed and placed in the garden immediately made him feel better. These young people, whose lives had been so tragically cut short, would at least live on in people's memories, and he decided that a memorial service be held every year in their honour, on the day he arrived in the parish on 14 September, the same day as his own birthday.

For the work of Open Family, numerous fundraising events were being held and planned for the future, everything from a rugby league lunch with H G Nelson and Tony Squires to a sponsored film night, from a corporate race day to a comedy night out. Father Bob spent a lot of his time racing around the country talking up donations, as well as working hard within the parish and the neighbouring areas, and coping with Costas's frequent outbursts. He kept up a manic workaholic pace and in 2002, it all came back to bite him.

He was rushing off to conduct a wedding, when he felt his heart racing at what he describes as 320 kilometres an hour. He tried to ignore it at first, but when it seemed to be getting even faster, he rang a priest friend to see if he could cover the wedding and drove himself to the local clinic. The doctor there sent him straight to hospital. After a number of tests, he was diagnosed with atrial fibrillation, an irregular heartbeat, and prescribed medication to keep it in check. 'I thought I was dying!' he says. 'But now I know it's the lowest form of heart conditions . . .'

He made an effort from that point on to eat more healthily, try to cut down on the amount of junk food he loved to eat and to drop his occasional whisky and Cuban cigar habit. 'I don't drink,' he told those offering. 'I'm on the pill, the girth control pill.' But it did nothing to slow him down and he continued on exactly the same mad round of appointments, meetings, seminars, conferences, charity functions, motivational and inspirational talks, and services at the church. One day at the pulpit, he embarked on a new grumpy old man routine. 'We're expected to do everything, be everything to everyone,' he told the congregation. 'We're sent here, we're sent there . . . but you never hear anything about priest abuse!' There was a gasp of horror from some, laughter from others.

Yet the tightness of finances was no laughing matter at all. Father Bob had been propping up the work of both Open Family and the Emerald Hill Mission, at times, with parish money, and then the parish in turn with his charity funds. He felt there was a mutual agreement among all three for giving and taking as the fortunes of each ebbed and flowed, and his bookkeeper kept a careful tally of what went where. While many onlookers didn't mind that, feeling all the work was being done in the name of St Peter and Paul's anyway, others felt they should remain entirely separate entities, each strictly quarantined from each other, and feared the records were now becoming intricately intertwined.

By 2002, tensions had built up in both Open Family and the parish about money. A number of prominent business-people from the world of finance were now sitting on the board of Open Family, and they were used to running companies along strict profit and loss lines, with every dollar spent carefully receipted and accounted for. It was quite at odds with Father Bob's modus operandi.

'If someone came to him in great need, then he'd give

them money if that was what they needed because we were all about helping the poor, the marginalised, the dispossessed,' says Richard Tregear, an experienced outreach worker who'd joined Open Family from Mission Victoria because he believed so passionately in Father Bob's vision. 'We were all about giving service 24/7 on the community's terms, not ours. It was radical social work, outreach work and service delivery. But the Open Family board was becoming more and more and more conservative all the time, and the rebellious essence, the creativity that was there when Bob started was steadily diminishing. The people who came in and joined the board didn't understand community service, they didn't understand youth work, and they didn't understand what we were trying to do. Outreach was the flagship of our work, and we were answerable to the local community, and then Bob, and finally the board. But the board wanted to come first all the time.'

That board certainly tended to see things differently. Phil Ruthven, the founder and chairman of IBISWorld, an international corporation providing online business information, forecasting and strategic services, was a veteran member of the board, and was later to serve as Open Family chairman for two years. He was a long-time admirer of Father Bob and his work. 'No-one would deny he has one of the smartest minds, or highest IQs, almost in Australia,' he says. 'He's a remarkably unique man, with a warmth that's very disarming.' But he also felt there needed to be changes in the nature of the organisation as a way of modernising it, where strict processes and protocols had to be put in place to satisfy increasingly stringent accountability requirements. He saw Father Bob, on the other hand, as suffering a bout of what he suggests was 'founder's syndrome', where the founder wants to continue to operate his way, and the way he always has, and retain most of the power and control.

'In some ways, you need a fairly big ego to be able to start an organisation like this and keep it going in the face of some pretty extraordinary difficulties, financial, with the authorities and with the type of work you're doing,' says Phil. 'You have to be stubborn and have an ego, and he's someone who likes a measure of adulation to feed the ego. But that can be both the strength and a weakness of an organisation as you move forward. Bob felt as if he owned Open Family in a sense. That's where founder's syndrome came in. I remember saying to Bob one time that it isn't something you own. He said, "But you own IBISWorld!" I said, "That's true but that's a private company and it's taken a lot of money to do that."

'The board had issues with Bob but he's not someone you could ever bring yourself to dislike. There were problems with administration and the proper accounting of funds but there was certainly never any defalcation. He may have been great at handing over money, but he never used it for himself. When you weigh up what Bob's achieved, it's a hell of a lot but when you go into the second or third generation of something, it can be difficult, the same as with any other company that's been founded by someone. But nobody could take away from Bob what he's achieved. He'd been recognised by the United Nations as having the world's best practice in looking after street kids. The world's best practice! He's a remarkable human being, he's a very popular figure and has become in a sense a beacon for good things, like Ben Chifley's "The light on the hill". But all the saints in the Catholic Church are flawed in some way, including Mother Teresa in India, because they're all human beings.'

But tensions continued to grow, arguments started and tempers flared. When finances grew tighter, the board started talking about cuts to services; Father Bob talked about putting more effort into fundraising. It was a complete difference of opinion and cracks began to appear in the organisation. Father Bob, as the founder and chairman, and CEO Nathan Stirling were on the one side, and the rest of his board were ranged on the other. It felt clear to Father Bob that the board was trying to sideline him, and he dug in his heels.

His long-time ally Frank O'Connor watched on. 'Phil seemed to express the board's view that Bob was past it,' he says. 'So clearly the rot had started to set in from their perspective. Bob, of course, always felt they'd lost direction and the organisation was moving away from its core of being very focused on the extremely marginalised and disadvantaged, and was instead becoming just another service to provide things to slightly disadvantaged young people. And I think Bob had that fundamental disagreement with them that they'd lost their way.'

But back in the parish, the situation was becoming even more fraught. By 2002, Father Bob had run up an overdraft of $300 000, and that had been brought to the attention of the new Archbishop of Melbourne.

Father Bob wasn't unduly worried about the state of the parish's financial affairs. He'd consulted a financial adviser and the pair had toured the parish, looking at the buildings the

Catholic Church owned there. 'He looked around and said, "You're not broke! Look at all these empty buildings!"' reports Father Bob. 'His advice was to liquefy some of these idle assets.' As a result, he'd sketched out a long-term plan to sell some of the buildings belonging to the Church, to lease out some and to develop others with a series of different partners. That would net him around $1.5 million, he estimated, which would help pay for some much-needed repairs to other buildings, renovate others, and keep all his projects, as well as the parish, going.

The financial adviser approved the schemes, saying the development plans would bring healthy cash flow into the future. It all seemed perfectly straightforward to Father Bob. After all, he wasn't in the business of building wealth for its own sake. 'There is a clause in Canon Law which says that the parish priest must use parish goods for the poor and needy,' he says. 'That's the Church's true work.' The Catholic hierarchy, however, had other ideas.

He received a letter from the Archdiocesan business manager saying there was a level of concern about the overdraft, and a need for some more independent financial advice. Father Bob's spending needed to be a great deal more accountable and, at the same time, much more modest. Some within the parish welcomed the intervention. Gerry Vaughan, the treasurer of Emerald Hill Mission, says an incorporated body 'has to be run correctly, which is where I had a few problems . . .' The priest, however, didn't take kindly to the edict from above. He instead had some stamps made with gospel and Vatican II references on them – including 'I was hungry and you fed me' and 'I was in prison and you visited me' – and then provided

Bobby with his father, James. Although his dad gave everyone a tough time, Father Bob still today feels affection for him.

Bobby and his mother, Annie. Until her death she was still taking in work as a seamstress to make ends meet, and a hard life had made her old before her time.

Bobby with his brother, Jim, who went away for lengths of time with the air force, missing out on much of his youngest sibling's childhood.

When Bobby (right) turned eight, he was delighted to be given the important role of altar boy with his best mate, Brian Harman.

Bobby during a trip with his mother to a Daylesford guesthouse. He describes the weekend as one of his happiest childhood memories.

Bobby with one of his sisters, Kathleen, who was struck down in her prime. 'As a kid she had always looked after me,' he says. 'When she was gone, it was a huge shock.'

During his teenage years, Bobby joined the school-based Australian Army Cadets. 'I enjoyed it,' he says. 'It got me out, as I'd never really been anywhere or done much in my life.'

Young Bob Maguire was trained at the seminary in Werribee. 'Imagine, in the priest factory, I'd not read a newspaper in six years.'

Father Bob's ordination photo from 1960. His family and friends saw his ordination as a new start after a tough childhood.

Bob in 1959, studying at the seminary in Glen Waverley.

Father Bob holding his first mass at St Cecilia's in Glen Iris.

Father Bob at St Peter and Paul's Church in South Melbourne. Upon his arrival in 1973, he had plenty of ideas and plans for the first parish he would run himself.

There was constant demand for Father Bob to conduct weddings, funerals and baptisms. He still loves the idea of tending to the whole circle of life.

Father Bob in 1989 with his sister Eileen when he received a Medal of the Order of Australia for service to the community. 'I don't know why they're giving it to me,' he joked at the time. 'I'm only the commander-in-chief. I'm not the one doing the bloody work.'

Father Bob has always connected with young people. He speaks to them in a very egalitarian way – never talking down to anyone – as if taking them into his confidence.

Father Bob in a shirt gifted to him by students of a Gippsland Catholic college after he gave a speech there. *[Courtesy Cameron Reilly]*

Father Bob on the motorbike of Justin Dickinson. He regularly works with Justin's organisation, The Big Umbrella, to help marginalised young people at home and abroad. *[Courtesy: Justin Dickinson]*

In 2005, John Safran and Father Bob began co-hosting 'Sunday Night Safran' on Triple J. 'I think some people want him for his shock value but they might not understand how interesting and substantial he really is,' says John.
[Courtesy Fairfax Syndication / Rodger Cummins]

Community support was overwhelming when the Archbishop of Melbourne said Father Bob would be seventy-five and the time for his retirement had come. *[Courtesy Fairfax Syndication / Luis Enrique Ascui]*

On April Fool's day in 2011, Father Bob grabbed headlines by setting up a drive-through confessional. As a priest, he liked nothing better than a good stunt to shock people out of indifference. *[Courtesy Newspix / Craig Borrow]*

While Father Bob has been able to meet and greet many high-profile people in his life, his preference has always been to mix with outsiders and lost sheep.

Left: The memorial card Father Bob gave out at the funeral of Costas Vasiliou.

Below: Brian Rudd, who first came to Father Bob for help in the 1970s.

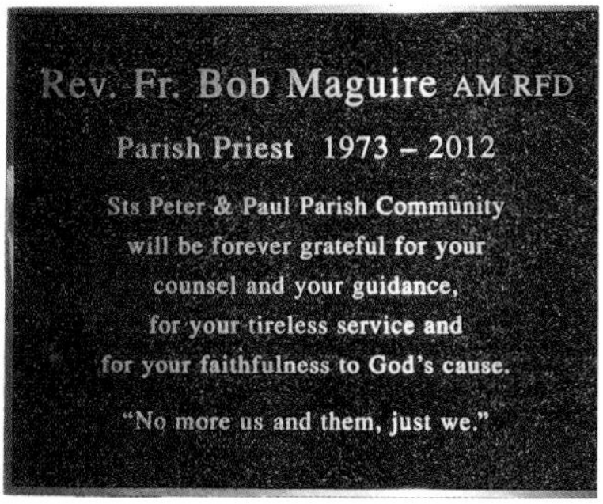

Left: The plaque that was installed in St Peter and Paul's after Father Bob's retirement.

'Football is often likened to religion,' says Father Bob. 'There's a ritual involved and while you go in hoping for the best, you know you're going to suffer along the way.'

Above: Father Bob wears his Melbourne Storm scarf next to Angry Anderson (left) and Les Twentyman.
[Courtesy Fairfax Syndication / Jason South]

Right: The priest proudly displays his allegiance to Collingwood Football Club.
[Courtesy Newspix / Fiona Hamilton]

Father Bob stands next to a portrait by Peter Ferrier, which was entered into the 2012 Archibald Prize. 'The superficial view of me is that I am a narcissist,' Bob says. 'The only thing I'm doing, in fact, is asking people to see past that and into [the real] me.' *[Courtesy Newspix / Craig Borrow]*

After 39 years at St Peter and Paul's, over 1000 people attended Father Bob's last service. He was presented with this pair of boxing gloves. *[Courtesy Newspix / Norm Oorloff]*

a set of accounts with such stamps next to each entry, and cheque butts with them on too.

The newly appointed Archbishop of Melbourne, Denis Hart, replacing his old seminary classmate George Pell, who'd become Archbishop of Sydney, was unimpressed. He had meetings with Father Bob about the finances.

His old friend Father Ernie Smith feared the worst. 'He's a complex sort of a person, and he can be his own worst enemy the way he goes about things,' he says. 'He doesn't like to be accountable to the organisation.'

Finally, Archibshop Hart, frustrated that they didn't seem to be getting anywhere, closed the bank account the priest had been using, and opened another that required a second signature to access any funds.

For Father Bob, that was a massive blow. From being a parish priest with a number of independent welfare organisations, being able to operate pretty much as he pleased, his activities were now being serious curtailed, and he was subject to a degree of control he'd never before known. 'That was completely unjust and unjustifiable,' says Father Bob. 'The small bunch of administrators who knew the whole story knew that. I'd arrived in South Melbourne when it was a bombsite and I'd worked for so many years to get it up to the stage where it was perfectly able to look after itself. Next on the plan was the sale of Emerald Hall, which was of no use to anyone, as it was heritage-listed and couldn't be used for residential and would have cost the Church more to repair than it could possibly afford. The tenant, Chris Apostolidis, was doing a great job of renovating it himself, and wanted to buy it for his Dance World, but then HQ said "No". So when it came to the next stage of feeding the poor and looking after people who had nothing, HQ started saying Maguire's attitude to both wasn't acceptable. They were saying crime, crime, crime.'

Yet his situation was about to become a whole lot worse. The South Melbourne parish chairman of the time, Brian Rochford, the operations manager of gas company Envestra, also wrote to the Archbishop, complaining about Father Bob. His letter ranged over a series of issues, including the level of general spending, the sale of church property, funds from the parish being spent outside the parish, personal growth programs that were developed by parishioners only and the priest's lack of socialising over a cup of tea after the Sunday mass. He also claimed Father Bob would routinely give money to 'a small, haphazardly selected group of people', and singled out particularly the amounts of money that were going to Costas and the young man's behaviour, which, the letter went on to say, was having an impact on the health and safety obligations of the parish.

'I don't have a lot of time for Father Bob but I don't want to press it,' says Brian today. 'My concerns were mostly about the money and where it went. But one thing I'll tell you about Bob, he never spent any money on Bob. But he spent a lot on other people, particularly with handouts to Costas.'

The letter was to prove a ticking timebomb for Father Bob. The Archbishop saw it as symptomatic of a growing dissatisfaction within the parish with their priest, and wanted to act on it.

Others within the parish, however, were appalled by the letter, and angry they hadn't been consulted before it had been sent in the name of the parish council. A number of them wrote letters of protest, including Frank O'Connor, a member of the parish at that stage for twenty-three years. He also wrote to Brian, calling his original letter 'most astonishing'. He mounted a vigorous defence of Father Bob, saying the priest had already given a number of undertakings about Costas, arguing that his ministry to the parish was consistent with his belief in the need to move from the clerical model of the Church to one based on individual and community responsibilities, and describing the priest's approach to finance as 'less than traditional'. He finished by writing that Brian should either resume his role of developing and supporting the parish in accordance with Father Bob's philosophy, or, 'If alternatively you don't believe that Fr Bob's view of Christ's message is correct then I am at a loss to understand how you can continue in your role as Parish Councillor of this Parish.'

They were strong words but, a decade on, and now a former local councillor and four-time mayor of Port Phillip and South Melbourne, Frank doesn't resile from them. Growing up in a hard-working Irish Catholic family in St Kilda, he built a successful career in IT and married and had two children, then he and his wife Ann volunteered to run a family group home for wards of the state, so he knew firsthand the kind of kids Father Bob had made it his mission to help. In 1980, after moving to Albert Park, he started attending St Peter and Paul's and became a huge admirer of the priest's Vatican II philosophy and an enthusiastic member of 'the people's liturgy'. He could see how people might be concerned by Father Bob's attitude to financial matters, but he didn't agree with them.

'Bob's always insisted that if you've got the money, it ought to be given to those who need it,' Frank says. 'If there was any money around, it went to what he saw as worthy causes and that's what was getting him into strife. He often sees money as the only lever he has to make change in the world. I disagree with him on this. I think he's got the capacity to change the world through what he says, and the inspiration he gives people by interpreting Christian gospel messages into modern-day living. But he likes to use money to solve the world's ills. He could always dispense money very quickly, but it's a philosophical thing. If you've got money, you've just got to hand it over because it's probably more meaningful and more relevant to the person at that particular time than it might be tomorrow or next week.'

Similarly, his CEO at Open Family at the time, Nathan Stirling, says to suggest that Father Bob can't manage finances is quite wrong. 'For anyone to portray him as a financial imbecile is the absolute inverse of what he's like,' he says. 'The impression that he's financially incompetent is ridiculous, and the trouble is then that mud sticks. But while I was never privy to the parish finances, he's quite competent. He simply chooses to spend money rather than save it.'

His old offsider Damian Coleridge agrees. It was simply an old-fashioned view of the Church and its responsibilities to those unable to help themselves, he believes. 'There's no point in being the richest person in the graveyard; it's about being creative with money,' he says. 'Bob is old-fashioned. You won't see his type again. He has a great belief in having personal responsibility for dispensing funds, and a real kind of love for the poor. It's generosity, giving done from the heart. Part of me actually rather likes that attitude. You don't have to go through these bloody mountains of paperwork to do it. But the times aren't propitious for that anymore.

'Yet I've seen that in other figures too. The old Archbishop Mannix used to walk through Collingwood on his way to the cathedral, dispensing coins as he went.'

At base, the clashes between Father Bob and his financial managers seemed to be a fundamental conflict of philosophies about the proper way for funds to be managed and spent. The priest had become well known for giving money to people who asked him for help, twenty dollars here, twenty-five there, and usually considerably more to Costas, but he was still rarely seen as a soft touch.

He could sometimes be heard chiding those asking for a handout, or telling someone to 'Get out of here!' One man once asked him for money, saying he was in need of fourteen dollars. Father Bob gave him a twenty-dollar note. The man insisted on carefully counting six one-dollar coins back into the priest's hand.

'And even if I am sometimes a soft touch, that's what the gospel is all about: If you give your cloak and they want your trousers, well, give them too,' he defends himself. 'And occasionally it might pay off. The people I've helped are often highly talented people whose lives have been wrecked by their childhoods or by drugs. Traumatic early-childhood experiences, like being abused, or being a state ward or having drug- or alcohol-addicted parents, can mess up your wiring to the point where you can't even aspire to do good things. But we should try to create equal opportunities for everybody. These people can still think, they still feel, they can still hurt . . .'

But the Archbishop, after trying to negotiate with Father Bob and having his approaches rebuffed, instead issued an ultimatum to his priest: either exclude Costas from the presbytery, stop spending money on him and allow the finance committee to supervise the accounts, or resign as parish priest. Father Bob tried to argue his corner, but Denis Hart, quietly, firmly and politely, held his position. Everyone knew that the Archbishop had the power to remove him from the parish, and doubtless some would have liked him to exercise that power, but in the end, Father Bob was the one to back down.

He sent out a note to real estate agents looking for alternative accommodation for Costas, and wrote back to his Archbishop to say all matters had now been attended to. Hurt, annoyed and affronted in almost equal measure, he desperately hoped that would be the end of the matter and he'd be left alone to conduct business pretty much as normal.

If Father Bob thought that times were bad, they were soon to become much worse.

In August 2002, the disgraced Father Vincent Kiss pleaded guilty in a Sydney courtroom to thirteen child sex offences. 'In my view, the offences are so serious that a custodial sentence is inevitable,' said Judge Penny Hock of the acts that had taken place between 1966 and 1973 in Albury, Yass and Sydney. The next month, he was sentenced to ten and a half years in jail.

There were then a series of revelations that suggested the charges were probably just the tip of the iceberg, and Kiss was a serial pederast who'd been abusing a huge number of boys, both in Australia and in the Philippines, for many years. A priest at his old seminary in the New South Wales Blue Mountains said a student had come to him one evening to disclose that Kiss had been taking him on trips into Sydney and to the Gold Coast as a young teenager, taking him to motels, abusing him, and then hearing his confession afterwards. The priest said, in retrospect, he should have gone straight to the police but back then, feeling bound by the confidentiality of the student's admission, and a sense of loyalty to the Church, he kept the terrible secret, all the while fearing what Kiss's 'missionary' activities might have entailed.

To Father Bob, this was all shocking news. If he'd ever suspected Kiss of abusing children, he would never have let him anywhere near his church. He was relieved, however, that Kiss had never been associated with Open Family or any of his work with children. But, predictably, Derryn Hinch went back on to the attack, linking Father Bob again with Kiss, and this time also adding the parish rows about money to the mix.

'He's never been good with money,' says Derryn. 'And he didn't care how he got it or spent it, even if that meant money laundering for a child molester. He made a pact with the devil. He said he needed the money for his children, but what about those poor children in the Philippines who'd been at the mercy of this man?'

Once again, Father Bob protested that he, along with the rest of Melbourne, had no idea what Kiss had been up to, and that he was only one of a long line of prominent and highly respected figures who'd been taken in by the debonair priest.

He feared the publicity might end up having repercussions on his organisations but it seems he was hurt personally by the attacks much more than his public persona or any of his work were. He continued to be as popular as he'd ever been.

But that wasn't always a good thing, he was soon to

discover. The publicity over the Kiss sexual abuse and allegations on the highly rating TV show '60 Minutes' that the Church had tried to cover up another instance of priest paedophilia had driven one of his parishioners to approach him with a horrendous accusation. As a twelve-year-old altar boy he'd been sexually molested, he said, at a holiday camp run by Catholic seminarians forty-one years before. And his assailant, he claimed, was a trainee priest known to the boys as 'Big George', a man he alleged was no less than the Archbishop of Sydney, George Pell.

17

Another New Project

The allegation that George Pell, the Archbishop of Sydney and arguably the most powerful person in the Catholic Church in Australia, had sexually abused one of his parishioners many years before presented Father Bob Maguire with a terrible dilemma.

On the one hand, he found this accusation very hard to believe. On the other, he'd worked with abused kids long enough to know that those in authority often didn't take their claims seriously and, in cases where they were telling the truth, scepticism and a refusal to investigate could cause them sometimes even more damage.

In addition, he wanted his beloved Church to be free of the taint of ever trying to cover up any kind of allegations involving the evil of child abuse. The Father Vincent Kiss case had been a sickening jolt for him, and he was determined that the Church always be prepared to be accountable for any past and present sins, however unlikely.

'What was I to do?' says Father Bob. 'I couldn't turn my back on the bloke who came to me. I was in a position of trust, and he'd come to me for help. I couldn't tell him to go away and just shut up about it. But I knew that if I supported him, I could be making a powerful enemy too. That could be the end of me, and my work.'

The man, a former member of the Federated Ship Painters and Dockers Union, told Father Bob he'd been driven in 1961 by members of the seminary at Werribee – the same seminary the priest had left the year before – to a holiday camp on Phillip Island, where one trainee priest known by the nickname 'Big George' had sexually assaulted him on several occasions. He'd recently been watching TV and had seen George Pell. He immediately recognised him, he claimed, as his assailant from all those years ago.

Father Bob listened in silence to the man. He'd known him for a number of years and admired him for having risen above a past riven by alcoholism and crime. These days the fifty-three year old was a respected figure whom he bumped into regularly at Collingwood football games and seemed genuine in his belief about what had happened. He said he wasn't after publicity or money – he'd been tortured by the memory of what he recalled having happened and wanted the Church quietly to acknowledge that, and perhaps have a private meeting with George Pell, to lay his demons to rest.

After the man had left, Father Bob made a phone call to the

National Committee for Professional Standards (NCPS), the body set up by the Australian Catholic Bishops' Conference to receive complaints of sexual abuse by Catholic priests. He told them what had happened, and arranged an appointment for the man who, for legal reasons, can't be identified. That took place in June 2002.

Two months on, however, events took a dramatic turn when details of his allegations were posted on a Sydney website, as well as the claim that the NCPS had decided it couldn't investigate because the case involved the Archbishop. The report further claimed that the complainant, frustrated by this lack of action, had decided to go to a journalist instead. At this, the NCPS agreed to hold a Church investigation. Then, in another shocking twist, aspects of the man's past criminal convictions were leaked to the media, as well as details of his alcoholism.

Two weeks later, George Pell held a press conference denying the claims, and saying the alleged events never happened but that he would cooperate fully with the investigation. He then took indefinite leave as the Archbishop of Sydney until the completion of the inquiry. That evening, Prime Minister John Howard defended him, declaring, 'I believe completely George Pell's denial.'

The inquiry took place during September and October of 2002, presided over by retired Victorian Supreme Court judge Alec Southwell, QC.

In his final ruling, Judge Southwell said the complainant's credibility had been subjected to a forceful attack but that it appeared the man had not had any problem with alcohol since 1979, and while he'd previously had thirty-nine convictions from about twenty court appearances, most of which involved drink-driving or assaults, the last one had been more than twenty years before; none had involved dishonesty.

In the end, with a marked lack of corroborative evidence, the case seemed to come down to the word of one man against another. The judge accepted 'that the complainant, when giving evidence of molesting, gave the impression that he was speaking honestly from an actual recollection'. But he said the Archbishop 'also gave me the impression he was speaking the truth'. As a result, he said he couldn't be 'satisfied that the complaint has been established'.

Melbourne lawyer Tony Joyce, who often acted pro bono for Father Bob, saw the verdict as a win for neither side. 'It was effectively a nil-all decision,' he says. 'Bob had supported the underdog, which is what he always does. It's one of his many good traits.'

The inquiry's conclusion was certainly less than the complete exoneration Archbishop Pell had no doubt been hoping for and Father Bob, reading the report of the inquiry on the Church website, felt nervous. His parishioner, he knew, would be devastated by the verdict but he also suspected George Pell might not be too pleased, either. 'I think this could be the end of Father Bob!' he told supporters. One of them nodded sagely. 'Yes,' he said, 'I don't know if Pell has it in him to forgive or forget.'

According to his biographer, Tess Livingstone, he certainly has, and she reports that after 'a little interval of time' George Pell prayed for his accuser. It is not known whether Father Bob was accorded the same blessing.

Father Bob had plenty of time over the next eight months to ponder that. Early in 2003, the sixty-eight year old was diagnosed with prostate cancer. It was his second bout of ill health in two years, and it took him completely by surprise. He was always so focused on others' needs, it felt almost an indulgence to be concentrating so much on himself and he felt very uncomfortable to be put in such an unfamiliar situation.

Happily, the cancer wasn't too far gone and he had daily radiotherapy treatments for a total of nine weeks over July and August for 'my prostitute problem', as he became fond of calling it. But he grumbled every time he had to go into hospital to receive the dose. It wasn't that he was particularly afraid of death; he felt he just didn't have the time to waste warding it off when there was so much still he wanted to achieve.

'As well, he told me he was having to walk around in one of those gowns that fasten at the back,' says John Cindric, who Father Bob helped, along with Costas, Brian Rudd, Chris Apostolidis and Mem River, and is today a good friend. 'He'd say he was being forced to walk around with his bum hanging out. He didn't think that's the way you should behave as a priest.'

But the treatment did give him plenty of time to sit and think, and it was then that he decided to start another charity project. He was still having rows with the Open Family board over how they were running the organisation and tensions remained within the parish and at the Emerald Hill Mission over the finances, so it seemed now was the time to strike out afresh. In addition, he'd been buoyed earlier in the year when he'd been awarded the Centenary Medal – an honour given to Australians who've contributed to the success of the nation's future in some way – in recognition of his long service to the congregation of St Peter and Paul's and the local community. A few months on, in a scenario he thought was ironic considering the criticism over his financial dealings, he was given the coveted Ernst & Young title of Social Entrepreneur of the Year for the Southern Region of Australia for a social, community or not-for-profit organisation. So as a result, the priest launched the Father Bob Maguire Foundation, a body set up to provide funding for about a dozen former clients of Open Family who were by then too old to qualify for its help.

'These were the survivors from the drug wars who no-one else wanted to help,' says Father Bob. 'They were former wards of the state who'd made it this far, but it was still very hard for them to keep going without any personal, family and community support. The prospects for this group of people, on the whole, weren't so good. Many had been terribly damaged by alcohol, drugs or their lifestyles. They were beyond care – beyond the kind of care other charities could give them. So I called the type of aid "futile care". It wasn't about giving them training or helping them learn new skills. It was about, simply, keeping them alive.'

Costas was to be one of the clients of the new Foundation. His position hadn't improved. He was losing weight, and exhibiting more signs of psychiatric problems. Father Bob, wondering at one point whether he'd also been abused at perhaps one of the state institutions he'd been in – Costas would never talk about any of them – persuaded him to make a submission to the Senate inquiry Report on Forgotten Australians, about children placed in institutions or out of home care. In desperation, he even sent him over to Cyprus to his family there to see if that would help. Costas returned a little quieter for a while, but still seemed deeply disturbed. The major problem was that the Archbishop had insisted Costas no longer be allowed to stay at the presbytery, or anywhere near it.

'I was caught short,' says Father Bob. 'I tried a little empty shop with a tiny kitchen and lavatory as part of it. I thought it was sad but he was becoming a hoarder by then, and could take most of his stuff in there. He wasn't a dirty hoarder, but a neat and tidy hoarder of pretty things. But the water wasn't on and I thought, I can't leave him out on street, so the only place left was at the back of my bloody premises. I thought that was getting a bit close to the bone, as HQ had said he shouldn't be there, but it cost nothing, he had a lavatory, a shower and a TV, and morally it was the only thing we could do. He was very grateful. He knew Denis [Hart] was after him, had declared a fatwa on him, and he knew that he was a pain in the arse. But he knew also that I couldn't throw him out as he had nowhere else to go. He stayed there till I found him somewhere else.'

Yet Father Bob was still heartened by the continuing successes of the kids who had turned out well.

Chris Apostolidis's Dance World, for example, was going gangbusters with students learning jazz, tap, classical ballet, hip-hop and musical theatre, and Father Bob loved dropping in to see how well everything was working out. He enjoyed seeing how passionate Chris was about dance, and how he managed to stir so much enthusiasm in his pupils. 'Once he came in here and said to me that what I was doing here was just as much a temple of God as his church,' says Chris. 'I was determined to set up a place of equality, where your gender, your race, your colour, your ideology, your religion, was not going to get in the way, where all that was left at the door. He liked that.'

Mem River, meanwhile, had been working with Open Family to help the priest get more involved with the Middle Eastern and African communities. 'I'd made a doco for schools about young Muslims after 9/11 for the Department of Immigration,' says Mem. 'There were a lot of tensions within and between communities in Melbourne and Father Bob wanted to get in touch with the Muslim community so we started working together again. He met some of the hardcore people, and created an atmosphere that made it all stop. It was pretty amazing!'

Afterwards, Mem took some time out to make another film, with Father Bob's encouragement and a bit of financial help. For this, he travelled to Iran and the mountains of northern Iraq to tell the story of an Australian Kurdish refugee who was returning there in a bid to find the love he'd left behind when he fled. 'If Bob didn't hear from me for two weeks, he was to tell the authorities that an Australian citizen was missing!' says Mem. After a long and torturous journey, along steep mountain ranges and over gorges with sheer 500-metre drops, the pair found the woman, who had since become an outlawed PKK (Kurdistan Workers' Party) guerrilla fighter, dedicated to regaining lost Kurdish homelands. The film, *In Search of Shilan*, directed by Mem and with the music also composed by him, ended up being shown around the world. Father Bob couldn't have been more proud.

Other kids of his were doing well, too. John Cindric had become a successful international aid worker and even Brian Rudd had managed to carve out some kind of independent life for himself. He'd moved away from Melbourne, and was shining shoes on the streets of Sydney.

Yet with his new Father Bob Maguire Foundation, there was also an element that was far more forward-looking than just the kids he'd helped in the past. It would include, he decided, a number of scholarships for disadvantaged students at various schools and colleges in Melbourne, paying tuition fees and buying their books and uniforms. He liked the symmetry of giving less well-off kids at the start of their lives access to the best start that money could buy, and helping those at the other end who hadn't fared too well.

'As a priest, celibacy isn't all bad,' he says. 'Instead, we're married to the Church and to the local people for the length of our natural lives. We have our ups and downs, the same as in a marriage, but you do your best to make sure everyone starts out as well as they can, then you stick together because you've made a commitment and, because when it does work, it's wonderful!'

Yet when it didn't work, just as in a marriage, breaking up could be hard to do. He was experiencing that firsthand with Open Family. The organisation was still expanding, with twenty street outreach workers in Melbourne, six in country Victoria, five in Canberra and six or seven in Sydney, but now it seemed he was being slowly but surely manoeuvred out. That was exacerbated by his great supporter, the CEO Nathan Stirling, working part time so he could study for a law degree. It looked like he might be leaving in the near future, too.

So at one board meeting, Father Bob took a proactive stand. He suggested that Open Family and his new Bob Maguire Foundation should merge to create a bigger, much broader organisation to look after people who were struggling for the duration of their lives, and proposed that veteran award-winning youth worker Les Twentyman, an employee of Open Family for the past six years, become the CEO of the new body. To him, it seemed the perfect fit. Les had very similar values to his own, and an enormous amount of experience in the field, having worked for over twenty-five years with kids for local government. He also had a high profile, having started the 20th Man Fund, which started a Care For Kids Program with well-known AFL footballers, a youth refuge and a back-to-school project.

The pair had known each other for years, bumping into each other from time to time as they both looked after kids on the streets, and then Les appeared on one of Father Bob's radio shows. Les reciprocated later, inviting the priest to speak at a conference he'd arranged during a one-time tilt for a seat in the Victorian Upper House. He's never forgotten it. 'The place was packed out and Channel 9 had their cameras going,' says Les. 'Then Bob gets up. He says, "My name is Father Bob Maguire. And I know what you're thinking: paedophile poofter . . ." Everyone was so shocked, there was absolute silence. They were hanging off every word. And the TV people were all shouting, "Cameras! Over here!" He certainly knows how to make an audience shut up and listen to what he has to say!

'Bob is very engaging, very entertaining. He's missed his vocation; he should have been an actor or a comedian. He's very quick-witted but sometimes he does and says things that put people offside. I remember on radio, something came up once about condoms. He called them sleeping bags for white mice.'

The Open Family board, however, weren't amused, and

turned down both Father Bob's plan to merge and also his idea to elevate Les. An alternative plan to have the then CEO of the not-for-profit Brotherhood of St Laurence, an organisation that works to prevent and alleviate poverty, take over as CEO in order to preserve, as he said, the cultural fit of the organisation was also voted down. Instead, with Nathan finally handing in his notice in July 2004 to accept a job with the Chief Justice of Victoria, the board hired a professional recruitment consultancy to find his replacement, and appointed a subcommittee of three to make the final decision on the successful candidate. Father Bob, the chairman, was not elected onto the subcommittee, and found himself having no say at all on the next CEO.

'He wasn't on the selection team. I don't know why. I suppose, in hindsight, it may have been a courtesy to have put the final two candidates in front of Bob,' says board member and later chairman, Phil Ruthven. 'He felt miffed about that. But we decided we should have a proper selection process.'

Yet some of the staff were appalled at the way valuable funds were being spent on that procedure. Les Twentyman was a major critic. 'Open Family was hijacked by the administration,' he says. 'It then went completely away from its original core values and was run along the lines of a corporate business. It was as if they'd completely abandoned what we'd been all about.' Outreach worker Richard Tregear was also angry. 'This was a hands-on charity that had its genesis in the street-people movement in Melbourne,' he says. 'Its great strength was that it didn't play by conservative rules. But the board just didn't understand the community in which they were working. They changed the nature of it completely.'

When Open Family finally appointed their new CEO, they paid the successful person an annual salary that some saw as befitting the post, and others saw as quite outrageously high. Ruthven says he can't recall the exact figure, but it was certainly over $150 000, while rumours claimed it was as high as $230 000. Ruthven, however, says they needed to pay a decent salary in order to get a good person and that salary was voluntarily reduced later when the charity ran into tough times. 'If you pay peanuts, you get monkeys,' he says. 'You might argue it was a high salary but we did go to a proper head-hunting organisation to do it and we went through a whole series of applicants. But for anyone who gets paid what a priest gets paid, it would have seemed horrendous.'

It did. Father Bob complained, he criticised the organisation publicly in the press and he was pushed further to the outer. 'They decided to go all businesslike and pay a new CEO an amazing sum of money,' he says. 'The theory being that if you have a flash CEO, that will be a recommendation to the business world that you're taking things seriously. So that's the option they chose, and they were sick of me anyway.'

They'd certainly been paying close attention to Father Bob's rows with the Catholic Church over his management of money. Just as some in the parish said that Father Bob spent too much money on his flock, and didn't keep it carefully enough accounted for, some members of Open Family echoed similar concerns.

Ruthven says the priest was having big problems with the Catholic hierarchy over his use of money. 'Bob was dangerous with a cheque book,' he says. 'It's almost ironic that he would criticise the folly of paying a new CEO when you saw the wastage that went on with him. He was ropeable that they'd taken the chequebook off him.'

But Nathan Stirling says to suggest Father Bob was wasteful or careless with money is to do him a grave disservice. 'That's rubbish!' he says bluntly. 'He's not a terrible money person. He's actually very astute with money; he's very good. He gets money in and then that money would go out. He didn't believe in building up surpluses or reserves. He would spend the money on things consistent with charitable purposes, which is a valid position to take. It's not necessarily orthodox, but it's valid.' Yet the new corporate regime at Open Family didn't seem much better with money. When Nathan left, the annual report financials show well over $1 million in the bank, an endowment fund with $500 000 and thirty-plus outreach workers. Three years later, records show the organisation had a deficit of $125 000.

Whatever the rights and wrongs of the situation, however, Father Bob was soon no longer chairman. Whether he jumped or was pushed is still a matter of some dispute. Phil Ruthven says the priest resigned; Father Bob says he was 'bumped'. The truth probably lies somewhere in between. But there's little doubt that Father Bob, although still on the board, was left angry, hurt and not a little bitter.

Even though the priest was still trying to find somewhere else for Costas to live, times back at the church seemed almost tranquil by comparison, and there were a few high points. British Prime Minister Tony Blair's wife Cherie made an unannounced visit on Palm Sunday and was reported to have been immensely impressed by Father Bob's service and his charity work. She even wrote to him afterwards, thanking him and expressing concern about a woman who'd passed out during the service, asking how she was. 'She survived,' Father Bob replied. 'That holy water always does the trick.' Cherie then donated some clothes to be recycled for those who needed them.

In 2004, the 150th anniversary of the founding of the parish, there was also a special mass followed by a barbecue and a supper dance at South Melbourne Town Hall. A plaque was placed in the garden honouring the Aboriginal ancestors, as well as the convict and free-settler forebears.

Melbourne Archbishop Denis Hart dropped in on St Peter and Paul's too, and attended the Wednesday breakfast barbecue out the back of the presbytery, cheered on Henry Nissen's football team, celebrated midday mass and visited a couple of parishioners.

There would be times in the future when Father Bob could barely believe they had once been so civil to each other.

18

Battle of the Gonzos

John Safran was a young man on a fast upward trajectory. The journalism student dropout turned advertising copywriter first found fame as one of the most controversial candidates ever on Australian TV's 'Race Around the World', where he streaked naked through the city of Jerusalem – except for his footy scarf and beanie – was baptised in Africa, put a voodoo curse on his ex-girlfriend and placed plaques in Disneyland about Walt Disney's alleged links with Nazism.

He then filmed a show for the ABC in which he notoriously rifled through TV current affairs star Ray Martin's bin, and later tried to tempt cricketer Shane Warne to smoke a cigarette to break his advertising agreement with a nicotine gum maker. In 2002, aged thirty-two, he debuted his award-winning documentary series 'John Safran's Music Jamboree' on SBS TV, complete with his, by now, trademark outrageously comedic stunts.

By 2004, John had become renowned as the enfant terrible of Australian TV. It was then that both a lawyer with whom he was having a meeting, and his manager's mum, said there was a man about town they really thought he should meet: Father Bob Maguire. The priest was still regularly appearing on radio, in newspapers and in the Catholic *Kairos* newspaper with his column, and increasingly being courted by the media for his opinions on everything from the footy and the weather to the meaning of Christmas. John was intrigued.

'It's unusual that you get two completely separate recommendations at the same time, so I thought I'd go to see this priest,' says John. 'So I snuck into one of his midday masses. I tried to sit in the background, but he spotted me and he started doing this shtick. He was very funny, and really warm, and he was interested in the kind of things I'm interested in. I thought, Here's someone I could work with.'

Father Bob also remembers that day well. 'I looked across the dance room [the church pews], and saw Safran. I recognised him from the TV. I thought, Why is he skulking around in the back of the bloody church? I don't like seeing strange people appear. He was obviously lurking with intent and I thought we might get robbed. Or I'd known he was running around Jerusalem without any clothes on and I was afraid he might start running around naked in the bloody church. I thought I should call security – if I had any!'

When Father Bob was asked to review Mel Gibson's religious blockbuster *The Passion of The Christ* ('self-indulgent' but 'a celebration of humanity'), the pair went together, John presenting the priest with flowers and chocolates ready for their 'date'. Father Bob was horrified. 'We're going to see Jesus being crucified, and you're giving me flowers and chocolates!' he complained. 'God Almighty!'

At the time, John was filming a new eight-part series for SBS, 'John Safran vs God', in which he scours the world looking for God, or talking to the people who say they've found Him. He decided to ask Father Bob onto an episode in which, despite being Jewish, he applies to join the Ku Klux Klan in California, holds a competition for Australian-Palestinians to win Israeli citizenship and road-tests Catholicism under the guidance of Father Bob.

The show launched on 30 August 2004, with Father Bob's episode airing the day before his seventieth birthday. In the show, the priest gives his host a crash course on the Bible, on lighting candles as an altar boy and on kneeling: 'All Catholics learn to kneel,' the priest instructs. Their trip to the cinema was also shown, with Father Bob complaining that Mel Gibson would have done better spending all that money on the real work of Jesus, 'in Bangladesh, Baghdad or Redfern'. John tests the fledgling relationship too when he does the reading at mass, and quotes from a hellfire-and-brimstone sermon in one of Morris West's novels, much to the shock of parishioners. The series, which also included a fatwa placed on TV star Rove McManus, the trial of a hallucinogenic plant and a disturbing exorcism by a fundamentalist preacher, caused a storm of controversy, but was also an immediate hit, and garnered a range of plaudits.

Father Bob's star turn, however, turned out to be the

highest rating of all the segments, with hundreds of emails and phone calls all congratulating the priest on his appearance. 'Bob was terrific in the show,' John says. 'Being a priest, he's got this authority about him, but that means the comedy is even funnier. He's also so smart. I can't believe how simultaneously smart he is, but then also worried about things he doesn't know. He relates to young people so well too. He's got a real thing that he thinks youth have all the answers and that does means he comes over really well to a young audience.'

At the conclusion of the series, John then asked Father Bob if he'd be his co-star on another TV project set to air the next year, called 'Speaking in Tongues', in which the pair would discuss a range of subjects. Father Bob readily agreed. 'I like that Safran's honest. He's an honest performer. And an activist, and I like activists. I thought it was about time I started doing something different too. I've always liked the media, and I thought that might be a good way to get my message out. We're not good at that in the Church, we tend to keep it all in-house and if we keep on doing that, we'll be buggered. A lot of his audience are younger too, and they're the demographic we have to reach for the future.'

Things were looking up, at least in one area of the priest's life. As he contemplated how quickly things could change, he received a call to say he'd won the 2005 Australian of the Year, Local Hero, Metro Award for Victoria. 'Father Bob is one of the unheralded and truly Australian heroes,' said the valedictory with the award, presented in November 2004 by the deputy premier of Victoria, John Thwaites. 'Father Bob is a strong, inspirational leader to both his congregation and the wider Australian community.'

Father Bob accepted the award and thanked everyone involved. But, privately, he was bemused at the irony of receiving an honour for, among other things, founding the organisation Open Family when he'd lost the chairmanship under such fraught circumstances. And he wondered if yet another award, the public acknowledgement and his rising visibility would help his cause, or simply make him a bigger target.

Suddenly, Father Bob seemed to be everywhere. Outside the Church he was being called upon to comment on everything under the sun, and he did so with a humour and plain language that appealed to the religious and the secular alike. 'As long as you don't mention God, you're all right with most Aussies,' he says. 'If you do, they run for the hills.'

At his church, where he felt much freer to talk about God and Jesus, his enthusiasm, irreverence and determination to include everyone seemed to know no bounds. A few years before, he'd copped criticism for conducting the funeral of career criminal Victor Peirce, shot dead in nearby Port Melbourne in what was widely suspected to be a drug-related killing. Victor's mother Kath Pettingill, at one time the most influential woman in Melbourne's underworld, had always predicted a violent death for him, and asked Father Bob to bury him. The priest agreed, farewelling him in a service in which he studiously concentrated on Peirce's finer qualities. When people asked what he was doing, burying such a villain, Father Bob replied simply, 'He's dead! Do we need a second opinion?' Later, he explained, 'It's our duty as priests. We're bound, without fear or favour, and the last thing we should do is judge other human beings. We're about all human life, the good, the bad and the ugly, and it's hard to say who's who as often the ugly are the most lovely inside.'

Now, Father Bob was introducing a range of ever-more daring events, including inviting Aboriginal people to come and perform a smoking ceremony in St Peter and Paul's and talk about their customs, and locals of every faith and creed, including Jews and Muslims, to take part in inter-faith services, with a Muslim imam – organised by Mem River – calling worshippers to prayer in the church. He also provided premises for a language school for the local Greek Orthodox church. 'He's a man of great depth,' says the church's Father Chris Dimolianis. One Christmas mass, a couple of rappers came along to perform a psalm from the Old Testament while a photograph of a mother and father and their baby on a life-support machine – a child baptised by the priest shortly before she died – was projected onto a screen in the background as a modern version of the 'Holy family'.

All of them, however, retained his informal, chatty, stream-of-consciousness approach, something he himself called 'Bobbywaffle'. His sermons covered an ever-expanding number of topics and contemporary references, all designed to bring the point he was making home to his congregation. Some days he'd talk about the situation in Darfur in Sudan, South Africa and Haiti all in one breath; other days he'd bring in news stories about bushfires, AIDS, sudden infant death syndrome and an earthquake in Japan. He never prepared notes, either. He'd read up the night before, have a think about the events of the week, sort out what he wanted to say, and then just wing it from the pulpit. 'Don't panic!' he was fond of saying. 'I'm a priest!'

He'd often interrupt a sermon, too, by asking if anyone was still awake or, spotting someone he knew in the congregation, asking them by name how they were. He once even had a long chat with a parishioner from the pulpit about his problems in the middle of a service. He'd offer toys to restless children to play with and regularly invite youngsters who were trying to raise money for a good cause up to speak, sing or play an instrument, and encouraged everyone to support them. Another day, a tennis ball bounced in from the court nearby and Father Bob stepped down from the altar, picked up the ball and went off in search of the boys who'd lost it.

When the Sydney Swans won the Grand Final in 2005, breaking the league's longest premiership drought since they'd last won as South Melbourne in 1933, he allowed the team's flag to be draped over the altar and their song to be sung by the congregation. At mass, he'd often give communion to an elderly woman he knew to be a fellow Collingwood supporter and, together with the wafer and sip of wine, he'd stealthily pass her a videotape of the last game, courtesy of his suppliers at Channel 7. When she later died, he tried to get permission to release a flock of magpies at her funeral, but he was told it wasn't possible. He released some doves, with black-and-white ribbons, instead.

He never minded a touch of controversy to get his opinions across, either. One day, he talked about the amount of discrimination that young people faced in their daily lives and the need to have a much more open mind when dealing with them. If that didn't happen, he warned, 'we'll create a generation of Amrozis'. There was a sharp intake of breath with that reference to the Bali bomber, but he carried on regardless. He said David Hicks, detained by the US in Guantanamo Bay on terrorism charges, should be brought home to Australia; that allied troops should withdraw from Iraq and pay the locals compensation; and that detention centres should be closed down. He bemoaned the increase in the number of poker machines.

Occasionally, he'd suggest having a service for a homosexual man or women, or a single mother, saying everyone should be afforded the same solicitude. 'We shouldn't lock Jesus into history,' he'd advise. He said sex before marriage wasn't allowed in theory but, in practice, people should make up their own minds. Another time, he spoke publicly about his doubt that Mother Mary was a virgin. 'I don't give a bugger whether she was or not,' he said. 'The Hebrew word means "a young woman of marriageable age". Then the Greek comes in and uses the word for virgin.'

That was still small fry, however, in contrast with his view on the vexed subject of contraception. 'I don't mind the Vatican,' he says. 'Every institution needs a bureaucracy. But we should butt out of the debate about it, leave it to the experts.'

He was also outspoken about drugs, and not just that they were a scourge of the modern age. 'Bloody drugs are the trouble. I hate them. We alleged disciples of Jesus of Nazareth fell asleep when drugs came in and claimed forty of our locals. I still feel responsible for that.' He also believed that drugs should be decriminalised, an attitude completely at odds with the Church's much more conservative stand. 'It's too easy to say we're going to wage war on drugs, we're going to cut off the supply and tell people not to use. We've tried that for years, and can you see any evidence we're winning the war? No? The only answer is to decriminalise drugs. That would stop people having to mix with the dealers and getting trapped, and committing crimes to get the money to buy drugs.'

His experiences with Costas had hardened his attitude to drug dealers. He'd seen how much Costas and most of the rest of his band of 'survivors' had suffered as a result of drugs, as well as a number of those who'd died, and desperately wanted the situation improved. Of course, he could never be sure when or if Costas was still using, but he was certainly exhibiting the type of psychotic behaviour consistent with drug-taking. Sometimes he'd be good, and would ask Father Bob what had been in his sermon that day, and the pair would talk quietly together about God and the gospels. These were times the priest came to treasure.

Costas also had moments of perception about his own situation and would apologise for not turning out a success like Chris Apostolidis, Mem River or John Cindric. 'If you put up with ranting and raving, you often ended up with a startling spiritual insight,' says Father Bob. 'It was worth waiting for. But as Costas and many of the other survivors got older, the more problems they had – health, mental health and legal – and they didn't want to leave the area. For them it was their sacred site.'

From time to time, Frank O'Connor would also call around to play chess with Costas. 'He had his ups and downs, and on some of the downs he hit the absolute depths,' Frank says. 'On some of the ups, he was a very personable, engaging young man and you could enjoy his company. But over the years the depths got deeper and lasted longer, and the ups were less frequent and less visible. But Bob never gave up on him. I remember Bob being constantly challenged by people asking, "Why are you still pouring money into him? He's got no future, he's got no hope."

'But Bob used to dismiss that. He said to me one day that at least when Costas is dying, he won't be able to say nobody was there to help. But I think eventually the cost to Bob, in terms of friction with Open Family and the Archdiocese, was huge.'

Predictably, with so many flirtations with danger, trouble would inevitably follow. Some parishioners complained to the Archbishop about Father Bob's support of Costas, some of the views he expressed, and the increasingly informal nature of his liturgy. Some of his TV viewers and radio listeners also voiced their disapproval. One of the biggest storms was when he became a regular guest of John Safran on the TV personality's new radio show 'Sunday Night Safran' on youth station Triple J in 2005, with its motto 'Everyone offended equally'. 'Most shows on a youth network would make fun of an old guy, but having a seventy year old who can really hold his own is great, and exactly what you wouldn't expect to have on a show on Triple J,' says John. 'That's appealing, and young people react so well to him! He's a great personality and I think a lot of young people see him as the grandfather they wish they'd had.'

But on one of his first appearances, the priest took part in a call-in confession segment, where listeners phoned, confessed on air to their sins and were given penance by the priest. One woman called to say she used the F-word too often, and Father Bob said the only sinful swearing was taking the name of the Lord in vain and told her to recite one 'Our Father' to atone. Another said he had used satanic powers to will to death someone in an internet chat room. Father Bob banned him from using chat rooms for twenty-four hours. The backlash from the Church was swift. Radio confessions were inappropriate, said one high-up clergy member, because a priest could never break the seal of the confessional, which included broadcasting it on radio. The punishment in extreme cases could even be defrocking or excommunication.

Father Bob's old schoolteacher Brother Leo Griffin observed his former pupil's progress with absolute horror. 'I couldn't believe what I was seeing!' he says. 'I thought, This can't be the same person! I was embarrassed by him. But I know he was very sincere, and when my brother was dying, he came to him straightaway, for which I was always grateful. But I didn't like the way he enjoyed the shock value of what he said. I didn't admire his foibles.'

Yet with all the extra TV and radio airtime he was getting, Father Bob was rapidly becoming better known to a wider audience all the time. On 'Sunday Night Safran', he was winning a devoted younger audience for the way he seemed to connect with everyone on air, no matter how different they were from himself. Psychic John Edwards, a guest interviewee one week, was so impressed, he sent Father Bob a personal family rosary as a gift; the world's most famous atheist, Richard Dawkins, came away from a debate full of praise for him; and both controversial US comedian Sarah Silverman and director Tim Burton refused their publicists' pleas to finish their star turns, so rapt were they by Father Bob's company.

'Everybody just seems to love him,' says show producer Serpil Senelmis. 'No subject is off limits, from porn stars to sex books, racism to homosexuality. He connects so well to a younger audience because he's so non-judgemental and is so energetic. One time when someone was talking about a gay club, he asked if there was such a thing as a celibates-only club, but we told him that kind of defeats the purpose of a nightclub! But he's irrepressible. When John and he engaged in a Twitter war to see who could get the most followers, he won hands down!'

Another breakthrough was his appearance on Andrew Denton's highly rating 'Enough Rope' show on ABC TV. In July 2005, Father Bob appeared alongside two other priests, Anglican 'boxing' minister Father Dave Smith and Aboriginal Uniting Church minister the Reverend Sealin Garlett. At one stage, Andrew persuaded the three to play 'Soul of the Century', in which they were asked various questions about the Bible. Father Bob's first on-air question to the host was a plaintive, 'Are there prizes?' The answer: 'There are, of an eternal nature.'

It didn't quite all go according to plan. Father Bob protested that he wasn't used to trying to beat anyone at pushing the buzzer first. 'Because we're humble, see, we usually let the other one go first.' Later in the game, he even accused one of the ministers of interfering with his buzzer, by pulling out its wires so it didn't work. But when he was asked how he continued to believe in God, even though so many young people died around South Melbourne from drink and drugs, he snapped to attention. 'It's you and me that let kids die,' he said. 'They died while we were sleeping. It's got nothing to do with God. I mean, once He got up onto that cross and was executed, that's good enough for me. His father got a hell of a fright because he thought this son was going to be a success.'

Things seemed to be finally sorting themselves out back in the parish, too. The Church authorities at last agreed to sell off Emerald Hall, which Father Bob had proposed to settle all the financial problems of the parish, as well as to enable him to continue with other work. The priest petitioned the Archdiocese to allow him to sell it to Chris Apostolidis for his Dance World but they refused at first. When it failed to sell to anyone else, however, they at last allowed Chris to buy it, a sale that netted the parish the funds Father Bob had always said it would. The parish accounts continued to be administered, however, by a business manager the Diocese had installed.

Encouraged by the success of the scheme to sell off the hall, Father Bob then worked with members of the parish council and his supporters to work out a vision for the parish 'block'. Next door to the church, on the corner of Bank and Montague streets, stood the Galilee Primary School, with a large part of the big old building still empty. Father Bob had the idea it should become an environmentally friendly community hub, and began talking to Friends of the Earth about what could be done in the space.

The rest of the vision for the future was more ambitious still. This involved converting the parish house to some form of aged-care facility, with a fully independent apartment for the parish priest; developing the original school buildings into residential apartments and the newer ones into supported accommodation; installing some kind of childcare facility along the eastern boundary; and continuing the meals service from the back of the church. These, Father Bob reasoned, would provide a continuous flow of rental income from the aged-care and childcare projects, a large capital injection from the sale of land for the apartments and an extension of the parish's work to help with supported accommodation.

The steering committee for this plan included Gerry Vaughan, the Emerald Hill Mission treasurer, Frank O'Connor from the parish and the lawyer Tony Joyce to handle the legal work, as well as a real estate agent and a financial expert. 'Potentially, even the present presbytery building could be turned into independent units for the elderly,' says Frank. 'There were a range of things. Father Bob liked the ideas, so he pursued that notion, particularly of the community housing units. He got frustrated a bit because he didn't understand that he couldn't just get on and get it done but there were always so many permissions and permits to get and any objections from neighbours to get over. The community housing project meant the land would be leased from the church, with that money going into a trust and the income going into the parish to make the parish viable, which is pretty far-sighted. There's another parish at South Yarra who have been building a smaller project, probably half a dozen units on some land at the back of their church, so we're probably not the first, but it's a fairly substantial example of what can be done.

'I think the lesson for Bob in all of that was always that

there are people around who can manage these projects perhaps better than he can. He's great at having the ideas but then he should sometimes just let others actually go and make the thing happen! But he was always so impatient and anxious because he knew it would be a good outcome for the parish, so he wanted it to happen sooner rather than later.'

With all these plans well underway, Father Bob felt he could finally begin to relax a little. There were still issues around Open Family but at least he felt the parish was now headed in the right direction. He could afford to spend a bit more time broadcasting his message about the importance of looking after kids and combatting poverty, without worrying so much about events back at the barracks.

John Safran's much-anticipated new show 'Speaking in Tongues' debuted on SBS TV on 7 November 2005, after a blaze of publicity in which John and Father Bob were dubbed Australian TV's newest, and oddest of, odd couples. No-one could quite believe the regular pairing of two people quite so different – a 33-year-old gonzo TV ratbag and his 71-year-old increasingly cranky gonzo priest sidekick – but the chemistry seemed to work a charm. Father Bob was eager to give it a go.

'Joy is increasingly rare in our culture and what I think we'll be trying to do is add a bit of joy to people's lives,' he said. 'An essential ingredient of joy is humour. Safran's good at a twisted sort of humour, and I'm a bit of a bloody fool meself. This show is a great opportunity for me to jump on the media bandwagon. It's a great way to market religion in a funny way of being serious. We're rescuing God from religion.

Even if people get interested in the cause in an indirect way, I can die happy.

'Safran is insightful and entertaining and I'm deep and meaningful as well as being vaudeville. I don't mind having a pie flung in my face.'

Billed as a current affairs–chat show 'with a spiritual twist', the weekly Monday-evening 'Speaking in Tongues' comprised the two men sitting at a desk before a background of stained-glass windows, talking over the topics of the day, interspersed with interviewing a variety of guests. 'So, say there's cannibalism in the news that week, I'll ask Bob what the Catholic perspective is on eating people,' John explained before the show went to air. Responded Father Bob: 'And I'll say it's all right in a desperate situation, as long as you don't do the killing. Just helpful hints, see, for everyday living!' On air, John enjoyed goading Father Bob on a huge variety of topics to see just how far he could push the priest. Father Bob usually managed to artfully duck for cover when he felt the need, or turn to humour to deflect the questions. When John pressed him on sexuality, for instance, he replied, 'I think celibate. I'm a retrosexual.'

There were also two regular segments: 'Matchmaker, Matchmaker', in which the hosts paired off young people from obscure religious; and 'Phenomenon', with guests who'd witnessed inexplicable events, like seeing a golem, a magic creature in Jewish folklore. Another feature to develop was viewers sending in their suggestions for the billboard outside St Peter and Paul's every week, with the winning phrase put up by Father Bob. They varied widely, from 'Deity Deeds Done Dirt Cheap' to 'Wake Up and Smell the Moses' and 'Get the

Flock Inside'. That week, 'Deity Deeds' won, replacing the sign already there: 'Trouble Sleeping? Try Our Sermons!' The show 'Speaking in Tongues' was also the first Australian program ever to be available afterwards as a video podcast.

The first episode kicked off into immediate controversy. John recounted that, in a private conversation with the head of World Vision, the Reverend Tim Costello – the man who'd slammed Father Bob for his Crown casino blessing – the Baptist minister had refused to appear on air with the priest, saying if he 'had as many skeletons in his closet as Father Bob has in his', he wouldn't risk appearing on TV at all. John grilled Father Bob about what he meant. The priest said he really had no idea but he'd like to congratulate Tim on his World Vision job and hoped he'd be able to do great work for the poor. They then went on to interview a retired sex worker discussing her religious clients.

The show was to continue in this fashion all the way through: risky TV constantly pushing the boundaries of both ethics and defamation law. 'And if we go too far, I'll blame Safran and just say, "Oh God! I didn't know it was going to be like this!"' said Father Bob.

19

Hatches, Matches and Dispatches

The love affair between Father Bob and the media showed no signs of cooling in 2006. With 'Speaking in Tongues' still on air, he was also asked to take part in a clutch of new shows, some markedly more successful than others.

The first of 2006 was the interview show 'Dream On', on community TV's Channel 31, appearing on a panel of celebrities helping decipher viewers' dreams. Then came an invitation to be the co-host of 'Good Samaritans', with barrister Michael Kuzilny, interviewing fellow kind hearts. But it was on the third project of the year where he had his biggest hit, as a chat show guest on the Ten Network's 'David Tench Tonight'. The show was already making international TV history when Father Bob went on. The brainchild of Andrew Denton's production company, it starred a host who was a complete animation in a world first, using the same capture-and-digital-enhancement technology as that which created the *Lord of The Rings* character Gollum.

'I didn't understand what they were going on about, when they asked me in,' says Father Bob. 'They wanted me to fly to Sydney to be interviewed by a cartoon? Then I said, Oh, all right then, I'll give it a go. But it was very odd being in a studio with just me and a screen.'

Yet the priest acquitted himself tremendously well. He started out complaining about someone who'd walked out of mass halfway through his sermon, when he'd been saying how Jesus said you can't have divorce. 'But if he'd have stayed, he would have heard the second half, when I said, If you can't avoid it, then you'd have to have it, but he missed it!' Then Tench tried to ask him about a dilemma the host had encountered while making love to a woman. Father Bob's eyebrows shot up. 'No, I'm not going there,' he said. 'No, not there.' Then, thinking about it, he smiled. 'Oh, all right then,' he finally agreed. Tench asked him, when the woman cried out, 'Oh God! Oh God!' should he reprimand her for blaspheming? Quick as a flash, Father Bob said he should tell her to get on the line to the local priest who'd immediately help her to get out of her dangerous situation. He'd advise her it was no good hanging around with blokes like Tench.

Shortly afterwards, John Safran became an even closer media collaborator, or, as Father Bob termed it, co-conspirator, too. In 2007, his 'Sunday Night Safran' radio show was extended to two hours on Triple J and the 71-year-old priest became his regular co-host. 'We'd been working together for a while by then, and we'd never had a fight,' says John. 'It was just this weird archetype of two people yelling at each other over a microphone. But I love working with him. He's so smart, funny, and yet so humble. But I think some people want him for his shock value but they might not understand how interesting and substantial he really is.' For Father Bob it had enormous value too, and not just in reaching a new, younger demographic. 'You learn how to be constantly ready for a barb, and for someone making a coarse remark about your most sacred truths,' he says. 'That was a very good lesson for me. I learned how to take attacks, not be offended and give back as good, sometimes, as I got.'

Father Bob's rising profile meant a constant flood of invitations coming his way, to make appearances at functions, to give speeches at dinners and conferences, and even to bless events. He was asked to review the TV show 'Underbelly' ('A good show about redemption. People should see it!' was his verdict) and at one Variety Club fundraiser, he was persuaded to perform a rap song he wrote himself, 'Finding a Better Four-Letter Word', with Tottie Goldsmith on backing vocals. It was an act that brought the house down. But he still never liked being called a celebrity. 'I'm not an actor, I'm an activist!' became his regular catchcry.

Yet he was pleased to discover his ease with the media, and it even inspired him to make videos of his own, appealing for funds to help with his Father Bob Maguire Foundation. Interviewed by Mike Ryan of the online radio and TV company Melbourne Business Now, Father Bob asked for thirty viewers to donate $7500 each in order to pay the annual costs of supporting the Foundation's 300 dependants: kids on scholarships, battlers and migrants without any other support. 'It's all about the security of the community,' he explained. 'If you're able to provide people without any connections in society with those connections, then the quality of your community will rise. If you want to beat terrorism, you only have to run around the countryside reconnecting the unconnected, and you'll be fine!'

The next year, in order to attract funds, he even dressed up as a nun and introduced himself as Sister Roberta of the Order of the Leaping Sisters of Saint Beryl, saying people were sometimes more willing to donate to causes introduced by women, as they assumed they'd be speaking from the heart, rather than by men who spoke from the head. 'Other Churches have women priests, but this is an opportunity to have a male nun,' he said. 'This shows how far I have to go to raise awareness and money for the Father Bob Maguire Foundation . . . I'm seventy-four, fat and bald but my face is my fortune, which is why I'm broke!'

His Emerald Hill Mission was working well, with various high-profile celebrities and sportspeople dropping by from time to time to go out with the food van. With Open Family, however, he didn't have much idea how they were doing as, despite still being on the board, he seemed to be more and more on the outer. He was alarmed by the continual talk there about spending cuts, still arguing that the board should be working harder to raise more funds rather than considering reducing services. By now, there were branches of Open Family in Sydney, Canberra, Albury/Wodonga, Shepparton,

Benalla, Seymour and Wangaratta, as well as the HQ in South Melbourne, and after working so hard to make it a national organisation, the priest felt it would be terrible to see it shrink. In 2006, board member and sometime chairman Phil Ruthven even made overtures to the Sydney street kids' champion Father Chris Riley of Youth Off the Streets, to discuss a merger in order to be able to gain some economies of scale. The approach, however, was rebuffed.

By the next year, 2007, Father Bob was off the board too. He was devastated. 'I'd started the thing and here I was, having no say in its direction at all,' he says. 'But it wasn't the same organisation as the one I'd started. It had moved in quite a different way.' Relations grew so bad that Father Bob, at one stage, went to his lawyer saying the body shouldn't be allowed to use the name Open Family anymore. He even trademarked it as his own. But eventually he dropped that. 'It was a very sad time for me,' he says. 'I would have liked to have kept Open Family with me till the end. But it wasn't to be. It was time to move on.'

Back in the parish, things were going well. The development plans for the block were progressing nicely, with a project control group being set up to determine goals and outcomes, invite expressions of interest, advertise and go through the assessment process. Information would be reported regularly back to the parish community, it was decided, and negotiations with the Archdiocese would begin.

Costas had quietened down a little too, and seemed to have beaten his addiction to heroin, although his behaviour was no less irrational. He still haunted the presbytery 'like the Hunchback of Notre Dame', according to Father Bob, but he'd adopted a dog, a Jack Russell called Rosie, and the pair would obsessively prowl around the neighbourhood. Yet he seemed a lot more settled. He took to giving people little presents he'd collected on the streets: a little flower here, a butterfly there, a pretty stone. At one stage, he took to giving away cigarettes, and buying ice-creams for people living in the Housing Commission flats. He also made friends with some of the tradespeople around the area, who didn't seem to mind the volume at which he lived. They liked him as he could play the clown very well.

Father Bob's then-secretary Judy Sampson says Costas always remained an enigma. 'I didn't understand him,' she says. 'At first, I thought he was just a crazy boy who screamed a lot. He'd be very loud and in your face like a puppy dog. Then all of a sudden, there'd be silence and you'd look up and he'd put a little flower on the desk.'

The priest tried to keep him out of harm's way, while still tending to the business of the parish. He was in constant demand to conduct weddings, funerals and baptisms, often now baptising the grandchildren of the people he'd first met as young couples in his congregation. He loved that idea of tending to the whole circle of life, and the way he knew nearly everyone in his church, and often their parents, grandparents and children too.

He certainly had his critics who longed for more traditional services and wished that, just for once, Father Bob would stay on track, and there were occasions when he couldn't quite meet parishioners' expectations. One time, a woman came to him crying, saying her husband was cheating on her and she didn't know what to do. One of the priest's helpers, Henri Ser, reports Father Bob gave her a tissue and a sandwich and then told her that a lot of people seemed to be having affairs these days. 'Bob said to me afterwards, "Look, what do I know about marriage? I've never been married; I don't know anything, really. I can give lectures on it and talk on it and toe the line on what I'm supposed to say, but, really, a priest giving advice on marriage isn't the best idea."'

Yet Father Bob was still enormously popular with others for the way he was happy to conduct ceremonies, and make them personal expressions of the people involved, not even seeming to mind the novelty elements that were being introduced more and more often. Over the year 2006 alone, he held more than 100 weddings at St Peter and Paul's, sometimes conducting as many as three a day. He said the main attraction was the magnificence of the church itself – although, 'I may be added value,' he conceded.

One of his more unusual weddings involved the bride imploring him to lock the doors of the church as soon as she was safely inside so her mother couldn't get in, while, in another, the couple had eight parents there. A big wedding between an Egyptian bridegroom and an Italian bride saw Father Bob standing waving all the guests to their correct seats. 'Egypt to the right! Italy to the left! You, sir, wrong side!' A dog came up the aisle in another, with the wedding rings in a pouch on her back. Father Bob had a bowl of water waiting for her at the altar. 'I don't care what they do,' he says. 'It's their wedding. The church is a living gathering. It's about what's important to the people at the centre. Our role with the

Church shouldn't be about telling people what they can and can't do!'

He always liked to use humour to make the ceremony more meaningful too. He would tell the single men in the congregation, 'Bad luck!' if they'd ever had designs on the bride. If the Amens weren't loud enough at the end of the prayers, he'd joke about everyone needing to eat at the wedding supper. The Amens would inevitably then come back loud and strong. But his blessing was still no guarantee of marital bliss. One couple he married had a blazing row at the wedding reception and parted just a few days later.

One funeral even turned into a wedding, when Father Bob asked the daughter of the deceased, who was there with her boyfriend, why she wasn't yet married. She mumbled an answer and the priest then suggested she get married, there and then that day. She and the boyfriend agreed, and Father Bob performed a marriage ceremony. It was a day of both great sadness and of great joy, with tears mingling with laughter.

Celebrity weddings were a little more problematic. He wasn't so keen on those, particularly where couples had added security or tried to barricade themselves away from photographers. But he happily married Australian swimming champion Michael Klim and his bride, Balinese princess Lindy Rama, and then Elise May from 'The Price Is Right' and 'Postcards' and her beau, Lee Turner. Later, he officiated at the wedding of his old Open Family mate Les Twentyman, who was in 2006 named Victorian of the Year for his work with kids. Les was finally to follow him out of Open Family. 'I think it was somewhat hijacked by the new administration,' he says. 'I ended up not liking the organisation, so I quit and went back to my own charitable 20th Man Fund that I'd formed years before.'

The other major booking for Father Bob continued to be for funerals. Some parishioners didn't like the way he conducted these, feeling they should be a great deal more solemn. Others liked the eccentric way in which he could behave, to lighten the mood. Father Bob officiated at the funeral of former boxer and referee Johnny Wheeler, calling it 'his last main event'. Carlton legend Adrian Gallagher, one of the mourners, said it was a glorious service, especially at the end, when someone rang the bell ten times. 'Half the congregation jumped out of their seats and started shadow-boxing!' he said.

In February 2007, Cardinal George Pell introduced new guidelines for family members speaking at funerals, saying that too often they made 'inappropriate remarks' glossing over the deceased's proclivities, like drinking prowess or romantic conquests. It was symptomatic of the new conservatism still sweeping through the Church in Australia, with people like the Cardinal working hard to exert their influence to retain traditional elements.

Father Bob was by now only one of a dozen or so priests actively living the Vatican II message, opening up their churches, encouraging their congregations to take the liturgy and questioning traditional teachings on issues like contraception, divorce and gay marriage.

'We've become divided,' says Father Bob. 'We're split between traditionalists, who like to stay inside the church, and modernists who don't mind going outside, where the people are. We have the physical church, and the church in our hearts.' Church authorities said the increasing traditionalism was down to George Pell's influence, and also a reaction to postwar and 1970s liberalism. As Father Anthony Denton, director of the Catholic Vocations Office, explained, 'It's a bit like the scenario from the English TV show 'Ab Fab', with a bong-smoking mother having a conservative daughter.'

Yet in a series of snubs of the Church hierarchy, it was usually Father Bob, much more than Cardinal Pell or Archbishop Hart, to whom the media went first for a comment on any issue of the day. They knew they'd always get a thought-provoking response, and often a humorous one, too. Asked in April 2007 whether everyone should pray for the drought to break, he said that they could pray for rain 'until they go black in the face', but it wouldn't solve the water crisis. 'Maybe our prayers need a creative spin, like, "Oh God, please turn this wine into water!" I know a lot of people won't like that, particularly if they have a nice bottle of Grange on the table, but this water problem is bigger than us all. We need to work on finding solutions ourselves.'

The parish also had a chance to sing Father Bob's praises the following year, when it marked the thirty-fifth anniversary of his arrival as parish priest with a special service. Yet favourite times of year for Father Bob still remained the traditional occasions: Easter and Christmas. He often felt Christmas was becoming over-commercialised, but was determined not to be a killjoy. 'You can be a stick-in-the-mud and complain, or you can just go along with it,' he says. 'I prefer the latter. But I do like to remind people about the real meaning of Christmas: do no harm and do a bit of good. Treat others as a facsimile of yourself. Make a change at the local level, in your homes, in your community, in your town. You don't have to have things to have Christmas. You need to have humanity.' Once, he recounted, a man asked him what he should be doing at Christmas. The priest suggested he look after others. 'What others?' the man asked. Father Bob sighs. 'He didn't even know what the word Christmas meant. I told him to go home and Google it.'

At home in the presbytery office, there were other changes taking place. Following the death of Father Bob's dog Rocky, he was offered a replacement, another standard poodle that had been ailing in a pound until rescued by an animal-lover who vowed to find him a new home. The first couple to take him called back two days later to say it was impossible; Franklin had proved an excellent escape artist and kept jumping over their fence. They brought him back and, desperate, the woman had phoned Father Bob. He hadn't hesitated to take him in. Franklin turned out to love being around people, which was just as well with so many people constantly staying around the presbytery.

Sometimes, those guests still could be troublesome, particularly if they were high on drugs, or desperate for money for their next fix. One of the volunteers claims someone there once chased her with a machete. Another time the TV went missing – presumably stolen and sold for cash. Father Bob had a screen door installed in his office, so he could see who was calling before they rang the bell, and a security keypad was put in, so visitors couldn't get access to the inner areas of the presbytery. The problem was, the priest could never remember the code number, and insisted on sticking a Post-it note on the keypad with the code number scrawled on it. 'He had a great mind, always active, always coming up with grand schemes,' says a parishioner. 'But he was never so good on the details.'

The other major change was the rapid advance of technology. Father Bob had been writing an internet blog since mid-2005, often dictating it to someone who actually typed it in for him, and he loved it as a way of communicating what he had to say about the world. He also had his own website, podcasts, Facebook and Myspace pages, was constantly on email and his mobile phone, and loved Google and Wikipedia on the net. 'It's a miracle to have so much information and wisdom at your fingertips,' he says. But now, at the start of 2007, he'd discovered something quite new: Second Life, the online virtual world, where users could customise an avatar, connect with others and socialise.

Father Bob said his main motivation for creating his odd-looking avatar Bob Aji – 'We had no money in the bank, so couldn't afford a better one,' he explained – was to build a spirituality centre and see if the 3D world would function better than the real one. Avatars should be able to take a break from their hedonistic lifestyle, drop into a faith centre and decide, if they wanted to, he said, to become a Second Life monk. 'And in our next life, hopefully we'll all be digitally enhanced and look so much better!'

In other quiet moments, he still read voraciously, and wrote letters or emails to people around the world to talk about their missionary work, and to those in the Australian news whom he felt were having a particularly hard time. One day, for instance, he wrote to the footballer Ben Cousins who was struggling with drug-taking, and to the retired Anglican bishop and Governor-General Peter Hollingworth, who was at the time under fire for the inappropriate handling of sex abuse allegations. 'He's a very compassionate man,' says Father Hal Ranger.

He also replied to the thirty or so letters he received every week. On any given day, there might be somebody writing to him to thank him for a past favour, to ask for a new one, to congratulate him for spreading the message about God, to give him news of a mutual friend, to say how much he'd helped them with a life dilemma or to complain about something he'd said. 'You make me realise how good life is when I listen to you,' said one Triple J listener. 'You help me get through everything.' From another: 'I felt like I'd touched God in your presence last week.' And from one atheist: 'I'm not a believer but people like you make me realise I might well be missing out.' There'd also be regular posts on news websites along similar lines: Father Bob for Archbishop, for Cardinal, and some even said for Pope. To any such suggestions made directly to him, Father Bob always politely demurred, pointing out he was merely a lowly parish priest who didn't have to wrestle with any of the politics of the Church, unlike men like Cardinal Pell.

Plenty of others, of course, weren't so glowing. 'I was appalled at what you said this morning on TV,' one viewer wrote to him. 'You made a mockery of the life and death of Jesus and you're likely to turn people away from the Church. Please do not cheapen Christ on TV.' One man phoned him up after watching him on TV's 'A Current Affair', where he'd appeared talking about British chef Gordon Ramsay's constant swearing. 'You've exceeded your use-by date,' said the man. 'Retire or go to Tasmania!' Other people branded him a narcissist or an egotist for speaking up publicly so often, and appearing so frequently on TV, on radio and in newspapers, accusing him of 'showing off'. But Father Bob weathered every storm. 'I always replied that I was putting in,' he says. 'Catholicism is a broad Church and we should be able to talk about what's troubling us, and discuss it freely. Church people should be actively engaged in building civil society, we should be putting ourselves out there, we should be getting the debate going at every opportunity.'

In the rest of his spare time, he was still devoted to Collingwood, often attending matches with his mate from the Painters and Dockers who'd made the allegations against George Pell. He rarely missed a home game and had become a well-known champion of the club. Its president, Eddie McGuire, was, in turn, an equally enthusiastic supporter of the priest. The pair had first met in the 1970s when Father Bob was taking services as a chaplain at his old school, the Christian Brothers' College. He made a huge impression on the then 12-year-old Eddie. 'Bob was a large breath of fresh air coming through CBC, with style and verve and a message that was always welcoming,' he says. 'He was the first priest ever to come in, hold a mass and finish it twenty minutes before the scheduled finish at lunchtime and say, "There's nothing worse than being in church when you could be out playing football." He made an impression on everyone! The boys all thought he was a legend.'

Father Bob was also invited to take on a role as an ambassador with the NRL's Melbourne Storm. The crises in the performances of each club, he reckoned, often balanced each other out, or at least took his mind off some of the most crushing losses.

The priest still liked nothing better than a good stunt to shock people out of what he saw as their lethargy about the poor and defenceless. A new ad highlighting the need for funds for his Father Bob Maguire Foundation this time had stickers of a knife, fork and napkin on the top of a rubbish bin to represent a dinner plate, to bring home the plight of those forced to scavenge for scraps to survive. 'For the homeless, every day is a struggle', read the message, created free of charge by ad agency Clemenger for Father Bob's foundation.

And when Australian workplace agreements were finally declared to be dead, the long-time committed union man even held a funeral for them, with the ashes held in an urn, at St Peter and Paul's for Channel 31's 'The Union Show'. 'May the burial of these AWAs remind us that death comes to us all – political and human – and it is the natural passage for all life,' Father Bob solemnly declared. 'May these AWAs sleep on and not reappear in an eternal slumber in your Godly care.' Then he scattered the ashes under the rose bush in the church garden.

But beneath the flamboyance of such attention-grabbing acts, there was always a serious message. He felt strongly about the rights of the disadvantaged, and was outspoken in their defence. When, for instance, the government moved to trial schemes cutting welfare payments for families whose kids didn't attend school, he spoke out forcefully against the experiment. It would merely force needy families to rely on charity, he predicted. 'We are going to create a social problem to solve another social problem and at the expense of those who are least able to articulate their predicament.'

As if to prove his argument, six weeks later he announced that he had to suspend his work on the streets because his charity couldn't cope with the rise in the number of people asking for help since the start of the global financial crisis. When he'd explain he didn't have the money to give, some of those people were getting menacing and threatening, he revealed. 'These people are desperate, poor and frustrated. Some have been marginalised for forty years.' He couldn't resist a jibe at the Church hierarchy, either. 'I'm living in a double-storey house on almost an acre and it's obviously worth millions. So when I say I don't have the resources to help, people don't believe me.'

But Father Bob's resourcefulness was still greatly admired by many and at the end of 2008, he was named as one of the top ten Victorian heroes of the year by the News Ltd newspapers. 'Father Bob inspires us because he is not afraid to speak out for the poor and disadvantaged,' said the commendation. 'After a lifetime of working with the poor and speaking out on social injustice, Father Bob is one of Australia's genuine heroes.'

It was a lovely sentiment, but still Father Bob couldn't help an uneasy feeling in the pit of his stomach. The next year, he'd turn seventy-five, the age at which priests were usually expected to offer their resignation to the Archbishop. Personally, he couldn't imagine anything worse than retirement. He still had so much he wanted to do, and so little time. He hoped the Archdiocese had forgotten his birthday.

They hadn't.

20

(Un)Happy Birthday to You

On 2 September 2009, the phone rang in the St Peter and St Paul's presbytery office. Father Bob Maguire picked up the receiver. There was a brisk, businesslike voice at the other end. 'Hello,' it said. 'Denis Hart here. Are you in? I'll be over in twenty minutes.'

Father Bob felt his heart sink; the Archbishop of Melbourne just didn't make casual calls. He felt a dark sense of foreboding. He called his secretary Judy Sampson into the office. 'The Archbishop is on his way,' he told her. 'Will you sit in and take notes of our meeting?'

When Denis Hart arrived, Judy showed him in and took

her seat, as the two men sat stiffly on either side of the desk. She then bent over her pad and took notes, not daring to look up. 'The Archbishop said Father Bob would be seventy-five in twelve days and the time for his retirement had come,' says Judy. 'They bantered to and fro, each watching their words very carefully as they both knew I was sitting writing everything down.'

Finally, Denis took an envelope out of his pocket and put it on the desk, saying it was Father Bob's invitation to retire. The priest looked at it and shook his head. 'No,' he said carefully. 'I'm not going to sign that.' After a few more words, the two men formally nodded and Denis stood up and walked out the door.

Judy stared after him, then glanced back at Father Bob. He was still sitting unmoving at his desk, his body hunched, a shell-shocked look on his face. 'It was like a bad dream, really,' she says. 'I couldn't believe what had happened and, I think, neither could he.' But then the priest lifted his eyes to the heavens, and she could see his lips set in a defiant line. 'And then,' adds Judy, 'all hell broke loose.'

The Catholic Church's Code of Canon Law dictates that, on reaching their seventy-fifth birthday, parish priests are required to offer their resignation to the Archbishop – although he doesn't necessarily have to accept. Usually, if he considers priests to be doing satisfactory jobs in their parishes, and if they are still in good health, then he allows them to stay much later, at least until eighty. It's a recognition that many just aren't ready to retire at that point and, with a critical shortage of new recruits to the priesthood, the Church is often more than happy to extend their tenure.

With so many priests being allowed to stay well beyond their seventy-fifth birthday, including Father Bob's predecessor at St Peter and Paul's, Father Lou Heriot, who had just that year been ordered to retire from his parish in Brighton East – at the age of eighty-two – Father Bob had considered himself pretty safe. He was far too busy to even contemplate retiring, with so much work still to be done. His Father Bob Maguire Foundation was by now supporting no fewer than twelve kids with scholarships, as well as several dozen older battlers, and he was feeding hundreds more each week out the back of the church. He was also one of the most popular, if not the most popular, priest in Melbourne to conduct baptisms, weddings and funerals, with people travelling from all over Victoria to attend his masses, and his profile was growing exponentially through the media. 'But when I'd first been invited to South Melbourne, it was for life,' he says. 'I thought I'd be safe from being made to retire so early. I thought the rules that were prevailing at the time I was appointed would apply, rather than those of a new regime, and I'd be exempt. I'd keep going indefinitely, until I was incompetent or incontinent, or both, and live out my years working for the parish, in the only home I'd ever known.'

So when the priest had received a letter from Archbishop Hart in January that year – ironically enough for him declared by Pope Benedict the Year of the Priesthood – saying he was due to turn seventy-five and that the Church would be expecting his resignation offer, Father Bob didn't take it seriously. He'd put it to one side, planning to reply to it later. But then he hadn't given it a second thought.

He'd always been careful, in any case, to not intentionally upset the Church. He made it a habit to be clear in the paperwork that any weddings conducted for divorcees were civil ceremonies, he often sent tapes of his shows with John Safran to the diocesan office before they aired and he was intent on trying to keep Costas in the background, after the Church hierarchy had told him to stop supporting the homeless former heroin addict. Now forty-eight, Costas was occasionally visiting the back room of the presbytery and filling it with the 'treasures' he'd collected as he roamed the streets with his dog Rosie, but for the most part was being billeted elsewhere. But the priest soon forgot the letter as the year quickly developed into another hectic round of commitments, with a huge diary of appointments, the growth of his Foundation, the food van – christened the Hopemobile – driving around the streets serving meals to the homeless, and the constant search for funds to keep everything going. After a while, he didn't even mind the fact that the Catholic diocesan newspaper *Kairos* had finally cut his column after years of publication, although he would later give that a more sinister motive as the first shot in the campaign to silence him. Yet at the time, he barely even had the space to think about it, he was kept so busy with work and his new mastery of tweeting with a Twitter feed, as well as the usual round of controversies.

This year, it was Easter that proved a flashpoint. It started out with the Victorian TAB announcing that, for the first time ever, outlets would be open on Good Friday for the placing of bets on races in Singapore and South Africa and on two NRL games. The move sparked immediate outrage, with anti-gambling advocate the Reverend Tim Costello, who'd criticised Father Bob for blessing the Crown casino, slamming it as being motivated by little more than corporate greed, and the Melbourne Catholic Bishop Christopher Prowse saying Good Friday was the day that should be reserved for remembering the death of Christ. Father Bob, on the other hand, said he had no objection to people gambling that day – as long as they went to church first. His comments did nothing to endear him to his more pious detractors.

Shortly afterwards, trouble flared again when his old TV partner and Triple J radio co-host John Safran was reported as having had himself nailed to a cross in a Good Friday ceremony in the Philippines, half-naked and wearing a crown of thorns. Safran endured a huge amount of criticism from those accusing him of trying to mock Christ's death until Father Bob stepped into the fray to defend him. 'He would not have done it contemptuously,' the priest said. '. . . it would have been for a forensic investigation of religious practices.'

The TV star has never forgotten Father Bob coming to his aid. 'He really stood up for me in the press and calmed things down a bit,' says Safran, who hung on the cross for five minutes before being taken away for medical treatment, as a segment on a new ABC TV show 'John Safran's Race Relations', to screen later in the year. 'He'll always stand up for you. He's very, very loyal.'

Father Bob's former Open Family worker Les Twentyman also discovered how deep Father Bob's loyalty ran. He'd gone into hospital for day lap band surgery but there were complications, and a serious infection threatened all his vital organs. The band eventually had to be removed and he was placed in a coma. Over the following weeks, he nearly died several times as fluid developed on his lungs, he needed a ventilator to breathe and his condition deteriorated.

'I was in a coma for over a month and in intensive care for two months, but Bob visited me every day and on two occasions gave me the last rites,' says Les, who finally rallied and recovered. 'It was quite funny to wake up and see Bob at the end of the bed. To have him there, as well as one of the sponsors for my charity, the 20th Man Fund, being Le Pine Funerals . . . you think if you're going to die, at least two of the boxes are ticked!

'He is super loyal. He knew I like Pepsi Max, and he'd bring it in for me. I'd look forward to that. He really polarises the Catholic Church, and annoys the rabid dogs of the right, but he's a great man. We've talked about merging our two charities to beef up our efforts for the poor and excluded.'

Both men were feeling similarly hurt by the changes to Open Family, the organisation they'd respectively founded and worked for, and watched keenly as controversy developed over how it was faring under its new managers. A report out in August said it had lost almost $1 million in the previous four years, axed one of its regions, had cut wages by 10 per cent and was demanding money from the Canberra operation to be allowed to continue working under its banner.

Chief Justice Terry Higgins of the Supreme Court of the ACT who was then the Chairman of Open Family Canberra, and had been involved with the organisation since 1988, says HQ decided his branch would only be able to operate as Open Family on a payment of $40,000. He refused and renamed it Youth Care Canberra instead, an organisation still running today. 'I think Bob is amazing,' he says. 'His mass at St Peter and Paul's used to be the best entertainment in town. He was always a very generous man, perhaps overly generous at times, but he had some spectacular success stories among others that weren't. He ran very effective programs. His knowledge of street kids and his understanding of them is phenomenal. He's an inspiration.'

Open Family management said the organisation had been hit hard by circumstances. 'We'd had a number of quite extraordinary situations – the 2007/8 drought, the bushfires and the GFC – which all drained probably $600 000 from us in just one year,' says Phil Ruthven. But others saw it differently. 'After Bob left, morale went down,' says former Open Family worker Richard Tregear. 'He was the heart and soul of it in many ways but the new people were much more about economic rationalism.'

But Father Bob still had plenty of other causes to champion, and not only for the poor. He spoke up on behalf of Richard Pratt, the billionaire philanthropist who was facing criminal charges after admitting in a civil trial to being part of a price-fixing cartel. On his deathbed, the businessman, whose wife Jeanne had once been on the board of Open Family, had asked that charges be dropped so he could clear his name. Father Bob always believed in speaking up for those under attack by the rest of society, like Peter Hollingworth in the past, however unpopular the stand might make him. This time, he was happy to pay tribute to the 'cardboard king'. 'Mr Pratt warned us all that we should be businesslike, as well as bleeding hearts,' he said.

Trying to take a leaf from his book, he was also always

looking for new opportunities to raise money and engage with the community. Jumping on the bandwagon of popular farmers' markets, he declared a new 'father's market', a series of arts, crafts and clothes stalls in the grounds of the church on Sundays, with the stall rents going to both the church and his Foundation.

It was no surprise, then, that when the Archbishop visited the priest and told him he'd have to offer to retire on his seventy-fifth birthday, after thirty-six years spent working in the parish of South Melbourne, he was absolutely devastated. 'By the time he'd gone, I felt more like ninety years of age,' he said. 'Not seventy-five – the age of statutory senility. They told me I should be out within a month of my birthday. It was, "Congratulations! You're seventy-five! Now get out!" That's not nice.

'But my view is, if the parishioners still want me here as their spiritual representative, then that's my contract. My role is to serve them; I can't break that contract. The Lord says to look after your sheep. As well, I have commitments to my associates through the Foundation. No-one else is going to look after them. What are they meant to do? I have responsibilities . . . If there was nothing to do, then maybe I'd start believing that old people should retire. I wouldn't be churlish about it. But with so much left to do, and having to make up for the sins of our fathers, I don't want to be dishonourably discharged and be sent to a retirement village. That's not what I signed up for. I'm a 1934 model. We don't retire. We keep going until the wheels fall off.'

Over the previous year and a half, his good friend Frank O'Connor had talked with him about the need for succession planning, but they'd both considered it would be a comfortable distance into the future. 'We'd had a few conversations around succession planning for Bob, before he got to seventy-five, and had started doing some work around documenting the parish, the way it worked, what its various ministries were and who did what, and so on,' says Frank. 'But there was no real urgency to it. It was just that the hierarchy had talked about parishes needing to be thinking about themselves and planning the succession of their parish priests, and so we did some work around that.'

But now it seemed that the end really was nigh, and it had come far sooner than expected. The Archbishop even issued his own statement, with an air of great finality. 'Father Maguire has for many years provided exemplary service to the Archdiocese of Melbourne and in particular to the people of South Melbourne,' it read. 'I am deeply grateful to him for his exceptional pastoral work over many years.'

Father Bob was appalled and decided, with the writing so large on the wall, that he'd better break the news to his parishioners. That Sunday, at mass, he told his 200-strong congregation that he might be forced to retire, even though he dearly wanted to continue. Even he was taken aback by the avalanche of outrage that followed.

Fury at the decision to oust Father Bob exploded throughout Australia, in newspapers, on TV, radio and social media, and even in parliament. Nearly everyone demanded he be given the right to stay on.

Visitors came flooding to the presbytery to pledge their

support for the priest, and voiced their determination to support him in 'fighting the good fight'. As he went on his daily walk – he'd long since given away his bicycle – locals and outsiders alike rushed over to shake his hand and tell him to keep going. Others shouted from across the street, 'Father Bob! We're with you! Hang in there!'

State Opposition leader Ted Baillieu, later to become the Victorian premier, was also onside. 'Bob Maguire is highly regarded as an icon and I'm sure he will attract a lot of support from his own community,' he said.

Others were even more forceful. 'I think Father Bob Maguire should become Archbishop of Melbourne,' one reader of *The Age* declared on the letters page. 'He is, after all, eight years younger than Pope Benedict and he does listen to people and his agenda is clear.' 'Father Bob is everything religion should be,' wrote another. 'If there were more Father Bobs in the world, it would be a far better place. Fancy even contemplating retiring such a vital man.' And the *Faithworks* blog's verdict: 'This is the kind of priest the Catholic Church ought to celebrate, not sack.'

People were quick to point out how many competent people over the age of seventy-five were still active in Catholic religious life. Apart from Father Heriot, there was Father Paul Ryan in North Balwyn, who retired at the age of ninety-three, while the former Pope Benedict XVI had been seventy-eight when he'd been elected Pope four years before. Media commentators were also called in to give their verdict: people like social researcher Hugh Mackay, who said forced retirement was 'a joke'. Then there were the lists of other various 'aged' experts in their various fields, like eighty-year-old horse trainer

Bart Cummings, parliamentarian Billy Hughes, who only left the House at his death at ninety, the 79-year-old chair of the Victorian Bushfire Appeal Fund John Landy, the 78-year-old football coach Tom Hafey . . .

'The irony is that Bob's probably even sharper today than he was in the old days,' says one of his workers, Henri Ser. 'It's a travesty of justice saying he'd have to leave at seventy-five. I always remember him saying he wanted to live and work in South Melbourne till he died there.' His former Open Family CEO Nathan Stirling also contends that the age issue was a furphy. 'That's obviously spurious,' he says. 'It's just that he won't play the game they want him to.'

Hundreds of bloggers vented their anger on sites around Australia, and the invitations to talk on radio and on TV poured in. To everyone, Father Bob's message was always the same. He hadn't yet finished what he'd started; he wasn't ready to give up just yet. 'It's like if you're in a hospital and the head surgeon is performing delicate heart surgery and then the clock ticks past a certain hour and the administrator demands he leave,' he says. 'Wouldn't the patient say, "Hang on a minute! I don't want a new guy who's never done this before! I want the bloke who's experienced, who's been doing this for years, who started the operation"? You can't just leave in the bloody middle!'

In Father Bob's mind, this enforced retirement was quite clearly politically motivated. When someone on Channel 9 asked him what he thought about Pope Benedict's ability to do his job at such an advanced age, he responded darkly, 'It's not what you know, it's who you know.'

And it was at that point that things started to turn ugly.

21

Give Priests a Chance

Melbourne Archbishop Denis Hart launched his first counteroffensive against the Save Father Bob Campaign on 8 September 2009, signalling that the battle really was on.

He wrote an editorial in the Melbourne *Herald Sun* newspaper defending his stance, saying the Church law on offering to retire at seventy-five applied to everyone equally. He would offer to retire at seventy-five, and even Cardinal Joseph Ratzinger, who later became Pope Benedict XVI, had submitted his resignation on his seventy-fifth birthday as Prefect of the Congregation for the Doctrine of Faith, although Pope John Paul II had asked him to continue in his role.

'Notwithstanding the good that Father Bob has done, he knows the rules of the Church, and is conscious of the vow of obedience he took when he was ordained,' Hart wrote. '. . . Priests, particularly parish priests, are generally available 24 hours a day, often seven days a week. It can be demanding enough for a 45-year-old priest, let alone a 75-year-old priest. The Church believes it has a great responsibility to its priests throughout their lives. The later years bring a heightened concern for their health and well-being. The Church chooses to err on the side of properly caring for its older priests . . .'

His words did nothing to convince Father Bob's supporters that he truly had the priest's interests at heart. With no indication from the Archbishop that he had any other intention than forcing him to retire, more and more people came out to express their solidarity with the campaign, joining the self-proclaimed 'Bob Squad'.

The parish council chairman of the time was Tony Long, an assistant commissioner in the Australian Taxation Office who'd become involved with the church after reading a eulogy there at the funeral of an aunt in 2005. He'd been impressed by Father Bob's approach when the priest had first arrived in the parish, and by his charity work since then. Tony saw him as specialising in all the hard cases, like drug addicts and substance abusers, 'the troubled and the troublesome'. Tony was also a great supporter of the more recent projects, such as the plan for the commons building next door to the church to become a community hub, and now the next phase of the plans for the parish precinct: the use of largely vacant land at the back, with the help of partners and government funding, to be developed for social housing. 'This represented a model which the Archdiocese itself hoped to roll out to other parishes,' he says.

But most of all, he'd come to really appreciate the kind of church that had been put in place in South Melbourne. 'With the help and kindness that Father Bob offers, many people have, for the first time, been exposed to active humanity and Catholicism,' Tony says. 'This has been the core of our parish ethos and is a template for all communities. He operates without borders. He wants the outside world brought in and the outsiders brought in as well. He wants "inclusive brethren". Services have always benefitted from an injection of his famous humour and his sense of mischief, always with the purpose of making a point. He has never seen value in allowing the gospel message to remain shrouded in the obscure and the metaphorical. Of course we want Father Bob to be allowed to stay on! He has the total support of the congregation.'

Father Bob had the support of many other admirers too. Les Twentyman, for instance, said he was horrified that the Church would be trying to pension off one of its most valuable assets. 'Bob's so alive and sharp, how can he be retired off?' he asked. 'I'm staggered by their decision. We need Bob!'

But the Church wasn't willing to concede any ground. Instead, on the evening of Saturday 12 September, a date that became known as 'The Night of the Long Knives', Archbishop Denis Hart re-entered the fray from a quite unexpected direction. In a highly unusual move, completely without precedent, he issued a damning statement about Father Bob direct to the press. The first the priest knew of it was when he started receiving calls from journalists to gauge his reaction.

The statement claimed that Father Bob had 'financially mismanaged' the parish, overspending on his pastoral work with his various charities. He'd only managed to keep everything going, said the Archbishop, by selling off church assets worth millions. Between 1998 and 2008, the parish had incurred deficits for eight of the eleven years, of a total of $1.191 million, but sold church property worth $1.5 million. These 'real facts' were being revealed to counter the 'extensive negative media coverage of this issue'.

The press release made headlines around the country, and Father Bob was quick to respond. 'I was amazed he came up with those claims at that point,' he says. 'It was very naughty of him; he must have been desperate. He knew full well we had a parish plan to liquefy some of those idle property assets that were empty and slowly crumbling and we didn't have any use for, and his office had signed off on our plans to raise much-needed cash instead. We can't actually sell off anything without HQ agreeing to it, and they get 15 per cent of any sale. They knew exactly where the money was going, too. We couldn't do anything without them knowing. What we've done, we've done with the supreme commander's signature, so if I'm guilty, he's guilty.'

His response was backed up by Catholic commentator and Church historian Dr Paul Collins, who confirmed that any sale of property would require the signature of the Archbishop. 'My personal feeling is that this isn't the way to conduct affairs within the Christian community, or for an archbishop to treat a priest, especially one who's done such sterling service as Father Maguire.' The business manager of another large Catholic parish in Melbourne, Mark Bennett, also chimed into the row, saying any sale of property had to comply with a rigorous process of control administered by the Archdiocese. That involved 'obtaining current market valuations, the consent of the responsible regional bishop, detailed application to the Archdiocese property services office, consideration by the appropriate Archdiocese committee for such matters and, finally, the authorising consenting signature of the Archbishop to conduct the sale . . .'

Father Bob's niece Peta Knights was privy to the parish's finances, having done the accounts for her uncle for years, and she insists it's terrible to say he's bad with money. 'There was never any financial mismanagement,' she says. 'He simply felt the parish should be helping the poor. He did sell properties and used the money in different ways. It seems to me, he did brilliantly.'

The priest's supporters rallied behind him even more strongly. Tony Long slammed the statement as 'an outrageous misdescription'. He said it was astonishing that the Archbishop 'doesn't believe spending money on the poor and homeless is a reasonable use of the Church's capacities. The statement had been on the Church's site and then it was taken down. It took us two more years to get a copy of it. Everyone was absolutely offended at the lack of fairness; that tripled my blood pressure in about two minutes. They must have known they'd get a fight from the bloke, he wasn't going to lie down and take it, but it really changed the whole flavour of the debate.'

The public at large also renewed their backing. 'He is a man of the people, everybody loves him, and he should be here regardless of what the hierarchy thinks,' declared one parishioner. Another wrote in to a newspaper: 'Archbishop Denis Hart's criteria for judging Father Bob Maguire are money and property – two reasons for religious wars. Mine are compassion, good deeds, selflessness and op shop clothing. Bob scores gold on all.' Even professionals beyond the Church and parish were agog. From the marketing faculty of Deakin University, lecturer Dr Paul Harrison said Father Bob was a more valuable agent of the Church than a million-dollar ad campaign. 'What he is doing is living the essence and values of the brand, and people can see that,' he said.

Father Bob wasn't totally without critics at this time, however. One woman wrote in saying the priest's 'lack of loyalty to his calling, his church and his archbishop should be a matter for his conscience'. Another old mate from his National Council of Priests' days in the 1970s, Monsignor Frank Marriott, Vicar General and Moderator of the Curia of the Diocese of Sandhurst, and the administrator of Bendigo's Sacred Heart Cathedral, always admired his energy and work, and felt he'd been 'something of a prophetic figure in those days, very heroic', but now felt he was behaving badly.

'It was being handled badly both by him and others digging in to help him stay on,' he says. 'He should have said, "Yes, I'll happily resign but then maybe I could stay on for one month or two or three." There are good retirement schemes for priests who have done a lot of service and we were all a bit offended when he talked about being chucked out onto the street. That was a bit disappointing, and hurtful to the clergy. Vatican II gave us the right to retire and there comes a time when we all have to ride off into the sunset and do something different, me included. None of us have the right to keep a job forever. But I think over the last couple of years he's made a few indifferent calls. He lost the plot a bit.'

But Father Bob was unapologetic. He felt the Church was simply, at that stage, looking for an excuse, any excuse, to get rid of him, and he was determined not to go. 'If an Armaguard van drove up and delivered a million dollars, it wouldn't have mattered,' he says. 'Thirty pieces of silver never saved Jesus.' Rather, he believed, it was all down to a fundamental clash of cultures between himself as a devout Vatican II priest, and the Australian Catholic hierarchy, who were on the side of a much more conservative orthodoxy. George Pell had been chosen by Pope John Paul II, after all, to be Archbishop of Melbourne, then Sydney, after being critical of the 'laxness' of Australian Catholicism and in favour of a return to traditional teachings.

'I'm the meat in that sandwich,' Father Bob says. 'They were targeting the model of Catholicism I'd installed in the parish, with the blessing of parishioners. It was about all of us becoming involved in day-to-day Catholicism and being out there, working for the poor and disadvantaged, about putting everything into practice. The model and the experiment were in good favour for thirty-odd years, they said we were doing marvellous work, then suddenly it falls out of favour to the extent that they invade the laboratory, steal the experiment and sack the chief scientist. They couldn't understand what was happening: My God! These people are getting enjoyment from Catholicism and they're not totally and permanently dependent on us! They didn't like that, so they turned dog. And I made them uncomfortable, so better to get rid of me.

'It was just my bad luck that the Church is all I've got. Others might have interests in life, or families, but for better or worse, richer or poorer, I've invested myself totally in the Catholic Church and its work in the neighbourhood.'

While some undoubtedly felt that Father Bob was simply too 'out there' for the Catholic Church, and he'd certainly upset some parishioners in the past, others saw considerable merit in his view. One former insider in the Diocese says it was all simply a stoush with his bosses who didn't want money spent on outsiders; they wanted it spent on the Church, and solely on the Church. 'He's certainly not Denis Hart's kind of guy,' he says. 'He's the full bottle as far as Catholicism goes, but it's the wrap around the bottle that gets up the authorities' noses. But when this all came out in the media, my sense was that the Church had gone too far down the track to back off. They were keen for him to move away and I think it just got to the point they couldn't backtrack. It all went too far, too quickly, and they'd totally underestimated the amount of support he had, and how good he is with the media, and how much the media was onside.'

He was certainly eccentric but that's precisely why it seemed so many people were so fond of him. On Neil Mitchell's 3AW show once, he came on to talk about a particularly controversial issue. 'I did an intro about how contentious this was and as Bob came on air he said "Jesus Christ!"' the radio host reports. 'And I said, "Bob! You can't say that! It's blasphemy and you're a priest!" His reply was something like, "Oh, can't I? I was just sending my regards to the boss."'

The secret of his success is simply his warmth, believes his former secretary Judy Sampson. 'Everyone recognised that everything he did was for the good of someone else, never for himself,' she says. 'And it's amazing that he never shows signs of fatigue or weariness. It's exhausting just watching him. He just plods on, and he never says "No". He's totally there for the people and that's why they love him.'

One commercial branding expert even approached the

Save Father Bob campaign offering his expertise in defining, refining and harnessing the 'Father Bob brand'. He hadn't realised, however, that the priest was almost impossible to control. 'I think it was only twenty-four hours before Bob was in the papers for something that was totally, totally outside the range of what he'd agreed to keep himself to,' says Tony Long.

One of Australia's most respected film production companies, Ghost Pictures, also approached Father Bob with a proposal for a documentary about him, *In Bob We Trust*. The trio running the company, Lynn-Maree Milburn, Andrew de Groot and Richard Lowenstein, had between them a number of acclaimed projects, including *Dogs in Space*, *He Died with a Felafel in His Hand* and feature documentary *Autoluminescent*. Most importantly, though, they'd met Father Bob when they were making 'John Safran versus God', and had never forgotten his charisma. 'He said a film about him would be boring,' says Lynn-Maree. 'But we knew he was an incredible subject. Every conversation with him is like mental gymnastics, ranging across history, theology, current affairs, culture . . . He knows everything!' Eventually, he agreed and for the next three years, Ghost Pictures became a regular part of his life.

All the publicity and attention didn't make it any easier for Father Bob, though. On the outside, he was all bluff and bluster, but inside, he was terribly hurt by what he saw as a complete betrayal. 'On the surface, they'd been full of praise for me, saying what a good job I'd done. But underneath, I was being nibbled to death by ducks. They put the word around I was financially irresponsible, which sowed the seed of suspicion and would completely undermine everything I'd done and was doing. I was being attacked by a smiling assassin, which is worse than being beaten over the head to death by thugs. They were after me. It was the poet Alexander Pope all over again: "Damn with faint praise, assent with civil leer, And without sneering, teach the rest to sneer; Willing to wound, and yet afraid to strike, Just hint a fault, and hesitate dislike."'

Frank O'Connor, after having watched, and worked with, Father Bob for so many years on the parish council, felt he could clearly see what was going on. On the surface, the Archbishop was talking about Father Bob's use of money, but underneath he believed there was a lot more happening.

'I think, at base, it was a culture clash between Bob on the one side and George Pell, Denis Hart and the hierarchy on the other who are all trying to drag the Church back in time,' says Frank. 'You heard about Pope Benedict criticising nuns in the US for spending too much time and effort on the poor rather than supporting the Church teaching on homosexuality, etcetera. And you thought, Oh dear, they've got it wrong. But that kind of attitude permeates so much through the hierarchy and of course they appoint their own ilk to those roles.

'So someone like Bob who's willing to speak very publicly and provocatively around what he sees as the proper message of the gospel is going to make them very nervous. They want to get rid of him, and the money perhaps became their ammunition in the end to be able to apply the seventy-five rule.'

Tony Long also believed there was a hidden agenda at play. He'd seen the axing of Father Bob's regular column in *Kairos* as the start of a predetermined campaign to oust the priest. 'There was nothing in those pieces and his understanding of religion that the Church could possibly find anything but admirable,' he says. 'So when they told him they had no need for further columns, some of us felt that this was Step One in the plan to get him out.

'The real reason for this has neither been given nor acknowledged. But one only has to observe that Father Bob has been the most vocal and most "public" of those priests and commentators who want the Catholic Church to practise what it preaches. For Father Bob and others schooled in Vatican II in the mid 1960s, they require a practical and active interest in the poor and needy. This is a concern that has driven him for nearly fifty years as a priest. Today, action for the poor and needy is not just out of fashion at an institutional level within the Church, but it is also being consciously placed behind an emphasis on the pious and the devotional, and a renewed emphasis on the role of the cleric. The lay believers are mere witnesses to the various ceremonies ostensibly conducted on their behalf. On the surface, the dispute with the Church was about style, but at a deeper and more substantial level, the institutional Church and he just didn't have the same view about what Catholicism was all about.'

The fact that one of the poor and needy people Father Bob was championing – Costas – was deeply unpopular in the Church hierarchy, also didn't help. 'Costas knew he was putting me in harm's way and he didn't want that, but he couldn't help himself,' says Father Bob. 'It was getting around that he was still about, and then they were chip-chip-chipping at my reputation.'

He says the atmosphere at the time was just like on the US TV show 'M*A*S*H', about a team of doctors stationed in South Korea during the Korean War. 'The battle's on and people are firing at you, but then your own HQ starts firing at you too and it's hard to pay attention and work out who's the real enemy. You just never know when and where the next volley is coming from. You never suspected your own side might turn feral, but it was their friendly fire, their treachery, that was finishing me off.'

The day after Denis Hart issued his statement, however, was Father Bob's regular Sunday mass, held the day before his seventy-fifth birthday. Over 400 people packed into the pews and, as he walked down the aisle to the altar, they all burst into spontaneous applause. He frowned to cover the emotion he felt rising up in him, and concentrated on the service.

When it was over, and he walked back down the aisle, everyone rose to their feet to give him a rousing standing ovation. He nodded to the congregation. 'It's *Crazy Bob, The Musical*,' he commented wryly, along the way. Outside the church, he was stopped by reporters. 'What's the message for today, Father Bob?' they asked him. He smiled. 'Always look on the bright side of life,' he told one, quoting the song from Monty Python's irreverent movie *The Life of Brian*. And when asked by another, he amended John Lennon's famous song line. 'Give priests a chance!' he said, grinning back.

He spent the next hour outside, surrounded by wellwishers chatting to him and relaying their admiration and thanks. But, in truth, he was feeling far from confident he would ever get that chance, which he both felt he had earned and craved.

22

The Dismissal

It's not the size of the dog in the fight that's important, Father Bob Maguire has always believed. It's the size of the fight in the dog. And he was certainly putting up one hell of a scrap.

'Well, I was fighting for my life,' he says. 'I was fighting for everything I've ever believed in, everything I've done and everything I still wanted to do. I didn't want to give up. I'm not a leader, I'm just a clown who confuses the Romans in charge. I'm an embarrassment and I can see their predicament, but I had too many people depending on me to give up now.'

On deadline day – 17 September 2009, three days after his seventy-fifth birthday – the priest finally replied to the letter Archbishop Denis Hart had given him. Politely, but firmly, he wrote that he did not want to offer to resign. Then he gave his blessing to a plan by his inner circle of supporters to organise a delegation to the Diocese, hoping to negotiate a better solution. He then held his breath, hoping against hope for a last-minute reprieve.

Head of that delegation was lawyer Tony Joyce, who'd acted for Father Bob for many years. The diocesan business manager Francis Moore had once been a law firm partner of his, so he reasoned he could be the ideal person to broker a deal. He saw the issue as a fundamental disagreement over the right way for a parish to be run: Father Bob plainly believed that the Church's capital, its old buildings, should be used as income, and spending on the poor and looking after people was what the Church should be about, rather than preserving huge edifices.

'That became the catalyst for the Church to say, We aren't going to give you any ongoing period of time because you don't manage money the way we feel you should,' says Tony. 'And Bob was always a burr under the hierarchy's saddle. He made them uncomfortable. He was an itch that wouldn't be completely scratched. But the Archbishop never wanted to get in a slanging match with him on a public stage. Bob's always been a great performer, and Hart knew Bob'd kill him. So we had meetings in private instead.'

Meanwhile, the public outrage at his dismissal continued unabated. Letters still poured in to newspapers, and the issue dominated talkback radio and social media, with daily updates on TV. 'It's a sin to mothball him!' was a regular cry. 'Isn't that what a church should be about: giving money to the poor?' asked others. A few even quoted Jesus, the 'founder of the firm' as Father Bob was wont to describe him. 'If you want to be perfect, go sell your possessions and give to the poor, and you will have treasure in heaven.'

Apart from Denis Hart, there was another loud dissenting voice against the general tsunami of affection towards the priest. Predictably enough, it was Derryn Hinch. On 21 September, he weighed in on radio with yet another spray against Father Bob, again bringing up his giving twenty dollars to someone who allegedly spent it on drugs, and the Vincent Kiss affair.

'For the past couple of weeks I have watched with interest the deification of Father Bob Maguire,' he said caustically on 3AW. 'The people's priest. The Mother Teresa of South Melbourne . . . Well, I know I bit about Saint Bob and money. Dirty money. I remember when he was laundering dirty money, stolen money, for a notorious paedophile priest named Vincent Kiss . . . Bob Maguire made a pact with the devil . . . you may understand why I have not joined the "genuflect at the feet of Saint Bob" crusade.'

He wasn't completely alone. Some onlookers did sometimes wonder how realistic Father Bob was being in his insistence that both the parish and his Foundation clients really needed him, and might well not survive with him gone. 'But in talking so much about how we needed him, you also have to realise that he needed us and this job,' says one parishioner, who asks not to be named. 'What else did he have in his life? Without us and his causes, his life would really be pretty empty . . .'

Yet Hinch and the handful of other critics seemed the least of Father Bob's problems. Their voices were almost drowned out by the clamour of those on his side. Helping it all along was also the priest's – quite coincidental – appearance on the

ABC TV show 'Compass' that Sunday, discussing the nature of charity, and on John Safran's new series 'Race Relations', talking about sex. Both served him well, and with quite different audiences.

In his quiet time, he took heart in pondering the fates of the various Catholic saints over the years who'd rebelled, but then finally been recognised, and celebrated, by the Church: people like John Vianney, the patron saint of priests and a champion of the poor, and Mary MacKillop, at first excommunicated but later exonerated. 'The Church wants you to be like these saints but, as soon as you do anything, you're under arrest,' Father Bob says. 'They want to have their cake, then eat it too. But I regularly talk to these saints, who worked tirelessly for the poor like Jesus, and I'm still here!'

The very next day, the Archbishop and Father Bob's representatives finally announced they'd reached a deal: he'd be allowed to stay on for an extra two years and four months, until February 2012, with, as a concession, the Diocese handling the financial side of running the parish. Father Bob was both pleased and dismayed. He'd been hoping for an indefinite stay of execution but instead had another firm cut-off point.

Tony Joyce says, however, that it was the best possible deal on the table. 'We wanted more but we couldn't get more,' he says. 'I know he wanted life, but he got two and a bit years instead. He was too much of a thorn in their side to let him go on for much longer. He's always been a great catalyst for good but he's a great challenge for the Church, which doesn't quite know how to handle him. He's always loved that but when it came to negotiations with the Church, it didn't help.'

Frank O'Connor was disappointed too. One of the

problems was that the lawyers, while they put a lot of time and energy into helping Father Bob, were acting pro bono so his closest circle had limited involvement in instructing them. 'I always had a bit of trouble accepting that our lawyers, including a QC, only negotiated two and a half years as opposed to a period of time with a review at the end of that,' Frank says. 'If the Church's excuse for getting rid of him was financial mismanagement, and that had been fixed with new processes in place, then a review might find everything's running smoothly, so there'd be no need to kick him out. I wasn't quite expecting a drop-dead day, and one that was signed, sealed and delivered. But still we hoped that, as we got closer to the deadline, we'd be able to get some kind of extension.'

The Archbishop was gracious in what, effectively, was something of a backdown. 'I am pleased that we have found a way forward, to our mutual satisfaction, that will allow Father Bob to continue his work in the parish and for the disadvantaged in our community,' he said. 'I believe this decision will be welcomed by Father Bob's parishioners and his supporters throughout Victoria. It's a win–win.'

In truth, the outcome felt like a win for no-one. But Father Bob also put a brave face on the situation as he fronted up to the TV cameras, reverting to his old military speak. 'I'm an old digger and I salute the Archbishop as a senior officer, and he acknowledges my competence as the unit commander,' he said. 'And if a two-year contract is good enough for [AFL player] Barry Hall, then I might settle for one too.'

Secretly, however, he hadn't given up on his dream of being parish priest of South Melbourne for life. By the time the deadline came around, he hoped that the Church might have relented. He just had to hope for the best, work hard and keep his head down. But that was always easier said than done.

Life was now busier than ever for the reprieved priest. There were appearances for the Melbourne Storm NRL club, for which he was the now number-one ticket holder, and he was a keen member of the campaign to have the Grand Final, late in 2009, shifted from Sydney to the Melbourne Cricket Ground. Although he blessed the team, and they ended up winning the match, that was another campaign that ultimately failed, followed by the disappointment of the Storm being stripped of the title for salary cap breaches. There was some consolation for the priest though. Each win, try and goal scored in their last fourteen games of the year raised money for various charities, including the Father Bob Maguire Foundation. There was also his other new campaign, no less ambitious: teaming with Les Twentyman and rocker Angry Anderson to curb the rise of gangs and the carrying of knives.

In between, his national fame brought him even more attention. He was invited to MC more charity events, with most of the funds being earmarked for his Foundation; he was asked for his opinion on everything from the weather to Christmas; he fronted a campaign for improving the care of older Australians; he was named one of Australia's favourite ratbags; he was again an Australia Day Ambassador; and he was ranked the eighth most loved and admired person in the country in an AGL Energy survey.

As a result, as 2010 arrived, he saw himself now able to play a higher-profile role in the wider community, taking initiatives like publicly calling on the teen killer of an Indian student to surrender himself to him so he'd have guaranteed safe passage to the police, joining the campaign to bring jailed drug smuggler Schapelle Corby home from Bali, and saying that Opposition leader and staunch Catholic Tony Abbott's views on asylum-seekers – 'Jesus didn't say "Yes" to everyone' – didn't sit comfortably with the Church's philosophy of 'Love thy neighbour'. 'As a preacher, Jesus always put himself with the outsiders,' said Father Bob. 'Jesus would have put himself on that boat with the boatpeople.' He had another skirmish with Tony Abbott a short time later, when the politician said he'd be giving up sex for Lent. Father Bob responded in Latin, 'De gustibus non est disputandum', or 'There's no accounting for taste'.

Yet he was still just as active back home, at his beloved St Peter and Paul's. Early in the year, he announced the start of the transformation of the old Galilee school into the community hub, South Melbourne Commons, and had a barbecue at the site, with a working bee to start on the demolition and renovation of parts of the building. At the same time, his Foundation was fully functioning, looking after both kids and his long-time older 'associates', some of whom were doing well, and some of whom weren't. One day, on his way from the presbytery to the church to open the doors as usual at 7 a.m., he was horrified to see one of his long-time charges, Steven Cooper, a 48-year-old father of three, hanging from a rope tied to a tree in the front garden. He raced over, but the man was already dead. 'He called me and asked me to come down quickly,' says helper Henri Ser. 'He was very upset.'

There was certainly always a dark side to his work. One

time, he was asked to conduct the funeral ceremony for Katie Peirce, the 24-year-old daughter of underworld figure Victor Peirce, whom he'd buried eight years before. The young woman's mother Wendy Peirce had been in jail when her daughter died of a suspected drug overdose and blamed both the police and her mother-in-law Kath Petingill for her death, claiming she'd died after someone had injected her with a 'hot shot' of heroin. There was even drama at the service when the two mourners with Katie's eulogy arrived late, and then Wendy confronted Katie's half-brother Chris and demanded he leave. Father Bob intervened and successfully calmed everything down 'for the sake of Katie's child', he said calmly. He even made everyone smile when, in a reference to the Formula One Grand Prix that had just taken place in Melbourne, he said, 'Just like the Grand Prix, Katie's run her last lap.' There was a sharp intake of breath, then laughter. 'That went down quite well,' says Henri Ser. 'He tries to make people happy, even at their darkest hour.'

At the risk of being dubbed 'The Gangland Priest', Father Bob also offered to bless the clubhouse of the outlaw motorcycle gang the Comancheros – a group that would come back into his life two years later with disastrous consequences. 'I'm a blesser,' he explained. 'I blessed the casino and got into trouble for that, but I still like to bless things.'

He had another controversial meeting, brokered by his childhood friend Brian Harman, with former leading gangland figure Mick Gatto, who was bringing over US comedian Jerry Lewis for a $1000-a-ticket black-tie show to raise money for muscular dystrophy and now also the Father Bob Maguire Foundation. That show ended up netting the Foundation

$80 000, and another the following year brought in $40 000. Mick Gatto attended school at St Peter and Paul's as a kid, so the place had always meant a lot to him. 'And I think Father Bob is a terrific human being,' Mick says. 'All he wants to do is help street kids and the homeless, and is out there beating the drum for them and doing the right thing. He's a little bit unorthodox in the ways he does it, but he can't do enough for people. I couldn't speak more highly of the man.'

To add to funds, Father Bob completed a 5 kilometre walk for the Run Melbourne event, giving up biscuits, increasing the number of visits to parishioners in hospital and walking around Albert Park Lake as part of his training regime. 'One time, I walked in the dark and nearly fell into the bloody lake, silly old bugger!' he said. He also had red Viva La Bob! T-shirts made and said anyone from his 'Bob-terage' who donated more than fifty dollars to his Foundation would receive one free.

One of the priest's greatest gifts was being able to express his faith in catchy secular terms and he showed that again and again. Talking about the haves and the have-nots, and the need for a little redistribution of wealth, he explained the problem as, 'Australian society has a case of "affluenza". The problem is not poverty but affluence. Most people have far too much; much more than they need. The other dangerous virus is "instant gratification syndrome"'. On Easter, he said people shouldn't get bogged down by the idea of Christ's crucifixion. 'That grim side of Easter is a lot to inflict on secular society, and people like giving chocolate eggs, which is still a symbol of renewal, so isn't that the best way the message can be expressed?' And when a church group performed a gruesome mock crucifixion in the street, sparking a storm of controversy, he tried to settle things down, saying they might have been better staging their stunt in their church. 'You don't have to use street theatre to get your message across,' he said. 'You can do good things, like caring for people who are socially marginalised. That's crucifixion, too.'

A highlight of 2010 came when a special Sunday-morning mass was held at St Peter and Paul's to celebrate the golden jubilee of his ordination. The church was packed with well-wishers, keen to honour his past and hear his plans for the future: to set up a new inter-faith centre servicing Southbank and the Docklands.

Meanwhile, he was still just as visible on stage and screen. He was a special guest of comedian Josh Thomas in his series of live stage shows on different topics. One performance misfired spectacularly, though, when Father Bob was put on with a cross-dresser to discuss gay marriage. 'The idea was that Bob was the conservative priest and he was set up to look uptight,' says John Safran. 'But that went down like a lead balloon. Firstly, he's not uptight, and secondly, people feel very warmly towards him and are very respectful to him, so making fun at his expense just doesn't work!'

More successful was his appearance on ABC TV's 'Talking Heads' with Peter Thompson, where he came up with a new word that described his own particular institutional orthodox but unconventional approach. 'I'm unconvenstitutional,' he proudly declared. It was on that show that he also first brought up the notion that he may have been bullied into signing up for retirement at the start of 2012. It signalled the beginning of the next phase of his campaign, to stay on well beyond the deadline he'd agreed.

Feeling he was on a kind of good behaviour bond with the Church in the interim, Father Bob was careful never to overstep the mark, even when he didn't agree with what the Church might be doing. He felt strongly the Melbourne diocesan authorities were wrong when they went even further than George Pell's new rules on family members making inappropriate remarks at funerals, this time banning footy anthems, romantic ballads and other popular songs from funerals. They also said celebrants 'should moderate any tendency to turn the funeral into a secular celebration of the life of the deceased'. But when asked for his opinion, Father Bob chose his words cautiously.

'My job is to salute and say, "Thank you for that, sir!" and then try to find a way of keeping everybody happy,' he said. 'If people want to sing "Good Old Collingwood Forever", then maybe I can suggest they get outside first and sing it out the front . . .' But in truth, he privately felt this was one more example of the clerics being hopelessly out of touch with what people wanted from their Church.

The recognitions for his achievements kept coming and, secretly, he was thrilled with each new award; perhaps these would make the Church rethink its position. At the end of 2010, he won the Council of the Ageing Award for helping the underprivileged and homeless, and was crowned Old Bastard of the Year by the International Society of Old Bastards. Then, at the start of 2011, he was honoured with a golden jubilee dinner at Crown casino, hosted by Australian TV presenter and Collingwood president Eddie McGuire with Les Twentyman, Denise Drysdale and John Blackman giving him a roast, with all proceeds going to his Foundation.

Yet he always seemed to be in the news for other reasons too, both good and bad. On the actual day of his roast, he hit the headlines for saying he'd conduct a gay ceremony held outside a church building, although not a gay wedding as that would be against Church and state laws. 'I can't break those laws, but if the law changed, I would be the first to perform such a ceremony,' he said. 'As Christians, we should be caring for outsiders.' He also organised a publicity-grabbing fund-raiser for victims of Queensland's devastating floods, with a circus show including performers even more colourful than he: a man who'd lie on a bed of nails with up to 100 kilo-grams of concrete on his chest being hit by a sledgehammer, and another taking a nine-inch nail from a train sleeper with his teeth.

But he unintentionally managed to fall foul of the Church authorities once again when his plans for the South Melbourne Commons, a partnership between Friends of the Earth Australia, the Father Bob Maguire Foundation and the Parish of St Peter and Paul's, were eventually submitted to council and it turned out the Archdiocese hadn't been informed. As a result, it lodged an objection with the council, to try to block the scheme. Father Bob was both frustrated and outraged that everything was dragging on slowly when it was so patently such a good idea. He couldn't disguise his impatience. 'The problem is, I've got a limited life here, according to HQ, so I need to put this all in place before they have their wicked, wil-ful and wanton way and kick me out.'

The parish council stepped in to try to mediate and discov-ered that all the arrangements to lease and retrofit the building along strictly sustainable lines had been made on an ad hoc handshake agreement. They then went in to negotiate with the Melbourne Diocese's Roman Catholic Trust Corp to sort out some of the necessary paperwork. 'It worked out all right in the end, except we couldn't convince the Trust Corp to give them a long-term lease,' says Frank O'Connor. 'So they had to stay on a short-term lease, and just hope for the best . . .'

Yet the resulting South Melbourne Commons finally developed into a huge community, and commercial, success. It became a meeting place for locals, with a children's space featuring playgroups, a gardening club, parties and after-school activities, an organic fruit, vegetable and groceries store, a cafe, a community garden, a hall that could be hired for functions and events, affordable office and meeting spaces for community groups and a playground. The whole enterprise was intended to become a model to motivate residents, community groups and facility managers to perform sustainable retrofits on their own homes and buildings, and was ultimately lauded by the Catholic Church at HQ as a wonderful example of an environmentally responsible project that could be a model for other parishes.

With Father Bob now such a media personality, nothing he did or said went without note. He'd attended a protest about the treatment of asylum-seekers at a detention centre but, when tensions increased and a man in a wheelchair was capsicum-sprayed by police, the fact that he'd been in attendance was reported in all the newspapers. Becoming the patron of InterAction, a multi-faith youth network, he called for a broader type of religious instruction to be taught in schools to encompass the ethos of all religions and for a system of community, rather than denomination-specific, schools; both ideas sparked instant controversy. He was a judge on the new ABC TV talent show 'Strictly Speaking', to find Australia's best public speaker, and pulling off his clerical collar on an episode of Adam Hill's chat program on the same channel 'In Gordon Street Tonight' also attracted a lot of attention. But setting up a drive-through confessional by the church on April Fool's Day drew the biggest newspaper headlines. 'All the media went for it, and had pictures of him standing outside the food bus with the sign for the drive-in,' laughs Henri Ser. 'I thought it was really clever. He was bringing the Church to the people, which is what he does best, but it caused a bit of a stink. There's not much of a sense of humour in Vatican City. Obviously the powers that be didn't like him being so out there, and being outspoken, but what he said and did was never anti-Christ or anti-Church. He was just a lot more open-minded than the people up above, and should be admired for making religion enjoyable.'

But everything came to a sudden halt in June 2011 when Father Bob attended one of his Foundation scholarship students' prize-giving. He was walking up the steps at the front of the school, when he felt a searing back pain and realised he was struggling to make it to the top. Fearing it might be his heart playing up again, he went to see his cardiologist. His supporters hoped for the best, but feared the worst. 'I dropped him off at the hospital that day, and I wasn't sure if he was going to come out again,' says parish council chairman Tony Long. 'But then when I went back in, there he was sitting up, chatting to all the nurses and having a ball.'

After a number of tests, he was diagnosed with an abdominal aortic aneurysm, where the large blood vessel that runs to the abdomen had ballooned, and he was rushed into surgery. There, he was given two stents and a clamp to fix the problem. Afterwards, he was taken to a respite home for priests for eight weeks to recuperate. 'I languished out there,' he says. 'But what to do, for God's sake? I didn't need intensive care, but I needed some TLC to get me back to an AAA rating, that was all.'

John Safran visited him, brought him a laptop and set up Twitter for him so he could keep tweeting. Tony also called by. 'He did find it hard as he was the liveliest bloke there,' he says. 'But he was exposed for the first time to what it was like to live a life for your own benefit entirely. He got up, he ate, he thought only things that were relevant to him, he didn't have anyone's needs to service other than his own. It was completely novel to him and I think it caused him a little bit of anguish because it was foreign, and also because in a way it was sort of enjoyable. I think he was umming and ahhing, should he come back to the parish, or should he have a bolt hole, a place that was just for him and not the presbytery with Costas and people always rushing around. But in the end, he came back, and just carried on where he left off.'

Father Bob couldn't resist a joke at his own expense, either. 'Hello children, it's your beloved pastor speaking to you from the other side,' he tweeted. 'i.e. Balwyn.'

In July 2011, Father Bob received what he imagined would be a massive boost to his campaign to have his stay of execution in the Archdiocese extended: he was named Victorian of the Year. In his statement accepting the award, he said it belonged to his parishioners, supporters and 'associates' of his Foundation. 'It was wonderful to be recognised like that, but only in so far as it gave the kind of work we all needed to be doing a higher profile,' he said. 'And, of course, unfortunately for my bosses, it will make me more determined to pursue the idea that we are all in this together, that the Messiah won't be coming to save us, we need to save ourselves first, with a DIY, BYO form of religion.'

It buoyed his spirits enormously, feeling that the title would make it much more difficult to move him on from his parish. He renewed his claim that he was 'pressured' into signing the deal to quit and said he needed to stay. 'Why break up a relationship when everyone seems to agree it's a bloody good thing?' he asked. In addition, work had finally begun on the next stage of his plans to develop the parish precinct, his community housing project of forty units being built on land close to his church, and he wanted to see that through. He knew that would net the parish enough money to keep it on its feet forever. Early signs from HQ even looked promising too. Archbishop Hart praised the priest's community work, saying he 'thoroughly deserved' the award, while callers to talkback radio, contributors to social media and newspaper letter-writers were stirred to start pressing again for Father Bob to be allowed to stay on.

The priest got together with his two closest advisers, Frank O'Connor and Tony Long, and they all had meetings with the Diocese, hoping to win them over. At the same time, they decided to start succession planning in earnest. While now hopeful of winning Father Bob an extra few years in office, they felt they should still start looking for someone suitable to eventually take over, with Father Bob perhaps staying on as an adviser, living in the little flat in the top corner of the presbytery.

Father Bob made a call to a priest he'd known who'd been working in Papua New Guinea, and someone else said they'd heard a monk from the Franciscan Capuchin order, the same group that had produced the first priest in South Melbourne in 1854, was interested in the parish. The trio agreed to ask the Capuchins in, to see whether their approach would be at all sympathetic with Father Bob's vision. 'They'd been working in Leichhardt in Sydney, so they came down and we started talking to them,' says Frank.

'And then, just twenty minutes in, with everything going well, Bob left the room. At that point, they casually mentioned that they'd already signed a ten-year contract with the Archdiocese to take over from 1 February 2012. We were just stunned.' Frank looked at Tony and Tony stared at him. 'Our jaws just hit the floor,' says Tony. 'And then Bob walked into the room, and we broke the news to him. He's usually good at disguising his reactions to things, but this time he didn't make any attempt at all.'

23

Let's Hear It for the Bogans

Father Bob Maguire was absolutely devastated to hear that arrangements had already been made to take over his parish. Suddenly, it felt as though the last chink of light in his dream to stay on in South Melbourne had snapped shut and the future now stretched ahead of him, empty and directionless. Even though he still should have been celebrating being acclaimed as the 2011 Victorian of the Year, it all abruptly felt worthless, and hopeless.

'I suddenly realised it wouldn't have mattered if I'd have won the Victoria bloody Cross, or Australian of the Year; they would have still wanted me out,' he says. 'Honours are good as they reassure people, but for the Church, nothing I did would make any difference. This was personal, and we were past the point of no return.'

His supporters on the parish council, Frank O'Connor and Tony Long, were equally shattered. 'Not only had Bob never been told that negotiations were already taking place with others, not only was he not told that a contract had been offered, but then he had to find out in those circumstances that a contract had actually been signed!' says Tony. 'The fact that it should emerge as almost, not quite an irrelevancy but almost an accidental disclosure, is astounding. Bob was treated so shabbily, I was really disappointed. Perhaps it was all about the dislike some senior people might have of Bob. Because Bob's not someone to curry favour. He only curries curry.'

Frank too could barely believe what had happened. 'The bishop a few years before had been telling us about parishes needing to plan for themselves and determine their own futures, and then it turns out that head office had already taken absolute, total control! It was something that had also been done in complete secrecy. We asked the Capuchins, "Don't you think it would have been worthwhile to have actually spoken to the parish first?" They got a bit embarrassed at that stage, and the conversation ended and we parted company.'

At that point, the trio went public. Tony in particular didn't hold back, blasting the Archdiocese's signing up of the Capuchins without a word to the parish as 'contemptible', 'tawdry' and 'distressing'. He said 'vacuuming Bob out' was like sending people who don't precisely conform 'to the gulag'.

Behind the scenes, Father Bob, now seventy-seven, was distraught. He claims he later found out that other priests had been offered his parish, but had turned it down out of respect for him. 'The Capuchins should have done the same,' he says, bluntly. 'Hart put the key in the ignition, but the Capuchins turned it.' He put the Church's treatment of him down to Cardinal George Pell's highly conservative Roman doctrine, and resultant disdain for his own Vatican II approach. Cardinal Pell used to work for the theologically hardline Pope Benedict XVI when the former Pope was head of the Congregation for the Doctrine of the Faith. Pope Benedict had, in the past, dismissed dissenters as 'cafeteria Catholics', then the Cardinal, just before the Capuchins were signed up, gave a talk over in Ireland on 'authentic' Catholicism versus 'cafeteria' Catholicism.

'So I suppose that's what he saw me as practising, "cafeteria" or "bogan" Catholicism,' says Father Bob. 'I was about a populist approach, taking the faith to the people, having them involved in a real expression of their faith, and ministering to them, and spending money on caring for them. The founder of the firm said it is better to feed the poor than install new statues in church. Jesus of Nazareth would say, "There's too much bloody ceremony around here!" But that approach wasn't in favour anymore. The current model is to be in the church and say prayers and be no bloody good to anyone. To think I was told off for spending money on the poor!

'It's all about the growing conservatism of the Church, with George spearheading a move to the right, starting this division. We're on different sides. We're split down the middle between traditionalists and modernists and we don't have much to do with each other. That's what did me in. I like to tell the truth. Like John the Baptist, he didn't give a bugger. He went on and on until they cut his head off.'

When approached through his representative, Cardinal Pell declined to comment for this book.

'I think it was just frightful,' says his old mate Les Twentyman. 'It was spiteful. Bob was part of the fabric of South Melbourne, he was popular, whereas Pell isn't popular and I think he's intent on taking the Church back to the stone ages. Bob does fall out with people, and people love him and hate him with a passion. But you don't become a leader unless you've got that. Try to please everyone, and you please no-one.'

Meetings took place with Archbishop Hart, looking for some compromise solution, where Father Bob could stay on in some capacity or other, even if just for an orderly transition between the regimes. He still desperately wanted to stay on, but for the first time, suddenly it seemed he might be fighting a losing battle. Yet he was still determined not to give up and likened his stand, just a tad over-dramatically, to the lone protester facing down a tank in Tiananmen Square in 1989. 'I'll keep going till I drop,' he vowed. 'You couldn't ask Field Marshall Montgomery when he'd retire. The job doesn't finish until the battle is over.'

From the wider community beyond the Church, the protests and the accolades continued to come. Father Bob's supporters urged the public to bombard the Archdiocese with letters, emails and tweets asking for the priest to stay, there was a full front page photo in the local *Port Phillip Leader* newspaper with the caption "Save Father Bob" and a sub-heading saying "display this page in your window and let the

Archdiocese know you support Father Bob", and a Facebook page, Save Father Bob Maguire, was set up. Father Bob's own Facebook page was sitting right on its limit of 5000 Facebook friends and his Twitter feed chalked up over 85 380 followers. In October, in the middle of talks with the Archbishop, Monash University presented Father Bob with an honorary fellowship for his services to the community. He made a joke about hoping his swollen head – from receiving so many awards – might still fit the cap, but that luckily his meeting with Denis Hart had shrunk it to size.

The former Victorian Premier Jeff Kennett even waded into the battle, saying age simply meant more experience and that he was convinced Father Bob wouldn't retire. 'For to retire is to prepare for death.' John Safran watched on, bemused. He couldn't understand why the Church objected to a few old properties being sold off, when they plainly had so many. But he privately doubted that the protests would have any effect. 'The Church authorities can be quite impervious as they don't actually need any more money, and they don't even seem to need a congregation anymore,' he says. 'They're not like Nike or McDonald's, who are careful of their reputation. They clearly don't care about bad publicity. But Father Bob is a great asset to them, and he's inspirational, passionate and very funny, coming at things from weird angles. It's unfortunate that he seems to have picked the one sector where he's not rewarded for having a great sense of humour.'

In the media, he had plenty of fans. Influential 3AW radio personality Neil Mitchell, who regularly had him on the show, regards him as a treasure. 'Certainly his pews overflow,' he said at the time. 'His services have been described as a combination of community meeting, religious worship and stand-up comedy. They hum along. How's that bad, when most churches think a full house is two confused old ladies and a wandering drunk looking for somewhere to sleep?'

Neil says now, 'He's magnificent, unpredictable, passionate, entertaining, and a little dangerous. The audience loves him and they will do anything for him and there are only a few of what I would call the old-fashioned Catholics who are critical. In my view he was treated differently to some other priests [by the Church], probably because he was seen as an embarrassment. The Church has been battered lately. Bob was one of the good things it had going for it and they trashed him. Absurd and inconsistent. In the first battle to save him we all turned up at the church on Easter Sunday. The place was packed. My audience had donated hot cross buns and chances are every other church in Melbourne was half full. Bob's was standing room only. I thought, It is madness to drive him out! I remember him breaking down on air one day in his final days at the parish, and that was rare. After that, a listener who had heard the discussion and was in the area drove to the church, hopped out and gave Bob a big hug and drove off. That is what Bob provokes.'

Ben Fordham of 2GB in Sydney is another big fan. 'I find every word he says absolutely enthralling. He steals my show every week. I'm attracted to rebels, particularly within such conservative institutions like the Catholic Church. The Church is sailing towards danger and the leadership is too rigid to see the rocks but there's Bob yelling from the back: "Beware!" He breaks down the bullshit and tells it exactly as it is. I can't believe how they're ready to let go one of their marquee players, a man who really puts bums on seats.'

Union leaders also queued up to sing Father Bob's praises. He'd always supported them – 'True Christianity is about union, solidarity, love for your fellow man, the same principles as unions,' he said – and now they saw it as their turn to help him. 'The Painters and Dockers think the sun shines out of his backside,' says his brother Jim.

Atheist and popular weekly *Age* blogger Dick Gross came to the party too, damning the Church hierarchy. 'The challenges of Catholicism are patent – eroding congregations, disappearing candidates for priesthood and scandals that would test the patience of Job,' he wrote in his column 'Godless Gross'. 'In the face of a major success story that is Father Bob, rather than build on that success, a demoralised organisation is tearing itself to bits. It is tragic to behold.' The priest's old helper, TV star Tony Barber, was similarly baffled. 'He has a wonderful profile and is more active than ever,' he says. 'I can't fathom why they'd be prepared to lose him. But the Church's loss is the public's gain.'

Of course, not everyone was on his side. 'Father Bob Maguire is not an employee of the Catholic Church but a priest subject to obedience of his bishop; obedience he swore at his ordination,' said one newspaper letter-writer. 'In my view he is an egotistical eccentric who is adept at preaching social justice but divorced from the rest of the body of Catholic teaching.'

But then on 4 November 2011, the final verdict was delivered. Archbishop Hart confirmed the now 77-year-old Father Bob would be leaving his church on 1 February 2012; there had been no stay of execution granted. Instead, the priest would be given the title of 'Pastor Emeritus', which would give him more freedom, and allow him to continue his community work and still say masses in parishes around Melbourne. 'I am deeply conscious of the day-to-day grinding demands which are there [for a parish priest] and I think that we can best use Bob and his wonderful abilities by providing him with a broader canvas, a bit of freedom, and a broader scope,' said Denis Hart.

If the Church hoped that would persuade the priest to make a dignified exit stage left, they were to be sadly mistaken. Instead, it was like a red rag to a bull. Father Bob blasted his new title as 'bullshit' and 'the kiss of death', and said he and his parish felt 'dishonoured' and that the Church was being 'bloody-minded'. 'Once they train that red dot on your forehead,' he said, 'you know you're gone. The Romans are ruthless.' What's more, he said he would seek canon legal advice before considering an appeal to the Vatican to overturn the Archbishop's decision.

But those who knew Father Bob well noted something change in him from the moment he learned his fate was sealed. From that moment on, he saw the clock as ticking down on his time as parish priest of South Melbourne, and barely said a mass without reference to that clock and his fate.

'That didn't exactly endear him to the Church, and gave them every chance to retaliate,' says Tony Joyce. 'Those kind of "Collingwood backhanders" didn't help when he was looking for an extension. He knows how to press the right buttons, and the wrong ones.'

It was just that he couldn't quite believe what was happening to him, believes Tony Long. 'For the rest of us, if an event was coming up, maybe we'd say we'd face it when it came, or make a Plan B, but not him. Some of us would try to get him used to the idea of the cut-off day and say, "Look, you can still do your work, you won't be in the position of parish priest, but you can still be effective. It could be an opportunity." But he'd just say "No!" in that definite way he has. In essence, he was saying he still needed the religious elements of his job. He felt that very, very strongly.

'He was very hurt. He said he was going to sleep in his chair as he couldn't face going to bed and then he'd wake up and be all crooked, which affected him badly.'

But then came an event no-one had predicted.

During all the dramas with the Church, Father Bob had enjoyed one success at least. After years of trying to get Costas – one of his first street kids turned now more-or-less-permanent troublesome case – professional help, the authorities had finally relented. With Costas up on a charge of making a public nuisance of himself, helper Henri Ser had intervened and managed to get him onto a diversion program through the magistrate's court, to be treated as someone with a mental health issue rather than as an offender.

Everyone was relieved that he'd be getting some skilled treatment at last. Many of the priest's supporters and parishioners admired Father Bob's determination never to give up on Costas, even though the man was given to violent outbursts, often appeared terribly psychologically and emotionally damaged, and had undoubtedly given both the Archdiocese and the priest's critics plenty of ammunition to use against him. Most, however, longed for Father Bob to be tougher on him, and saw Costas as an expensive problem they wished would become someone else's.

'I think Bob could have done things differently to support him, perhaps without incurring the costs that he did,' says Frank O'Connor. 'But then Bob would say, "Why should he go without compared to anybody else? What right have we got to say he shouldn't have access to a car, and why shouldn't he live normally with all the regular comforts?" Bob always had a good answer, and he'd never give up on any young person who needed help. I think Costas not only cost Bob a lot of money over the years, but he probably also cost him Open Family and some of the support he would otherwise have had in the parish. But then if it hadn't been Costas, someone else would have come along. Bob would have found another cause, another reason, another person. He never wanted anyone to be able to say that there was nobody to help them when they needed it.'

Tony Long says it was always impossible to ask Father Bob simply to cut the difficult people loose. 'We might say, "Ignore those people because there would be a benefit to your core group in concentrating your energies elsewhere,"' he says. 'But that's never going to be him. He comes with a package of beliefs, whether it's helpful to him or not. He wanted to help whoever was in need.'

Father Bob frequently said how much he regretted not being able to 'exorcise' his father of his demons; at least now he was working to do that for others. For his mantra was always that old cry from the World War I battlefields of France: 'Don't forget me, cobber!' 'Jesus of Nazareth was about inclusion, about the family of humanity,' he says. 'It's about making sure no-one gets left behind, everyone gets help when they need it. I may be a pain in the arse, but at least I'm a productive pain in the arse. I've done things for others, I've invested in social capital, which a lot of clergymen haven't. It's not their style. Costas deserved a chance at life, just like anybody else, even though he was getting madder all the time, with a great sense of injustice in his life and yelling about people who'd done him wrong.'

After a further eviction, Costas had come to stay for another short period in the back room of the presbytery, while the priest tried to arrange somewhere else for him to stay. He'd wake up early in the morning, then roam the streets, drinking coffee and collecting trinkets either to hoard in his room, or to present as gifts for people.

'He'd put little tokens of love on Father Bob's desk or on [secretary] Judy's desk or in the hall or kitchen,' says Lynn-Maree of Ghost Pictures. 'Many people saw beyond the gruff voice, the loud outbursts, the strange behaviour, and shared moments of beauty and love.'

Father Bob says Costas liked sharing, and he liked people sharing with him. 'By 2011, I think a lot of people had got used to him and his ways. The locals would be protective of him and make sure others didn't pick on him. Everyone knew, for better or for worse, richer or poorer, that I supported Costas. As the parish priest, I had to look after others, many of whom didn't want me to look after Costas, so there was always that conflict of interest. But to those who told me to get rid of him, I wanted to ask, "What if your child went off the rails? What would you do?" It's important that everyone is looked after. But he knew I was getting kicked out, and he knew he was partly responsible for that, and he felt bad and blamed himself.'

But on the afternoon of Saturday November 19 2011, in between preparing for a wedding, Father Bob went to check on

Costas across the courtyard in the back room as he hadn't seen him all day. There, a shocking sight awaited him: Costas lying, dead, on the floor. The priest fell to his knees beside the body, and felt a great wave of grief envelop him. This was somehow worse, much worse, than anything else he'd ever been through. He'd buried forty of the people he'd tried to look after over the years, but he never thought he'd be burying Costas in his lifetime.

Distressingly, he didn't even have time to cover Costas's body. The bride was just about to arrive, and Father Bob didn't want to ruin her day too. 'Instead, I had to go straight into damage control,' he says. 'I called the police and an ambulance then had to go and do the wedding. But I really hated the thought of the poor bugger lying there on the floor. He deserved more respect than that.'

Talking about him afterwards was one of the rare times anyone had ever seen Father Bob with tears in his eyes.

The Victorian coroner ruled that Costas died at the age of forty-nine of heart failure, while others were insistent he died of a drug overdose, either accidental or deliberate.

Father Bob, however, was firmly on the side of the coroner. 'It does him an injustice to say he died of a drug overdose,' he says. 'Others might say they know he was using drugs. I don't know. But it's like an old drunk dying of alcoholism; he had health problems I presume had accumulated over the years and he just laid down and died. He was caught short, laid down and died. [Radio host] Neil Mitchell rang up and said, "You must be very sad." But it was so sad because all these people suffered so much. We couldn't save them.'

Everyone around the priest was stunned by the news of Costas's death. 'It was a huge shock,' says Father Bob's former secretary, Judy. 'In the end, I think he just wore himself out. He was so skinny. But his death affected Bob greatly. Costas was like his son. He'd looked after him nearly all his life. Bob was the only person in Costas's life, really, he was the only one he'd talk to.'

When others found out about Costas, the presbytery received dozens of phone calls from locals offering their sympathy, and around forty emails. Everyone had a little story to tell about him, an unexpected kindness or thoughtful moment. Many told Father Bob that he'd known him so many years, it must be like losing a son. 'But I'm a priest,' he replied. 'What do I know about having sons? I'm a priest, I'm socially handicapped, I'm psycho-socially challenged, I don't know the right way to feel.'

Instead, he threw himself into a frenzy of activity. He had a card made with Costas's face on it, and a photo of his dog Rosie, as well as his outstretched hand holding a multicoloured butterfly he'd once found, his signature and a saying Costas had loved: 'Not for you to ask the reason but to find a reason big enough.'

Lynn-Maree says the priest then raced around giving everyone a card. 'It was like he was on speed!' she says. 'He raced from place to place and spoke to everyone Costas had ever accosted. We found it really hard to keep up. He had tears in his eyes the whole time. I think emotions make him uncomfortable, so he covers it up with activity.'

Father Bob was adamant that Costas have a proper funeral

and so he was farewelled at St Peter and Paul's in a service with an Aboriginal smoking ceremony organised by Henri Ser, at which everyone held red and white balloons. Later, there was a remembrance service in the parish garden after the 10 a.m. Sunday mass, with a kaleidoscope of butterflies released into the air.

Father Bob wrote his obituary, remembering him as 'Respected member of Sts. Peter and Paul's Parish and founding member of the Father Bob Maguire Foundation'.

There was a maelstrom of plans and projects on the go, but no-one was quite sure what the future would bring for Father Bob. He continued his work at a frenzied pace, as if he was trying to solve all the problems of the parish in what limited time he had left.

He kept a close eye on the building of the new community housing block by the church, which had, as he'd forecast, put the parish accounts in the black for about $1.6 million, and he auctioned a giant Lego mural of Flinders Street Station to raise money for his Foundation. He appeared as a guest panellist on a new gay radio show in Werribee, he was on the Nova 100 Christmas show with Dave Hughes and Kate Langbroek, and he put out calls for a warehouse from which to continue his charity work after his time as parish priest expired. At the same time, he sat for a portrait by stencil and aerosol paint artist Luke Cornish for the 2012 Archibald Prize, which became the first piece of stencil art ever to make it into the finals. The process was even documented in a short film entitled *Me We* – after boxer Mohammed Ali's poem, the shortest ever written, proclaiming the power of one – for the Tropfest short film festival.

There were also a few surprise visitors to St Peter and Paul's: a crowd of young people from the protest group Occupy Melbourne. They'd been occupying the City Square from the middle of October 2011, as part of the worldwide Occupy movement protesting social injustice, poverty, corruption in the financial sector and corporate greed. The group had been continually moved on by the City of Melbourne and Victoria Police, and had set up camp in a number of other sites as well as the city centre. This offshoot group had been staying in Flagstaff Gardens but had been threatened at knifepoint by a passer-by and, fearing for their safety, visited Father Bob on the day before Christmas Eve to ask if they could set up twenty tents in the grounds of his church instead. 'I felt sorry for them, and said they were welcome to stay as individuals rather than as a political group,' he says. 'They were all thoughtful twenty-somethings, very nice people wanting to make a genuine protest and I said they could use the kitchen in the presbytery and the power. After all, it was Christmas!

'It was a nice experience coming at such a difficult time for me. It was like the arrival of twenty or thirty angels coming to reassure me. I could never have designed it.'

One of the members of this group, nineteen-year-old apprentice cook Michael Carlyon, was making some coffee in the kitchen at 3 a.m. on Christmas Eve when Father Bob came down to get some food out of the fridge. 'We started talking and he told me about his history,' says Michael. 'We exchanged stories, and our friendship grew from there.'

Michael had been born in Ireland but had come to Australia as a young child with his family. He'd had some issues at home, and later spent three to four years on the streets, until he was attacked there, a knife puncturing a lung, and at sixteen went back to stay with his mother. 'I'd seen the dark side of life in Australia,' he says, 'and I felt that shouldn't be happening. We have such a rich country, and yet we have so many people really struggling, so that's why I joined Occupy Melbourne.'

Father Bob was enormously impressed with the young man, and offered him a job with his Foundation, to restart the kind of work that Open Family had previously been doing with kids on the streets. 'Michael was like a soldier from God,' he says. 'It was an epiphany, a bright spot in the gloom. He seemed to have a vocation of his own to work with homeless teenagers, whereas our work had gradually become partly palliative, critical care and burying the dead. So it was a revival.'

Gradually, the priest was trying to work out a future path, in case he didn't receive that final reprieve from the Archbishop. With his old Open Family organisation just having announced a merger with youth organisation Whitelion, he felt there was now a fresh need for more work to be done among homeless young people. One worker still at Open Family, from just after Brother Alex left, says that it had shrunk a lot since Father Bob was at the helm. 'He was such a great figurehead and was so motivating and attractive to people, and under him Open Family was constantly growing,' he says. 'But now it's totally different. It's much more conservative and more corporate. At its height, we had thirty to forty outreach workers in Melbourne. Now there's just a dozen or so. It's very sad.'

But as Father Bob prepared for his last Christmas mass, he still hadn't given up hope that he might be able to stay on and continue his youth work as the parish priest. After all, the Australian ambassador to the Holy See Tim Fischer had reported that he'd been flooded with emails in Rome asking for Father Bob to be allowed to keep on. 'Who knows what Santa might bring me?' the priest told reporters. 'Maybe there'll be a letter from the Pope saying I can stay . . .'

He'd always seen the Church as his metaphorical mother and father, and after most of his lifetime spent with them, he was finding the break very hard. Andrew de Groot of Ghost Pictures says, despite his bravado, it was heartbreaking to see his pain close-up. 'He was angry but he also had that imprint of children whose parents divorce and then abandon them. The Church had taken him in as a fourteen year old and he'd given his whole life to the priesthood, but now it was booting him out. He thought it was a home, but it had turned out to be just a business. And he was never prepared to have the carpet pulled out from beneath him. He had no Plan B.'

That Christmas Eve mass, and the Christmas Day mass following, the church was packed both times with wellwishers, as Father Bob delivered a message about 'saving each other' rather than waiting for God to do it for them. 'We are all in this together,' the priest told the congregation. 'The mystery of Christmas is that humanity is the safest place for God to be.' As he left the altar, a number of his parishioners broke down in tears.

'It's not right,' one woman sobbed. 'He married me and he baptised all my kids. The Church is crazy to kick him out. He's a wonderful man, a saint.'

Father Bob walked out of the doors, and didn't look back.

On Sunday, 29 January 2012, Father Bob said his last mass at St Peter and Paul's as parish priest of South Melbourne. Over 1000 people crammed into the pews, including faithful parishioners, celebrities, Comanchero bikies, fellow priests, even the separated conjoined twins Trishna and Krishna.

There were standing ovations for the priest who had just entered his thirty-ninth year of serving the neighbourhood, and floods of tears amid the accolades, the prayers, the songs and the pipers playing. Lynn-Maree, like the rest of the congregation, was overcome with the emotion of the occasion. 'There was a moment you could see, from the set of his jaw and his lips, that he was saying, "This is it!"' she says. 'And I couldn't help a quiet sob and then feeling the tears streaming down my face. There was such sadness. It was the same when he was up in his room, packing up ready to leave, and he was trying to make sense of it all. It's like when you're on the phone and someone hangs up on you and there's no recourse; it's a very different energy to just having a row. There's such disappointment and sadness that he can't do everything he wants to do.'

After the service was finished, he was presented with boxing gloves, inscribed with the words: 'Father Bob, God's Own' on the left, and 'Father Bob, Keep Punch'n' on the right. As he draped them over his shoulders, he suddenly looked as if all the fight had drained right out of him. As he bustled away, everyone looked after him, wondering how he was going to fare.

One of his most loyal parishioners, Mavis Keighery, felt as though life would never be the same without him. 'He said he was heartbroken,' she says. 'I don't think he'll ever recover from this. I don't know if he'll be able to keep going.'

24

Leave 'Em Smiling

The phone rings in the office of a former real estate agent's shop on a busy street in Albert Park, and Father Bob Maguire snatches it up. He listens intently for a minute, then rises to his feet. 'I'm coming, Mother!' he barks, slams the receiver down and races out the door.

A minute later, he's behind the wheel of the large motorhome a corporate admirer has lent him for six months, steering it cautiously towards a low bridge, then changing his mind about whether it'll get through and doubling back on himself to take an alternative route instead. 'That was the devil's work,' he's mumbling to himself. 'That could have taken our bloody top off!'

Ten minutes on, in between answering his phone and

reading texts at traffic lights – 'The things we do for Jesus!' he exclaims – he's manoeuvring the large vehicle gingerly along the railings outside a hospital where one of his parishioners lies dying inside, waiting for him to perform the last rites. As he shunts back and forth to move out of the way of oncoming traffic, he bashes into the rails, halts, then bashes into them again. A woman standing at the entrance to the hospital dabbing her eyes with a tissue looks on horrified.

'That's her daughter,' declares Father Bob, grabbing his bag and leaping out of the motorhome with an agility that gives lie to his seventy-eight years. 'Here comes the ready response unit! All for one and one for all!' He then scurries off towards her, along the way throwing a quick look back to assess any damage to the back of the vehicle. As he reaches her, he asks urgently, 'Is she still with us?' The daughter nods, and races back into the hospital, the priest in hot pursuit. The pair then run down a corridor, up two flights of stairs and down another corridor until the woman stops finally at the entrance of a room. 'There she is,' she says finally, indicating a comatose figure on a bed, wired to various monitors, with three nurses standing in the corner.

Father Bob opens his bag and whips out his long green and white stole, the symbol of ordination for priests, and throws it on, while rummaging for his battered old Bible and his pot of oil. Then he approaches the bed and stands by the woman, gently touching her hand. He reads softly from the Bible, recites a prayer, then solemnly anoints the woman's forehead, drawing the sign of the cross in holy oil, while saying her sins have now been forgiven.

After the last Amen, he turns to the room: the nurses

looking solemnly on, and the daughter softly sobbing. The air of tension and misery is palpable. 'Right!' says Father Bob, decisively. 'She's now cleared for take-off!'

There's a sharp intake of breath from everyone in the room, and a silence that feels like it will never end. Then the grieving daughter, through her tears, starts laughing, and the nurses, relieved, all join in.

'Father,' says the woman. 'I want you to do her funeral. I don't want anyone else. Will you do it?' Father Bob smiles. 'Yes, of course,' he says. She hugs him warmly.

As he troops back out to the motorhome, he grins. 'It's good to make people laugh, even at the worst times of their lives,' he says. 'Do you say something mealy-mouthed, or do you use secular humour to cheer people up? I try not to add to the horrors of death. I try to highlight the bright side and people seem to appreciate it. They like a clown; they like to have permission to laugh. I always prefer to leave 'em smiling.'

It's been seven months since Father Bob packed up and left St Peter and Paul's on 1 February 2012 and, despite the grief of losing his home, the anger, a fair deal of bitterness, and the confusion over what his next steps should be, he now seems almost as busy as ever he was.

After a few weeks in a hotel, he and his dog Franklin set up home in the tiny back room of an office whose rent has been paid for the next three years by the Victorian Electrical Trades Union. 'He's always been there for us over the years, and after he was kicked out of his church we thought it was very important to keep him going,' says union boss Dean Mighell. 'We love his sense of social justice and how he uses his celebrity gloss to help the downtrodden and working people, and to promote good causes.'

The room's only just big enough to hold a single bed, a rug for Franklin, a few shelves of books, a TV and an easy chair, with a back door leading out to the yard where the motorhome parks, but it's enough. In there he wakes up every morning at about 6.30 a.m., reads his Bible and all the newspapers, watches the news on TV, raids the fridge in the tiny nook just beyond for his breakfast and finally emerges to walk down the corridor, lined with three small offices and a wider open area that serves as a conference space, to the main room near the front of the building, where he sets up behind a huge desk to work for the day.

It's now from this desk, with a framed signed Collingwood jersey behind him, that he sees a steady stream of people coming in to talk over their problems, to pay their respects, to make bookings for him to talk to various groups, to plan finances or to work out a way forward. The phone rings constantly, picked up either by a secretary or volunteer helper out front, or by Father Bob himself. The callers range from those keen to book masses, weddings, baptisms, funerals or last rites, to those asking him to visit schools, speak to organisations, participate in interviews for newspapers or magazines, or appear online, on radio, or on TV.

'We love having him on, not only for his razor-sharp wit, but for his warmth, his kindness and his integrity,' says 'The Project' co-host Carrie Bickmore. 'He's one of the most genuine souls I know. He shows us that religion needs to move and adapt with the times, and that it's our humanity, and our relationships with other people, that we should hold most dear.'

Ben Fordham on Radio 2GB says he's keener than ever to have the priest on regularly now he's lost his church. 'I want to make sure he has a congregation every week on radio to share his wisdom instead,' he says. 'That the Church sacked him is sad, but the tragedy is that they're the losers. He's such a forward thinker. We don't have enough rough diamonds out there, and we can't let him slip through our fingers. Our listeners just love him.'

As for Father Bob, the banner over the front of the office says what he dearly hopes the next phase of his life might lead to: The Father Bob Maguire Foundation: The Next Generation. 'Yes, it does sound a bit Star Trekky, but I'm now looking to the younger ones to continue the work,' he says. 'They're the ones with the energy, the optimism, the foresight and the wisdom to keep going what we've started. The future is theirs. Beam me up, Scotty!'

The priest, however, in all his alternate joviality, cantankerousness, gruffness and compassion, is still always at the centre of everything. Two of the kids he first started out helping, Mem River and Chris Apostolidis, are now giving him a hand with the Foundation, while others drop in to help as and when needed. 'He helped us when we were young, now it's our turn to help him,' says Slav Civcic, who got to know the priest as a kid after his father died and who now, together with his wife Trish Apiti and son Evan, also turns up regularly to give him a hand. 'He's a very good man, and it's a real privilege to be able to give back to him, even in a very small way.'

His new recruit Michael Carlyon is spearheading a return

to youth outreach work helping kids who don't so much sleep on the streets anymore, but squat in derelict factories and warehouses around town, while old mate Henri Ser looks after the food van, Henry Nissen keeps in touch with senior clients, and support comes from his inner circle of past parish chairmen and councillors Frank O'Connor and Tony Long, together with a variety of parishioners all now eager to give back after a lifetime of being cared for.

While there's an air of frenzied chaos – 'That's creative chaos,' protests Father Bob – still everything, somehow, seems to get done. 'Maybe people on the margins would find it too confronting if something were too organised,' suggests Father Joe Giacobbe of the Doxa Youth Foundation. 'Bob goes about things in a different way, but he makes things happen, he's effective. A lot of organisations come and go, and he's been doing it for fifty years now.'

The 'futile care', or 'triage', support for old associates continues as well as the pastoral work, the ceremonies Father Bob is still allowed to conduct back at his old church, the masses and services he's invited to hold elsewhere, and the scholarships for both boys and girls. His major financial supporter for those scholarships, businessman Pat Lohan, got to know Father Bob during the early years, while working as the local bank manager, with the priest a regular visitor trying to raise funds for his various projects. Their friendships endured even despite one of Father Bob's 'unfortunates' holding him up at gunpoint at his bank. 'I just belted him, grabbed the gun and took out the bullets,' says Pat. 'I still have those bullets as a memento in my briefcase today. But we're old mates. I'm happy to help support Bob's work. You have to be Christian and be charitable, and I believe in what he's doing. He'd give anyone the shirt off his back. I don't always agree with the way he does things, and I do think he gets taken in sometimes, but if that's a fault, is it a bad one?'

Ideas for new schemes are constantly coming up and being debated, too. Father Bob played himself in an independent movie, *Palio*, and took the role of God in a comedy debate at Melbourne Zoo about conservation. 'I put in an appropriate performance,' he says, modestly. Meanwhile, Chris Apostolidis is working on his own idea for a TV show to broadcast on YouTube, connected to the priest's 86 000-plus Twitter followers. 'My personal belief is that the world needs his insight,' says Chris. 'I think he's such a unique human being, his opinion on things will help shape the future.' With Father Bob's interest in new technology and futuristic ways of doing things, the priest also loves the idea of a 'pop-up church' where he can say mass any time, anywhere he likes. In addition, he tweets constantly to his massive following as his own 'parish church without borders'. 'Twitter is perfect for him,' says his radio partner John Safran. 'He can sit alone but still connect with the world and let the world know he's there.' With his film *In Bob We Trust* due to premiere at the Melbourne International Film Festival, he's also embraced an online religious service, Church.tv, through which he live-streams sermons on a Sunday via a computer and webcam to a huge audience all over the world. 'He may not have his own church or pulpit to stand behind anymore, but this gives him a much greater presence and reach,' says CEO Mark Crosling. 'He's a natural on the screen. He makes a lot of these Hollywood gods look second-rate.'

He's attracted some unusual allies along the way too. As well as Mem, who's able to liaise directly with the Muslim community, he's also forged a strong link with a young Buddhist, Freeman Trebilcock, who started the multi-faith youth network InterAction, of which he's the patron. InterAction now borrows the Foundation's food van once a week to deliver food from a food rescue charity and a Hare Krishna temple under the banner The Fast Supper. Freeman's now also helping Father Bob in his bid to set up an inter-faith centre, catering for all denominations and beliefs, in Melbourne's Docklands. Their rival bidders for the space include the Hillsong Church and, ironically, the Catholic Church.

'I absolutely love working with Bob,' says Freeman, twenty-four, who's organised for Father Bob to have a meeting with the Dalai Lama in June 2013. 'I think of him as what we in Buddhist terminology call the bodhisattva, which is an enlightened or heroic, wise one or, in my favourite translation, "an ambassador of love". The Christian equivalent would be a saint. Some people just love him for his larrikinism and his no-bullshit matter-of-factness but there's a profundity behind what he says, a meaning and a wisdom and knowledge. Being around Bob is like you're in a slipstream; you catch a ride on his energy and enthusiasm.'

Another partnership is with Justin Dickinson, the founder of The Big Umbrella, a not-for-profit organisation that helps marginalised children and young people, both locally and internationally. One of its biggest schemes is a refuge, partly funded by Father Bob's Foundation, set up in Nepal for kids who've been the victims of people-traffickers and who now live on the streets. The pair also set up the Father Bob

Maguire's 4-Life Academy together, providing a community leadership program, vocational training and a mentoring system for schoolkids in Melbourne, with the support of the National Australia Bank, who provide premises and corporate volunteers to help train the children in finance, governance, marketing and public speaking. With the Academy's encouragement, one group of children at a local school managed to raise $6000 in just three months for the Nepalese street kids. 'When I think about it, this program goes all the way back to the kind of character-training programs we did in the army in the old days,' says Father Bob. 'It's incredibly effective, and it seems the children really respond well.'

With the organisation growing fast, Justin sees Father Bob as having a big future with it. 'Father Bob is everything, he's our mentor, everything,' he says. 'If I get stuck on something, I ask myself, "What would Father Bob do?" Or I just ring him. He has a way of making things so logical and straightforward. But I especially love it when I'm tired of fighting the never-ending losing battle that comes with running a charity and he pats me on the back and says, "Now get back out there, they need us." And, as usual, he's right. It's not about us. It's about them. I hope that one day our academy will run all year round, and his name will be immortalised forever for every generation; the next Fred Hollows.'

Yet there have been setbacks along the way. The idea of appealing to the Pope in Rome over the loss of his church was an attractive one, until he discovered the cost of hiring experts in canon law to take on the case. Going to Rome to appeal in person also wasn't so attractive to someone who'd never before been overseas. 'It sounded good, but I don't think that was ever going to happen,' he says sadly. 'It'd need a miracle now to persuade people that South Melbourne wasn't *terra nullius* when the Capuchins came.'

Then there was the loan of the mobile home, with the notion that he might become a roaming priest, wandering up and down the highways and byways of Australia to minister to people wherever he found them. 'It was a nice idea of a nomadic priest on the road, but I personally never subscribed to going up and down the highway having cups of tea,' he says. Besides, for someone who hadn't had a single day's holiday since he was ordained in 1960, and whose only day off lasted forty-five minutes before he rushed off to deal with an emergency, he was never much of a one for travel.

The need for funds remains a constant in his life. A planned major injection of cash into his Foundation vanished when a special-edition solid aluminium gnome donated by the team on the TV show 'The Block' (who had been working close to his church) raised over $45 000 in an eBay auction but the winner was found to be a hoax bid by a fourteen-year-old boy. Later, Nine Network CEO David Gyngell donated $10 000, the amount of the highest legitimate bid, and gave him the gnome to auction himself. Father Bob suggested it was a heist worthy of a Batman movie itself – *The Return of the Dark Gnome* – after a kidnap by the Joker. A limited-edition bobble-head doll of the priest, with one of his favourite slogans, 'Who Cares Wins', underneath, raised a small sum, at least.

There were also the daily irritations and indignities of living without his parish: having to organise everything for himself after so many years of having a large institution behind him; managing with all his papers, books and tapes in boxes since moving out; and often having to rely on parishioners' generosity even to eat. 'What the hell's this?' is a regular cry in the office when he looks in the fridge to see what a parishioner may have brought him in for lunch or dinner. 'Moroccan soup? What the hell's that? What's wrong with a simple sandwich? You don't want gourmet meals when you're an ex-pauper, you just want square meals.'

There's the people constantly phoning him with offers of old clothes, shoes and donations of food, all of which he no longer has the space for. 'Sorry, comrade,' is his regular refrain. 'I'm the mad priest and I've been thrown out of my church, you see. I don't have the room anymore, even the dog's going mad, staring at all the spots on the carpet in the new place. Try the Salvos?' Another caller who wants to volunteer to help with his Foundation, but can only spare 6.30 a.m. to 8.30 a.m. on weekdays, is also turned away. 'What on earth can we find him to do at that time? We just don't have anywhere to put him!' On a single day recently, 20kg of powdered soup was delivered, only to be discovered it was past its use-by date so had to be disposed of, and then came the donation of a coffin. It was the first time anyone could remember Father Bob lost for words until he regathered his thoughts in time to ponder whether someone was wishing him dead.

That daily grind he can't resist using for comic purposes. 'Thanks, Denis!' he regularly cries, citing the Archbishop at any new annoyance. 'Thank you *very* much!' It is never an expression, or indication, of any kind of grudge, though, he insists. Just like Hamlet, so often quoted by his dad throughout his childhood, he likes to think of it more as a continuous running monologue, partly shared with his 'audience' for their interest, but tinged with a dark humour.

Naturally, others can hold grudges against him. Father Bob's old adversary Derryn Hinch returned to the scene shortly after his liver transplant to blast the priest yet again for his association with Vincent Kiss. This time, Father Bob hit back, accusing the former radio broadcaster of hating priests, and demanding an apology. 'It's a pain in the arse,' said Father Bob. 'You can't defend yourself against mischief.' Radio supporter Neil Mitchell joined his call for an apology.

Derryn now says Father Bob has done a lot of good stuff over the years but 'he's a media whore. He knows how to play the media. He got thrown out of the parish, but it was time for him to go. He tried to justify money laundering. But I don't dislike him. He's an engaging old coot but I wonder how much is performance.'

However, when it is put to Derryn that while Father Bob did accept money, then write cheques for Kiss's ultimately non-existent Vanuatu charity, so did many more people – and people much wiser and higher up in respectable financial institutions – he backs down a little. 'Maybe I accept that,' he says. 'But he didn't defend himself very well at the time. But, yes, I can be like a dog with a bone, that's true. It's probably true too that I've kept on attacking him over the same thing. But I'm not trying to paint him as the devil incarnate. Anyone who had anything to do with Vincent Kiss gets tainted. He was one of the smoothest operators I've ever seen . . .'

Yet it's not been unknown for Father Bob to hold a grudge, either. 'He's extremely non-judgemental and takes people genuinely as they are but with one tiny qualification: he can hold a small grudge if he thinks you've been disloyal,' says Tony Long. 'He hopped into one person at a meeting who wasn't there, which makes me want to come to every meeting ... He can say it exactly as he sees it.' He also tends not to put much effort into keeping up friendships with his peers. A number of his old Vatican II mates bemoan the fact they've lost touch with him, and he's so hard to drag along to any kind of social gathering. Father Bob concedes that, but has his defence ready. 'Well, what can you expect from me?' he asks. 'I'm a priest, I'm psycho-socially challenged.'

It's a line that came in handy again when the Comancheros outlaw motorcycle gang put a banner up on the Hopemobile food van he was using after a group of tradesmen updated the van for free, and the priest invited them to put their advertising materials on it in return. When the van's owner discovered the 'Support Your Local Comancheros' sticker, he was ropeable. Father Bob started off defending the gang – he'd tangled with them once before when Mem had the misfortune to bump his car into that of a gang leader's wife – then looked them up on the computer. 'Oh dear, oh dear,' he said. 'Shootings ... drugs ... It doesn't look so good, does it? But I suppose you could argue that there's always an opportunity for redemption, and you don't want to mess with a bikie gang ...' The owner ended up taking the van back, and the priest appealed to supporters to help him buy one. They quickly obliged.

The announcement of the Royal Commission into child abuse by the Church and other public institutions Father Bob saw as a positive move. After years of apologising on behalf of the Church for past ills done in its name, and subsequent failures to investigate claims fully, he hopes this might mean a more open, accountable and democratic Church into the future. 'This could even be Vatican III!' he declares.

But his own personal major difficulty hit in the middle of December 2012, when he suddenly began losing feeling in his hands, arms and legs, and then lost the use of them completely, forcing him to cancel his Christmas Eve liturgy, a big blow for him. After three weeks, he was reduced to spending days and nights sitting in his chair in the back room, unable even to manoeuvre himself into bed. It reached the point in January 2013 where he believed he might be dying. 'I can't do anything!' he complained. 'The doctors don't know what's wrong with me. I started off shuffling like a penguin and then I couldn't move at all. I had an MRI the other day. I thought, "Jesus! They're putting me in a shredder!" I was sure the doctor would say I was a goner. Someone suggested it was the stress and grief of everything that's happened catching up with me. I don't know. I'm only a priest . . . I'm meant to be running a battleship here, but it's looking like a hospital ship . . .'

He finally agreed to go into respite care, from where he was transferred a day later to hospital. There, he was diagnosed with the rare illness chronic inflammatory demyelinating polyneuropathy (CIDP), in which the immune system attacks itself. Stress can indeed be a factor. Father Bob was put on an immediate series of blood protein injections to treat the condition. But lying in hospital, with a constant stream of visitors of friends, parishioners, supporters and media, he still couldn't help himself using the setback as a way to focus public attention on other, worthier, causes.

'I thought I should try to spin it for blood donations,' he

says. 'I wanted to say, "Don't cry for me, Argentina", but let's see if we can use this to persuade more people in Australia to give blood. There's a huge shortage. So I came up with the idea of giving to Bob's Blood Bank, because I was worried about depriving other people of blood just to keep the fat priest alive.'

A number of Father Bob's supporters would love him to be content with just doing good works, but at that, he rolls his eyes. 'I can't!' he protests. 'I'm a priest. I need a church. It's part of who I am.' Losing his home was hard enough, but losing his church was perhaps even harder. 'I do miss the church. I miss opening the doors at 7 a.m. in the morning and closing them at 7 p.m. I miss the sun rising in the east through those beautiful windows installed in 1912, and the sun shining through the rose window in the evening. I miss meeting the people there and sharing in the life of the church . . .'

He's retained a toehold at St Peter and Paul's, however, being allowed to say an informal mass at 6 p.m. at the back of the church on a Sunday for a small congregation and – somewhat incongruously, given his Vatican II approach – holding a highly formal traditional Latin mass at the altar at 7 p.m., with his back to the congregation as was the historical way. 'He's the only priest here who can do it,' says parishioner Helena Bieletsky, one of a group of people who travel from all over Victoria to attend. 'When we asked him, he began holding a Latin mass for us in 2011. Even though he hadn't done it for forty years, he remembered it perfectly. He has an incredible mind.' Unfortunately for other devout traditionalists, he's not been allowed to advertise his weekly celebration of the Latin mass.

Most of those who come along revere the priest, but there are some who would love to see a return to Church values of old. 'He does lead with his chin and is deliberately provocative,' says one, Michael. 'He's a thorn in the side of the Archdiocese but his role should be to sacrifice himself for the Church and the faithful, not to man the barricades and throw grenades at the establishment. He says it's all about the poor, the destitute and homeless children, but it's not. His role should be to defend the Catholic faith in society. I think this Latin mass will be his salvation; through that he should see the shallowness of much of the rest of his advocacy.'

Father Bob does also conduct occasional weddings, baptisms and funerals at the church when specially asked, but lives in constant fear of that option being closed off to him by his successors, the Capuchin friars. Their principal, the new South Melbourne parish priest Father Julian Messina, says that may well be the case at some point.

'There's still a little group of people who need time to bring closure to what was before,' he says. 'It's not going to hurt us to accommodate them and not disrupt things too much. But that's always up for review. If it comes to the point where it's dividing the parish because a substantial number of people were isolating themselves from the main community, I would have to review that. Quite obviously, we don't want to have little exclusive groups of people . . . A number of them are fond of Father Bob and have known him for many years, and were married by him, and their parents were married by him, and we have to take into account his special situation. But it is under review.'

The friars, a branch of the Franciscan order that broke

off in the sixteenth century seeking a simpler style, dressed in medieval brown tunics and sandals, say it was difficult taking over, but the Catholic Church is a hierarchical organisation and they were acting under orders. After the initial troubles, they say, the parishioners have generally welcomed them. They have continued Father Bob's initiative of feeding people out the back of the church, but will not be renewing the Friends of the Earth's lease of the South Melbourne Commons community hub, a move against which Father Bob immediately declared his opposition, on moral and environmental grounds.

'I've always admired Father Bob's way of doing things, and his ideals and vision aren't so different from ours,' says Father Messina. 'But we draw strength from a universal perspective, whereas his was a local parochial perspective.' When Father Bob fell sick with CIDP, Father Messina was among his first visitors but he also took that as a cue to press his claim even more strongly. 'The Archdiocese decided that Father Bob had reached a certain age and the security of his tenure wasn't as great as it had been,' he says. 'And that's been proved right now.' No-one brought up the possibility that the stress of Father Bob losing his church may have precipitated his illness.

Father Bob is often invited to say mass at other churches within the Archdiocese, however. His services are always immensely popular, but invariably confronting. 'I admire and love Bob greatly, but he's not easy,' says his great friend, Father Kevin Burke. 'I had him here saying mass a couple of weeks ago. I was a nervous wreck because you don't know what he's going to say next! One woman walked out as Bob does provoke people, probably more so when it's in a one-off situation. But you've got to close your eyes and see beyond the facade and front and gimmicks and jokes, and there's a pretty good message coming out. You just have to try not to be distracted.'

He's also in huge demand from schools. He'll go along to hold a service or simply to talk to children about his life, the Church and the lessons of religion. 'How old are you?' one six year old asks him. 'I'm ancient!' he roars back as the entire hall dissolves into giggles. 'Does anyone have any baby brothers or sisters back home?' he asks another class. A forest of hands shoots up. 'Well, when you go back tonight, have a look at their hands,' he says. 'Babies today are born with longer thumbs,' he explains. Everyone leans towards him, intrigued. 'It's so they can text much faster!' he says. There's a pause for the kids to digest this, then the sound of children's laughter fills the hall.

'He relates to children so well,' says one of the teachers, watching on. 'They all adore him.' Before he leaves, entire classes line up, determined to high-five him before he goes. And when an alarm outside suddenly goes off, he feigns panic. 'Oh no!' he cries. 'They're coming to get me!' It takes a full five minutes for the class to be quietened back down.

At the office, though, things are now quiet. Back with the full use of his arms and legs, although still having rehab sessions, he says he's now kicking goals for Collingwood, although he feigns worry about being accused of using performance-enhancing drugs. Still sleeping at the office, he's been offered a small flat in the community housing block he initiated close to the church, and can't decide whether to take it. He says the place is so full of memories for him, it might be painful living so close. Yet since he so regularly drives by the church, looking mournfully over, it might not really be so very different.

His youth worker Michael Carlyon suggests getting some pot plants for the backyard by his room, in case he wants to stay there instead. 'Pot plants!' echoes the priest with disgust. 'Pot plants! We're waging a war on poverty here, and you're talking pot plants!' Michael retreats, grinning, from the room.

While he still lives in constant fear of being given 'the red card' from the church, to say he won't be allowed to say masses anymore – 'They just refuse to give me a list of indictable offences,' he complains – it's unlikely his bosses will go much further. In public, at least, Melbourne Archbishop Denis Hart praises his aberrant priest. When asked for a comment for this book, he chooses his words carefully, but doesn't hesitate. 'Father Bob Maguire was ordained in 1960 and he's worked very hard for the poor and the underprivileged,' he says. 'For more than thirty years he was parish priest of South Melbourne where a large number of people enjoyed his compassion and work. He's a well-known priest and he has an inimitable style.'

Others, of course, are a touch more effusive. Over at Father Bob's beloved Collingwood ground, Jeff 'Joffa' Corfe, the leader of the Collingwood cheer squad and frequently described as one of the best-known sporting fans in the world, is full of praise. 'He's just a wonderful person,' he says. 'He was the shining light of the Church, but they were the only ones who couldn't see it. He's a man of the people, well respected, dearly loved, and just an amazing person, a wonderful human being.'

Collingwood president Eddie McGuire similarly counts

himself among the priest's great fans. A scholarship boy himself at CBC, he loves it that Father Bob continues to offer scholarships to give others a good start in life. "Bob's one of a special group of philanthropists keeping that program going, with education the greatest gift you could ever give a young person,' Eddie says. 'Throughout my career, we've worked on many projects together, and we want to work together on projects for the future, both privately and through the club. He's always been a fantastic Collingwood supporter and he's been a great mentor for the club and a steady source of inspiration over many years. It's been an honour and a pleasure to have worked with him, and I've been affected by him enormously. Bob is a real doer. He always looks on the bright side of a tough world and gets in and makes things happen, and gets stuck into the action. He may not be everyone's cup of tea but he focuses on a problem and finds an answer that will provide the quickest way to solve it.'

Likewise, his supporters come from all walks of life, from Appeal Court judge Bernard Bongiorno and retired judge Sally Brown, now at the International Commission of Jurists, to ex–heroin addict Linda, to stand-up comedian and radio host Meshel Laurie. 'Father Bob's inclusiveness and kindness are what draws me personally to him,' says Meshel. 'Father Bob seems to me to be a man who lives very simply by the teachings of Jesus Christ. I'm not the first person to note how few proud Christians seem to be able to do that, and I'm sure I won't be the last.' Even the Reverend Tim Costello, who'd criticised him in the past, has come round. 'Bob's lifelong commitment to the battler and the poor is something I admire,' he says now. 'His humour, courage and irony have been a source of inspiration to many people.'

Of course, Father Bob would be the first to admit he's made mistakes along the way, but says his driving force was always to try to do good, and not cause harm. He's still mourning the loss of his church, but will eventually come to terms with that too. His old mate Father Ernie Smith believes there were faults on both sides in the way his forced 'retirement' was handled, but believes Father Bob is certainly no closer to giving up. 'He's a survivor, Bob, he's a survivor. He'll get on with it.'

That's echoed by Monsignor Tony Toms. 'He'll be engaged in pastoral work until the day he drops dead,' he says. 'He's never thought of himself, only of others.'

And while being kicked out of his church has pushed him to the limits, believes John Safran, 'He is still a really positive person and an inspiration. He's had a lot of disappointments along the way, but he tries to leverage that into something else each time, and come up with a different strategy.'

Even the announcement in February 2013 that Pope Benedict XVI would become the first pope in nearly 600 years to resign didn't faze Father Bob. He foresaw that he'd merely be replaced by someone remarkably similar in conservative outlook, with little change to the global Catholic Church. 'Those in power are still the descendants of those who tried to cripple Vatican II and it'll just be a bit of an anomaly having a bloke in the back room while another fella goes up front to drive the bus,' he says. 'But I don't believe the balance of power will change. It would be silly of them to give that up.'

However, with the Church still in the throes of the global child sex abuse scandal, he does see a possibility of forces at work beyond Pope Benedict's stated reason for giving up the helm, which was ill-health connected to old age. 'The collective probably wants to move him out of the eye of the storm because he's got baggage in terms of being in Hitler Youth as a boy, and the sexual abuse and cover-ups that have happened in the past,' says Father Bob. 'This could then be a smart move in terms of moving him out of the firing line, and being seen to start again with a clean slate with someone else in charge. But that might be just my Dan Brown conspiracy theories coming out! And Jesus of Nazareth does still run the Church.'

As for Father Bob himself, the only way he knows how to continue is to simply keep going. He looks around his office and sighs. 'I'm buggered if I know what to do,' he says. 'I don't know. What can I do? I only know one way. There's this persistent myth now that Australia loves me, which is strange; it's too much for me. I think some disenfranchised Christians have fallen in love with the myth of the crazy priest.

'But I don't know. Some people have called me a maverick or a larrikin or a renegade, or they say I'm plain mad, and whether I was mad before I got to this stage, or whether I was driven mad by circumstances, I don't know. People'll have to decide for themselves. But just one thing: Don't ever make me a saint. Because that is something I'm most definitely not.'

Acknowledgements

First of all, I'd like to thank the people of South Melbourne and Port Melbourne, including the parishioners of St Peter and St Paul's, for revealing to me more about heaven on earth than I ever could have taught them.

I'd also like to commemorate the forty who died in the 1980s and 1990s on our watch, because a lot of good people did nothing.

And to the victims of abuse by institutions, both religious and secular, by those entrusted to their care, I would like to pay tribute to their struggle to be heard, and recognise their battles.

I would like to thank the women in my life – the mothers, sisters, nieces, and all those women over the years in the parish – who've given so much time and energy to our common mission to build a caring community, at one with the Church.

Thanks to Sue Williams for putting herself in harm's way to spend time with an eccentric priest.

Finally, to everyone who has helped us along the way, thank you and God bless.

Bob Maguire

Read on for a sneak peek of

Brought to you by

PENGUIN BOOKS

CHAPTER 1

Dad, Have You Ever Climbed Everest?

It happens just three days into one of the world's most gruelling treks.

Eight-year-old Alyssa Azar is almost halfway along the rugged Kokoda Track in the remote wilds of Papua New Guinea, and she knows that when she completes it – *if* she completes it – she'll have the world record as the youngest person ever to do so. But suddenly, she stops dead. The mud beneath her walking boots oozes up over her ankle gaiters as she sinks into the quagmire and lifts first one foot, then the other, to try to free them, but makes no attempt to continue.

The local porters look at her curiously. Over the past week they've learnt to expect the unexpected from this tiny little white girl, with her gap-toothed grin and mop of blonde hair tied into a rough ponytail. When she'd first been introduced to them as the youngest member of a new expedition along the historic trail, they'd shaken their heads in disapproval. She was far too young, and much too small, to embark on such an arduous challenge.

But she's already taken them by surprise many times, striding along the track through dense rainforest, heaving herself up giant steps hewn into the mountains that most fully grown adults have trouble with, scrambling up the steep sides of valleys and trotting down the other side. A couple of times, as they reach for her arms to try to guide her across a raging river crossing, or help her along a particularly precarious mountain ridge, she politely but firmly asks them to leave her be. She already has dark bruises on both elbows where the guides, terrified of losing such fragile cargo, grabbed her so hard she winced. She wants to do this with as little help as possible.

Alyssa seems to be coping well. In every village they pass through she causes a sensation. Little children hide behind their mothers as they regard her shyly; it's the first time they've ever seen a girl their own age who doesn't share the same dark skin. Then, as she smiles back at them, they grow in courage, running over to touch her face and hair to check that she isn't some kind of doll. Alyssa laughs and plays with them while the other trekkers in the party rest.

But now, in the middle of the track, she has stopped and the guides stand back to see what's going on. She looks over to her dad, Glenn, who is quickly catching her up. 'What's up?' he asks casually as he draws level, trying to keep any note of alarm out of his voice.

If she's hurt herself, or suddenly decided she doesn't want to go on, he doesn't know what they'll do. The only way back to civilisation is either to return the 40 km they've already slogged along, or continue onwards through the 56 km of mountainous country ahead of them. In his mind he's already hauling her onto his shoulders and carrying her on the marathon that lies in wait. But she doesn't look as if she's injured, exhausted or ready to give up. He's expected tears before now, either because the trek is much harder than she imagined, or because the conditions are so tough, with the oppressively steamy heat during the day and mind-numbing cold at night. But Alyssa has shown no signs at all of not being able to cope.

'Dad?' she asks softly.

He moves closer to her. 'Yes, mate?'

'Dad,' she repeats, 'I was just wondering . . . Have you ever climbed Everest?'

Glenn looks at his daughter with astonishment. He has no idea she's even heard of Everest, let alone been thinking about it as they've all been struggling up this part of the track.

He shakes his head. 'No,' he says. 'No, I haven't.'

Alyssa beams. 'Oh, okay,' she replies. He has no idea why she looks so pleased. 'I just wondered . . .'

And then she pulls her boots out of some of the thickest, stickiest mud on the planet and stomps off, leaving her dad, motionless, behind. As he watches the tiny figure disappear through the thick leaves and branches of the overhanging forest, he feels, as well as his usual pride, a vague sense of foreboding.